Free to Run the Race

FREE TO RUN THE RACE

Undoing the Burdens of Parental Disregard

by
Gary Ventimiglia, PsyD, PhD

Foreword by
Brad D. Strawn, PhD

WIPF & STOCK · Eugene, Oregon

FREE TO RUN THE RACE
Undoing the Burdens of Parental Disregard

Copyright © 2016 Gary Ventimiglia. All rights reserved. Except for brief quotations in critical publications or reviews, no part of this book may be reproduced in any manner without prior written permission from the publisher. Write: Permissions, Wipf and Stock Publishers, 199 W. 8th Ave., Suite 3, Eugene, OR 97401.

Wipf & Stock
An Imprint of Wipf and Stock Publishers
199 W. 8th Ave., Suite 3
Eugene, OR 97401

www.wipfandstock.com

PAPERBACK ISBN: 978-1-4982-9873-5
HARDCOVER ISBN: 978-1-4982-5917-0
EBOOK ISBN: 978-1-4982-9874-2

Manufactured in the U.S.A.   09/16/16

Contents

Foreword by Brad D. Strawn, PhD | vii

Introduction | 1

PART I—THE NORM OF CHRISTIAN LIVING

Chapter One
The Freedom of the Kingdom | 17

Chapter Two
The Boundless Affection of God | 33

PART II—OH, YOU GOT TO CARRY THAT WEIGHT

Chapter Three
Knowing, Being, Doing | 49

Chapter Four
(The) Father Knows Best | 68

PART III—ALL IN THE FAMILY

Chapter Five
Training Up Your Child | 87

Chapter Six
Help from "The Study of the Soul" | 110

Chapter Seven
The Embittered Christian and Trusting in God | 138

PART IV—ON THE ROAD AGAIN: UNDOING THE BURDENS

Chapter Eight
A Path to Healing | 159

Chapter Nine
The Power of Witness | 173

Conclusion | 193

Bibliography | 199

Foreword

The shelves of our local bookstores (if you can still find a bookstore) are lined with self-help books, which promise to assist one live a better life, raise lovely children, lose twenty-five pounds and even enhance spiritual flourishing. And while some of these books become best sellers, I often wonder how many readers stop reading beyond the first chapter. I have a sneaking suspicion that readers become disillusioned with these books because they simply don't work. They don't work because they suffer from over generalizations and because they are not grounded in deep meaning making systems. Their categories for what needs "help" are too broad and the explanations for why one should get better are vague and loosely anchored in a kind of generic ethic (e.g., everyone agrees that people should be happy, or thinner or have more well-adjusted kids) or spirituality (e.g., everyone agrees that people should be more centered, more connected or more mindful).

On the flip side, academic libraries are also full of scholarly articles and books written about transformation and increasingly the intersection of psychology and theology. The frequent problem with these scholarly tomes is that only a handful of academics read them due to the narrowness of focus, the complex jargon utilized and the lack of practical application. Rarely, and unfortunately, does one find a book that combines scholarly work in both theology and psychology and presents it in a way that is useful. *Free to Run the Race*, the book you hold in your hands, does both and does it well. Gary Ventimiglia has written a book that strives to be *helpful*. It is a book that is both deeply psychological and theological while endeavoring to make a difference in the reader's life.

Free to Run the Race is an act of love. It is a book that emerges out of the author's years of training in and practice of psychotherapy. Ventimiglia

Foreword

dares to look childhood trauma squarely in the face—to speak the unspeakable—with an eye to healing and restoration as well as prevention. In this sense it is a book for the traumatized and for the prevention of future trauma. This is the kind of book that the Christian community needs.

Ventimiglia avoids the shortcomings of so much of the self-help literature by first avoiding over generalizations. He writes about a *specific* process of childhood trauma, and its aftermath, captured in the work of psychoanalyst Bernie Brandchaft. This process of trauma emerges in the interaction of a missattuned child-caregiver experience resulting in what Brandchaft calls *pathological accommodation* and what Ventimiglia calls *parental disregard*. In this misattuned experience, children and later adults, learn to deny their own particular voices/personality/strivings and instead accommodate to whatever their environment (i.e., caregivers) has told them they must become in order to be loved. The brilliance of Ventimiglia's use of parental disregard is that it offers a specific kind of child-caregiver trauma that is both process-oriented while also applicable to particular individual experience.

Secondly, this book avoids the generic explanations for why we should get better by grounding its argument in the deep meaning making system of Christian theology and thoughtful biblical exegesis. With degrees in theology and psychology, and pastoral experience, Ventimiglia knows the psychology of religion research (e.g., how God representations come into being) but he doesn't fall into the reductionist trap that all religion boils down to psychology. He holds to a true God, as revealed in Scripture and most profoundly in the life, death and resurrection of Jesus Christ. And Gary knows that good theology makes a difference. While the psychology of religion can be incredible helpful in understanding the impact of religion on human experience, theology too may become a corrective dialogue partner to psychology. *Free to Run* traverses this dialogical back-and-forth with a well-informed and practical touch.

Finally, *Free to Run* is a book about love, and life. The trauma of parental disregard, coupled with problematic theology, can lead to a life of unhealthy accommodation, depression and even deadness. By understanding and owning one's history as well as engaging in the transforming love of God, *Free to Run* offers a pathway or invitation to engage in the abundant life that Jesus came to bring.

Brad D. Strawn, PhD
Evelyn and Frank Freed Professor for the Integration of Psychology and Theology
Fuller Theological Seminary, School of Psychology, Pasadena, CA
June 8, 2016

Introduction

> It don't really matter to me
> Everybody's had to fight to be free
> You don't have to live like a refugee.
>
> "Refugee"
> (Tom Petty, 1980)[1]

Tom Petty, the rock musician and prolific songwriter, once wrote: "Somebody somehow somewhere must have kicked you around some; who knows why you wanna lay there and revel in your abandon." Human beings suffer psychologically for so many reasons. Life is hard, relationships go bad, loved ones die, we get sick both physically and mentally, we make bad choices that have life-changing impacts. The economy goes south; people lose jobs; money pressures mount. We get abused, ridiculed and misunderstood. Sometimes we suffer through no fault of our own, such as from underestimated hurricanes and unanticipated earthquakes. We just get tired, run out of gas, get depressed and despondent. Petty expresses the depths of this when he says (in the same song): "Who knows? Maybe you were kidnapped, tied up, taken away and held for ransom." Though no patients in my psychotherapy practice have ever been literally abducted, for many of them this image rings true figuratively and emotionally.

The "hostage mind-set" can be manifested clinically when, as children, we are restrained from being who we are; when we are refused permission

---

1. "Refugee," by Tom Petty and Mike Campbell (1980).

to express ourselves spontaneously in matters that seem vital to us. Perhaps we are prevented from becoming physically active, or having a mind of our own, or figuring out puzzles, or expressing ourselves musically, or acting inquisitive or funny; any of the myriad qualities that could be fundamental aspects of being in the world. Simply put, a child becomes deeply conflicted when parents or other authority figures reject its essential self-expression. The child can feel that its own capabilities and inclinations are somehow "wrong" or alien to itself, even though those capacities are at the core of its self-cohesion.

Some mental health professionals call the child's self-directed actions (and the feelings that accompany them) the building blocks of a "sense of self," or a "felt self," which develops into a self-concept that is crucial for personal identity. The child feels joy in self-expressions because they arise from an awareness of internal capability and competence, a gratification in the living-out of its natural propensities and aptitudes. Early on, that sense of joy is bundled up in the child's connections with people he knows and loves. He "wants to" act on, or accomplish, or simply experience these things while his parents are watching and enjoying and approving.[2] What children do not desire attention and fundamental affirmation from their parents?

Eric Liddell, the British Olympic runner profiled in the movie *Chariots of Fire*, did not receive universal approval for his chosen path. His older sister believed he ought to forgo the Olympic Games and embark on greater goals in the Chinese mission fields. Liddell's response was simply, "God made me fast—and when I run, I feel his pleasure."[3] He saw with complete clarity that his speed, his talent for sprinting, was God-given, a quality and blessing intrinsic to his nature. Not to run would be a travesty, a denial of who he was.

Few of us are blessed with Olympic-level abilities, yet each individual has aspects of his life that share a kinship with the Scottish sprinter's brilliance. We may call this a "bent," a natural talent, an aptitude, an internal capacity or an innate endowment. Christians may call it giftedness, as Liddell did.

---

2. Fonagy et al., *Affect Regulation*, 54. They make a pertinent statement concerning parents at the beginning of their meticulously written volume:
> The caregiver's perception of the child as an *intentional being* lies at the root of sensitive care giving, which attachment theorists view as the cornerstone of secure attachment. (emphasis mine)

3. *Chariots of Fire*, written by Colin Welland, directed by Hugh Hudson (1981).

INTRODUCTION

The perceptive reader may ask, "What does this talk about following one's way or natural bent have to do with my ability to live a mature Christian life?" A reasonable question. The answer lies in the drastic consequences experienced by persons who, because of parental injunctions, are forbidden from developing their own particular way(s) in their lives. They see no choice except to accommodate themselves to the intrusive, mis-attuned, and even condemnatory injunctions of their parents. A child under these constraints easily comes to believe that his ordinary feelings and actions are "bad," because he has been emphatically told that they are bad.[4]

Psychoanalyst Bernard Brandchaft says of this,

> The first caretakers occupy the role of reflector of an ultimate reality and the absolute definer of who the child is. Their constructs, communicated in a thousand ways—verbal, gestural, and attitudinal—impart meaning to the child's experience. Enduringly negative or positive, hopeful or despairing, nourishing or depleting, these meanings continue to shape the quality and direction his inner life takes.[5]

Later in this book (chapter 4) I will demonstrate how these defining actions by the caretakers can permeate the breadth and depth of a child's life. It is not simply that parents may oppose, for example, the energetic/athletic expressions of their daughter, or the emotional sensitivities of their son. More profoundly, they may reject and subvert the child's intrinsic motivation, the internal feeling-state that drives him to uniquely communicate and express himself.[6] Brandchaft describes the pain induced into children

---

4. I am referring to behavior that would be considered circumstantially appropriate or age-appropriate, such as active play (running, jumping) or quieter types of "passive" play (such as reading, by an older child). The parent tells the child that he/she is being bad for not obeying injunctions against that behavior, though the parent's primary motivation is reducing their own anxiety or attending to other emotional needs.

5. Brandchaft, *Toward an Emancipatory Psychoanalysis*, 138.

6. Please note from the beginning that this book is not a "parent bashing" treatise. My concern here is with specific attitudes and philosophies of child-rearing that believe children's enjoyments or desires arising from their own subjectivity are somehow wrong, unsafe, or selfish. This mentality essentially violates, on principle, the *Children's Bill of Emotional Rights* described by Eileen Johnson. Johnson provides an excellent guide for understanding the emotional needs of children, demonstrating how parents can inadvertently violate their child's sensitivities when they do not understand the nature of childhood. She lists various mistakes parents make in reacting to their children's words. Here are the first four:

by caretakers (mostly parents, but also grandparents or other relatives, nannies, etc.) who desire the child to be something other than itself:

> This failure has momentous consequences. It renders the individual permanently the hostage of the responses of another for the determination and definition of who he is. He is imprisoned by a feeling of responsibility for the state of mind of another, and he is utterly unable to use his own unfettered volition in the choices he makes in the fulfillment of his attachments and in the interest he attempts to freely pursue and fully enjoy.[7]

This "hostage situation" can start very early in the child's life, most often by preschool age. The mother or father, for whatever personal reasons (i.e., those not pertaining to the child's legitimate safety concerns), refuses to recognize the actualities of their child's basic bent or way.[8] Brandchaft describes the internalizing of the parent's belief system within the child as the development of "structures of pathological accommodation."[9] We will explore the psychological and theological dimensions of this more completely later in the book. For now, I will posit that the parents' denial of the

---

- Adults misinterpret what children are saying.
- Adults fail to understand that children are often confused.
- Adults do not take the time to understand what a child is saying.
- Adults do not give importance to the thoughts of children. (2)

Johnson's book certainly does not criticize all parents or styles of parenting; instead it serves as a corrective for addressing hurtful mistreatments caused, for one, by parental disregard. See Johnson, *Children's Bill of Emotional Rights*, 1–28.

7. Brandchaft, *Toward an Emancipatory Psychoanalysis*, 141. See also Shabad, *Despair and the Return of Hope*, 195:

> Eventually such children grow up to feel their lives are not their own but instead the playthings of powers far greater than themselves. As the active initiative of developing their own lives gives way to the despair of a reactive passivity, such individuals are unable to liberate themselves from the bondage on which they feel their life depends. They perceive themselves as having no freedom of choice to say yes or no or love or hate, much less the freedom of movement to come and go as they please.

8. The rejection or disapproval may remind the parent of a painful experience in their own childhood, or an injunction they were forced to obey in order to maintain attachment to their own parents.

9. Brandchaft, *Toward an Emancipatory Psychoanalysis*, 193–220. Cf. Eigen, *Toxic Nourishment*, where the author describes, in vivid case studies, examples of deleterious parental relationships, situations intended for emotional sustenance that have become poisonous instead.

Introduction

child's expressions of essential aspects of the self engenders a deep-rooted mistrust in the child. The parents' (at best) misguided attempt at doing what is best for their offspring, or (at worst) purposely abusive denunciation has profound consequences for the child's life.

When the parents' "misconstruction" of their child springs from a need to alleviate their own anxieties or to use their children as some sort of extension of themselves, the exploitation becomes unremitting. It may be that the particular proclivities of the child remind the parent of some unacceptable aspect of themselves. It may be the parent is adhering to dogmatic precepts from a so-called biblical or even secular understanding of the parent-child relationship.[10] Regardless, the impact of the consistency and the longevity of these parents' actions cannot be overstated. Forced to curb expressions of temperament or behavior that feel fundamental to its existence, the child can easily fall into a depressive state of self-denigration. Many times this leads to an identity of self-rejection: a person ashamed of being himself, both who he is and what he has become.

I am calling this ill-treatment "parental disregard." The disregarding arises when the parents reject something unique and natural in the child's makeup while dismissing something that, if allowed to grow, would bolster the child's confidence and self-acceptance. This disregard could be as distinct as not allowing a young person to develop his artistic inclinations; or it could be as indistinct as not letting the preschooler explain her actions with her burgeoning command of the language, thus denying her the ability to self-regulate by "using her words"; it could be a parent not paying close enough attention to their child's particular capabilities in a certain area. The outcome of this can be that the child feels there is something wrong with him/her; that their mom or dad knows better what they are good at, or what feels satisfying to them inside. The corollary to this would be the belief that what they want to do must be silly or even wrong. The conflict usually causes some kind of shame, some kind of self rejection. Psychiatrist Andrew Morrison describes this appalling subjective state:

> I think of shame as that feeling of self-castigation which arises when we are convinced that there is something about ourselves that is wrong, inferior, flawed, weak, or dirty. Shame is fundamentally

---

10. For examples of philosophies of parenting that seem to center on the supposed necessity for training/disciplining the child away from their expressed needs (and the behaviors associated with those expressions), the reader may refer to the enormous volume of publications by Michel Pearl and Gary Ezzo. Pearl's *No Greater Joy*, vols. 1–3, and Ezzo's *Growing Kids God's Way* are useful as starting points.

a feeling of loathing against ourselves, a hateful vision of ourselves through our own eyes—*although this vision may be determined by how we expect or believe other people are experiencing us.*[11]

In childhood this sense of shame, a by-product of disavowing essential aspects of one's self, is primarily driven by the machinations of one's parents. As we will explore more fully in chapter 6, the child complies with the conditions of the parents' care because he intuits that otherwise he will suffer great harm or even death; not physical death necessarily, but certainly the excruciating pain of a psychological death. Carl Goldberg, psychologist and clinical shame expert, addresses this:

> The younger and the more often the child is shamed, the more pliant he becomes to unfair and abusive treatment from his caretakers . . . shame represents a special fear . . . the issues that evoke shame in the child are experienced as threatening to the survival of the child at a period of development in which the child is not capable of an accurate assessment of reality. During adult shaming the person returns to the feelings of fear of abandonment by his caretakers that he experienced as a child. At that excruciatingly painful moment—whether in adulthood or childhood, the shamed person feels small, helpless, and worthless. Time seems large and endless. He experiences no way to escape because he senses no moment in the future when he expects to be beyond the present painful moment.[12]

As we will see in chapter 4, this profile of the shamed-centered person is consistent with the Apostle Paul's description of children damaged by a caustic relationship with their fathers (parents). Paul admonishes fathers in Colossians 3:21 not to exasperate their children so that they do not lose heart. We will examine the dimensions of this "exasperation" (as translated

---

11. Morrison, *Culture of Shame*, 13, emphasis mine.
12. Goldberg, *Understanding Shame*, 18. Goldberg goes on to discuss recent research findings concerning the experience of shame in the infant:
> We can summarize the findings on the influence of self-consciousness and shame by indicating that the early experiences of shaming in the infant are moments (or just representations) of the loss of the safe-and-certain in the infants. Feelings of shame monitor the infant's relationship with significant, loving, and protective others. The anxiety of shame provides a sense of danger to the infant's physical and emotional safety. In short, the experience of shame comes from a threat to the infant of its loving bonds to its environment, particularly its caretaker's. (31)

Introduction

by the NASB)[13] in light of the resulting experience of the child's loss of heart.

Since much of the child's mistreatment occurs very early in life, he comes to believe that the feelings engendered by the mistreatment are self-generated. Even if by adolescence the teenager begins to blame his parents for his problems, deep in his spirit he continues to feel miserable about himself.[14] By adulthood he becomes, at best, a divided man who masks his sense of inadequacy even as he considers himself culpable for his own poor self-image. A Christian brought up in this manner will be hobbled by various levels of self-rejection and shame regardless of her cognitive belief that she is loved and accepted by God through Jesus Christ. She will find it difficult if not impossible to affectively gain a personal sense of who God is to her and what he has done for her; the "joy of his salvation" will rarely be part of her experience.

Does growing up from early childhood with this kind of parental diminution mean that a person is trapped in a life of self-contempt, with an unrelenting certainty that he will never get it "right"? Is this struggle permanent? My response is no; but it is a qualified no. For too long Christians have blamed this experience on the ones who suffer from it, believing they are solely responsible for the way they are or how they feel. Too little attention has been paid to developmental woundedness. In scriptural terms, we can call this woundedness "the sins of the fathers" (and mothers) with the assurance that it really does take place in this fallen world. More will be said about parental responsibilities for diminution in chapter 6 and illustrated by the case studies in chapter 7.

Biblically speaking, I see this woundedness as a very specific and very heavy burden in the lives of many Christians, hindering their capacity for living the Christian life in a trusting relationship with our Heavenly Father. As Hebrews 12:1–2 says,

---

13. All Scripture quotations (unless otherwise noted) will be taken from the New American Standard Bible.

14. Terry Cooper, in *Sin, Pride & Self-Acceptance*, 4, says concerning children with low self-esteem,

> Most kids act out, do destructive things and become self-centered because they have never felt accepted or accepted themselves. Rigid expectations and demands of children create strong feelings of inadequacy. When children don't like themselves, they are often damaging to others. Kids respond to support, encouragement and *the freedom to be themselves*. (emphasis mine)

> Therefore, since we have so great a cloud of witnesses surrounding us, let us also lay aside every encumbrance, and the sin which so easily entangles us, and let us run with endurance the race that is set before us, fixing our eyes of Jesus the author and perfecter of faith, who for the joy set before Him endured the cross, despising the shame, and has sat down at the right hand of the throne of God.

To live life in a manner pleasing to the Lord we must do two things, according to this scripture. First, keep our eyes (our heart and our mind) focused on Jesus, knowing who he is and what he has provided for us. Second, we must "lay aside" or release the encumbrances that weigh us down and the sin that can so easily trip us up. These two types of disturbances are distinctly different; we misunderstand the passage if we see them as identical.[15]

Much of the teaching around this passage centers on the issue of sin in a believer's life, and rightly so. Sin entangles us and distracts us from keeping our faith in Christ viable and present in our minds. We fall because our sin trips us, ensnaring us in some pursuit that detours us from the path of following Jesus. We fall because we forget who we are in Christ, deceived (willingly or not) into thinking that other ways of living may offer us more advantages.

By contrast, the "encumbrances" referenced in the verse are not acts of sin. They may generate opportunities for sin but they are not sinful in themselves. Encumbrances slow us down, make it difficult to keep going, make it painful to continue. They are like a load on the back of a person on a journey; a heap of stuff that saddles the person and drains his strength. For a runner, any extraneous weight will make the contest more grueling and may even cause him to lose the race.[16] One only has to consider the of-

---

15. Bruce, *Epistle to the Hebrews*, 349.

16. See Pfeiffer, *Epistle to the Hebrews*, 107. He describes these weights (encumbrances) by saying,

> The preparation for the race is all-important. We must lay aside "weights" (12:1). The illustration is intentionally ridiculous. What runner would think of carrying weights? Everything superfluous must be put aside if he hopes to win. So it is with the Christian. Sometimes we ask, "Is such-and-such a sin?" There may be instances where opinions will differ. Some things are known to be evil, and others may be on the borderline. The Christian must ask a further question, however: "Are they weights?" If they will slow our pace in running the race set before us, then they must be cast aside.

The experience of parental disregard (or, as Brandchaft calls it from the child's

Introduction

ficial track attire for Olympic athletes to see how important issues of weight have become!

Personal and spiritual encumbrances may be circumstantial, such as involving or over-involving ourselves in activities that complicate our ability to do what we are called to do. They may be relational, such as allowing a friend's concerns to dominate our time and energy, to the point of becoming unhealthy for us and for our friend. Encumbrances can even be ideas or standards that have little to do with following Christ and more to do with impressing others. In various ways these hindrances tear at our confidence and undermine our trust that God knows what he is doing when he allows difficult events and personal episodes to impact us.

In the lives of believers, I see encumbrances also manifested as adult responses to childhood mistreatment. Many times the mistreatment was experienced as parental neglect and rejection of fundamental aspects of the child's life or "bent"; or in terms of Proverbs 22:6, of the child's own "way" (ch. 5). The effort required to manage the conscious or unconscious pain of this rejection, even after many decades, sadly impacts the lives of many Christians. They find it very difficult to trust others they see as supporters or benefactors; even more challenging is cultivating a faith relationship through trust in our Heavenly Father. Parental (fatherly) woundedness cuts to the bone of our existence.

The Bible often references the relationship of the father to his children as an illustration of God's actions and intentions for us (ch. 4). Scriptures such as Psalm 103:12–13; Hebrews 12:16; Luke 11:11–13; and Matthew 7:9–11 actually anticipate much of the thinking in contemporary attachment theory about healthy child development. And as I've mentioned, Colossians 3:21 is equally crucial in this regard. The earthly father's intense anger causes his children to *lose heart*. In Hebraic thought the heart, among other aspects, is the primary locus of our self-understanding and so the mediator of our experience of others (Prov 4:23). The *loss of heart* therefore has a profound effect both on the child and the adult. As we will see in chapter 4, Paul uses a unique word for this kind of damage, employed only here in the New Testament. It may be literally translated as "being without heart, or soul." As a descriptor it could be rendered as having "a crushed or ruined heart."[17]

---

perspective, "pathological accommodation") creates in the Christian a weight of emotional conflict that can "slow our pace in running the race set before us."

17. I will have much more to say about this word (*athumosin*, translated as "lose

How do people deeply compromised in their ability to trust those who claim to care for them approach a God who says, as a father, that he loves his child in so many incredible ways? How can a believer genuinely receive the truths of Scripture if he can manage only an abstract acceptance of its validity? How can she trust that she is loved by a Person who says he is "intimately acquainted with all her ways" (Ps 139:3) when no one has ever loved her in anything like that manner? The Holy Spirit communicates the truth of God's intentions toward us, but we receive that communication through the template of our past experiences (Prov 23:7). A heart that has been crushed, ruined, or "lost" through the human phenomenon of child abuse (as impingement or rejection) hobbles the outworking of the mind of Christ in the believer. The encumbrances of the past make it very difficult to experience the truth of who we are in Christ.[18]

Modern Christians have typically undervalued the importance of feelings or gut-level affects. We necessarily apprehend real-life events, relational and otherwise, first of all through "right brain" emotional modalities. Emotions such as joy, fear, confusion, love, security, terror and others define the meanings of our experiences before we apply a cognitive, interpretive understanding.[19] (We will explore the implications of this in ch. 3.) Scriptures such as Nehemiah 9:17; Romans 14:17; Jude 20; and Psalm 51:12 among many others declare that coming to God through his wonderful grace should enliven us into a state of joy, a robust sense of vitality. How many people who come to faith in Jesus Christ feel next to nothing instead? Perhaps a sense of relief, but nothing on the scale of the biblical images of our reception, when we are justified, redeemed, regenerated, and reconciled to the King of the Universe—"things too wonderful for words" (Ps 139:6).

---

heart" or "be discouraged") in ch. 4. In my view the experience Paul describes cannot help but severely impact the long-term emotional health of the child; especially when this experience becomes continuous in the life of the young one. For reference, see Eadie, *Commentary on Colossians*, 256.

18. See the pertinent statement by theologian Klaus Issler in his *Living into the Life of Jesus*, 95, where he says,

> On that matter, our view of God may probably be much too puny and distorted. Distortions in our God-image can prevent us from receiving God's gracious love—in effect, *rendering various aspects of God's character as nonexistent*. For it's hard to assign the word love to a relationship with God when God feels like a judgmental parent who criticizes us without any display of affection. (emphasis mine)

19. Thompson, *Anatomy of the Soul*, 91–99.

Introduction

The joy of our salvation is the entirely natural result of being forgiven of sin, welcomed into the family of God, and given our vocations as "little Christs." Scripture describes us as lights in the world, salt, ambassadors, heralds, sweet fragrances, soldiers, Olympic athletes and much more in our service to Jesus.[20] It is for him that we expectantly wait, the blessed hope of our Savior's final appearing. All of this encompassed in an active, nourishing, and admonishing relationship with our Heavenly Father who adores us!

With so much at stake, how can we not seek to heal the damaging encumbrance of a lost heart, of struggling with an embittered, exasperated self-identity?

Clarifying these issues requires us to delve into "the study of the soul," contemporary psychoanalytic thought regarding the development of a damaged identity, noted so explicitly in Colossians 3:21 but also implicitly in Proverbs 22:6. I will reference (in ch. 6) the works of three important clinicians in the second half of the twentieth century: John Bowlby on attachment, Donald Winnicott on parental impingements and the development of a false self, and Bernard Brandchaft and his "structures of pathological accommodations."

To lay the groundwork for these insights I will first present my image of a maturing Christian (ch. 1): how she lives her life in the real world, how he confronts the pain of living in a fallen world, what kinds of attitudes, beliefs and actions accompany the believer who is living a "normal Christian life";[21] and how these qualities may be sustained. The life of the Christian matters here and now, and we must understand how to live out the kingdom of God in joy within the present world.

Following that (in ch. 2), we will see that walking in a manner worthy of our calling (Eph 4:1) requires a trusting relationship with God as Father; i.e., a biblical faith rather than an abstract belief. Scripture powerfully expresses the incarnation of Jesus Christ as "the radiance of His (God's) glory and the exact representation of His nature" (Heb 1:3). The Gospel of John depicts Jesus as the eternal Word of God who "became flesh and dwelt among us" (John 1:14). John tells us that by his actions Jesus explained

---

20. Matt 5:14; Matt 5:13; 1 Cor 5:20; 1 Tim 1:6; 2 Cor 2:15; 2 Tim 2:4; 1 Cor 9:24, 25.

21. An obvious reference to Watchman Nee's classic work on living the Christian life. Though I do not agree with all of Nee's teachings (such as his view of Rom 7), his emphasis on the importance of "knowing" and "reckoning" the truths of our salvation in Christ, and the work that this entails, fits well with my thesis. See Nee, *Normal Christian Life*, 33–58.

(or exegeted) God himself. He did this by dwelling with us, so that "we beheld his glory, glory as of the only begotten from the Father, full of grace and truth" (1:14). The disciples entered into a flesh-and-blood relationship with Jesus of Nazareth, hearing his words and observing and participating in his actions. Their faith in him was existential (that is, an actual trust in the present moment). They laughed, cried, argued, and rejoiced with him. They had the supreme privilege of living as witnesses to the reality of Jesus Christ.

Like the disciples, our faith must grow into an affect-laden reception of our mental acknowledgement that Jesus is Lord, our Lord, with a living awareness that he is alive and present in our hearts (by faith as an enduring felt-presence), through his Spirit who indwells us.

In the final section of the book we will consider how a person may radically change their understanding of what it means to be loved (in its affective experience and significance), as well as accepted and empowered to live for Christ. The process requires both a deep self-examination (ch. 8) and a willingness to receive help from others (ch. 9). The believer must work to recognize internal attitudes that are continually self-abrogating and self-destructive to the point of self-rejection. Careful, relentless development of self-awareness and self-understanding are the primary keys to laying aside these painful encumbrances.

The New Testament describes Christians as "not of this world" (John 17:14–16); that they are "strangers and aliens" in this corrupt world (1 Pet 2:11) because the world does not know him who was sent (see 1 John 4:6). By following Jesus we join a kingdom that is not of this world—at least for the time being. But Christians are never called "refugees"; that is, those who do not belong at all in the country where they reside. These are people who have fled from one country to another; they are refugees because they have taken refuge in a less-dangerous place. As far as this world is concerned Christians are actually liberators, bringing in God's rule and reign wherever the church gathers in the power of the Holy Spirit (see Rom 8:19–23).

In Tom Petty's song "Refugee," Petty says to the sufferer: "It don't make no difference to me, everybody's had to fight to be free. You don't have to live like a refugee." Too many believers live their lives in quiet defeat, with a gut-sense that they don't genuinely belong in the redemptive community of Christ. They cannot find freedom in their inner selves to step out and live a life of "righteousness peace and joy in the Holy Spirit" (Rom 14:17). They are too afraid to do this; they do not feel worthy, let alone capable of

Introduction

living this way. They live like refugees in a creation that "eagerly waits for the revealing of the sons of God" (Rom 8:19).

We know that every believer must fight the good fight to overcome encumbrances and the sin that so easily trips us up. Those who carry the painful weight of parental disregard, even to the point of rejection, have a particular fight ahead of them in order to get free. This book is about that fight. By God's love and grace you don't have to live like a refugee any longer.

PART I

The Norm of Christian Living

CHAPTER ONE

The Freedom of the Kingdom

> You have given all there is to give
> What can I give for you?
> You have given me life to live
> How can I live for you?
>
> "What Can I Do For You?"
> (Bob Dylan, 1981)

The lives of Christians can be severely impacted by developmental woundedness of a particular kind. When parents disregard essential aspects of a child's personhood, the adult believer's ability to internalize and experience the truth of God's love may be compromised or damaged beyond their own capacity to comprehend and repair.

In the Psalms, David tells us that God is a father to the fatherless, and he knows that God will take care of him even if "my father and mother have forsaken me" (Ps 65:8; 27:10). David does not describe how his parents' abandonment might have affected him. However, he does not hesitate to compare God's compassion and understanding for humankind to that of an earthly father's for his own children (Ps 103:13–14). The simile illustrates in kind (certainly not in degree) the ways that our reception and experience

PART I: THE NORM OF CHRISTIAN LIVING

of the worldly helps define and shape our experience of the heavenly.[1] Scott McKnight, explaining why Jesus described God as Abba, says:

> In *Abba* Jesus chooses a term from the home because love originates in the home where an *Abba* dwells. Not only does love begin there, but our first understandings of God begin at home and are *transfers* from both parents to God. We are wired this way. This is not something we do rationally and intentionally. It is something we do instinctually.[2]

The most important commandments that Jesus shared with his followers (Mark 12:38–41) were to love God with all their heart, soul, mind and strength (Deut 6:5), and to love their neighbors as themselves (Lev 19:18). How thoroughly may a person's capacity for love be constricted when her template for love was (and perhaps is) deeply and emotionally compromised?

Since Christians are called to live in this world reflecting the life of Jesus Christ, it is essential for us to understand how our developmental woundedness can impact this calling. Jesus "went about doing good" (Acts 10:38). He put others' needs before "His own and did not please Himself at their cost" (2 Cor 8:9; Phil 2:6–8; Rom 14:3). In the second chapter of Philippians Paul tells us we should "have this attitude in yourself as was in Christ Jesus." The Christian should imitate his Master, particularly in the attitude of self-sacrificial love.

So how can we go about living life in this world as Christians? What should the follower of Christ *do* after she has met the Savior? Or as Bob Dylan puts it, "You have given me life to live, how can I live for you?"[3] This indeed is the real question: How can I live for you in this world right now and for the rest of my life? How can I show you in deep gratitude that I love you, Lord?

LIVING IN THE KINGDOM

Jesus of Nazareth came to the people of Israel proclaiming that the kingdom of God was now at hand (Mark 1:15). He claimed that God, the great God of Abraham, Isaac and Jacob was uniquely his Father, and that he was

---

1. See Fowler, *Adult Development and Christian Faith*, 48–76.
2. McKnight, *Jesus Creed*, 26, italics original.
3. Dylan, "What Can I Do for You?"

calling all of the people to a new relationship with God. He described this new reality as being "born again" (John 3:3; cf. 1 Pet 1:23). He called out individuals to become members of his Father's kingdom, to live and reflect in their very lives the truth of God before the entire world (Matt 5:16). By doing this in the midst of what Paul would call "a crooked and perverse generation" (Phil 2:15), Christians emulate the goodness of God to his glory (1 Pet 4:16). They live as God intended humankind to live from the beginning.[4] As the Apostle Peter describes the believer in 1 Peter 2:9–10:

> But you are a chosen race, a royal priesthood, a holy nation, a people for God's own possession that you may proclaim the excellencies of Him who has called you out of darkness into His marvelous light, for once you were not a people, but now you are the people of God, you had not received mercy, but now you have received mercy.

After this the apostle instructs these grateful children of God to live in a manner that demonstrates the greatness of God's love and power. As unbelievers witness the transformed lives of the followers of Christ, they would confess that God has done amazing things and thereby glorify him (1 Pet 2:12). The believer's character and deportment, particularly in the face of suffering from persecution, showed that something profoundly different had occurred in the lives of those submitted to the Spirit of Christ. As N. T. Wright describes it:

> What the earliest Christian were struck by, and what they returned to again and again, was that in Jesus they had seen a way of being human which nobody had ever imagined before. This was a way of generosity and forgiveness, a way of self-emptying and a determination to put everyone else's needs first. . . . Jesus came, in fact, to launch God's new creation, and with it a new way of being human, a way which picked up the glimpses of "right behavior" afforded by ancient Judaism and paganism and, transcending both. . . . God's

---

4. Stibbs, *First Epistle of Peter*, 104. Lenski's comment on this verse in *Interpretation of the Epistles of St. Peter, St. John, and St. Jude*, 108, is relevant here:

> Because of what we are it is our great function that by word and by deed, by our confession and by our conduct we at all times and under all circumstances publish in our own midst and to all men about us him who called us out of darkness, etc. . . . True believers cannot keep still, they simply must speak out with lip and with life. They thus function as a royal priesthood and ever offer up sacrifices of praise and thanksgiving. This is the confessional and the missionary spirit and activity of God's people; for the sake of this God lets us remain in the world.

kingdom was bursting in to the present world.... Human beings were called at last to rediscover what they had been made for.[5]

In the ministry of Jesus Christ the kingdom of God was "bursting" into a world that did not know him and did not worship him as Lord (John 1:10–11). In their changed lives believers expressed the reign and rule of Almighty God; the kingdom of God was in their midst (Luke 17:21; 18:21; Mark 1:15; cf. Rom 14:17).[6] Theologian George Eldon Ladd said of this kingdom:

> The mission of Jesus brought not a new teaching but a new event. ... Jesus did not promise forgiveness of sins; he bestowed it. He did not simply assure men of the future fellowship of the Kingdom; he invited men into fellowship with himself as the bearer of the Kingdom. He did not merely promise them vindication in the day of judgment; he bestowed upon them a present righteousness. He not only taught an eschatological deliverance from physical evil he went about demonstrating the redeeming power of the Kingdom, delivering men from sickness and even death.[7]

Jesus said of his ministry that "the Son of Man did not come to be served but to give His life a ransom for many" (Mark 10:45; Matt 20:28). Writing some twenty-five years later, Paul elaborates by saying: "namely that God was in Christ reconciling the world to himself, not counting their trespasses against themselves" (2 Cor 5:18); and that at the cross God "made Him who knew no sin to be sin in our behalf, that we might become the righteousness of God in Him" (2 Cor 5:21).

It is worth noting that Jesus and Paul both spoke their words in the context of exhortations to right living and servant ministry. Jesus encouraged his disciples to become servants to others, to live and serve as he lived and served. Ultimately he offered his life in sacrifice, a ransom, a payment for others so that God could bring the believer back from sin and death. Ben Witherington says of Mark 10:45,

> The crucial word in the second half of the verse is *lutron*. The basic idea of this word is "deliverance by purchase," and it is used to describe an act of redemption, the buying back of human beings. The price of this ransom is not money, but the life of *bar enasha*

---

5. Wright, *After You Believe*, 131.
6. Ibid., 13.
7. Ladd, *Theology of the New Testament*, 80.

... a substitutionary suffering or giving of a life that frees others is in view.[8]

In this incredible salvation event, Jesus as the "son of man" (*bar enasha*) demonstrated the way to live, a way of ordering one's life in relation to others. Christians do not give their lives in order to redeem the sins of others, but to proclaim and glorify the One who did!

Because this ransom was paid for us, Paul says, we have been given the "ministry of reconciliation." We are "ambassadors for Christ entreating others to be reconciled to God" (2 Cor 5:17–21). We evangelize, sharing the good news by our words and by our actions. This was the reason Peter extolled his readers to "keep your behavior excellent" (2 Cor 2:14–15) and our lives should express the life of Jesus Christ in everything we do. As the Apostle John says so succinctly: "The one who says he abides in Him ought to himself to walk in the same manner as He walked" (1 John 2:6; cf. John 13:15; 1 Pet 2:21).

Living on this earth as redeemed men and women, sons and daughters of the living God, we are to increase the kingdom of God by the manner we live our lives. Scott McKnight, in his helpful book *The Jesus Creed*, describes this by saying:

> By virtue of entering the Kingdom of God, we Christians make the astounding claim that we live under a different order—God's order. Living in that order should make a difference in our day-to-day living and in our society. After all, the kingdom Jesus describes is a *society* and not just a personal nest.[9]

BEHAVING WITH BEATITUDE HEARTS

So how then do we live "in society" as members of his kingdom? Jesus addressed this question in a preaching episode popularly called the "Sermon on the Mount." As John Stott put it, Jesus words in Matthew 5–7 are nothing less than a description of the "Christian Counter-Culture."[10]

Jesus begins the sermon with "the Beatitudes," described by R. V. G. Tasker as "a kind of mosaic of the Christian character."[11] They are qualities

---

8. Witherington, *Christology of Jesus*, 255, italics original.
9. McKnight, *Jesus Creed*, 143, italics original.
10. Stott, *Christian Counter-Culture*.
11. Tasker, *Gospel according to St. Matthew*, 61.

of life that motivate specific behavior in particular kinds of circumstances—not only in the community of faith, but in the entire world. These forms of "blessed" thinking and acting would draw the attention of the unbeliever to God's work in the follower of Christ (Matt 5:16). One author says of the beatitudes,

> The beatitudes should be thought of as be-attitudes. This is in reality a deeper life sermon. . . . Here Jesus is probing the inner being, raising the question of motive. As has often been said, the larger question in ethics is not what a person does, but why he does what he does. And motive is the source from which our acts issue. As C. H. Dodd has pointed out, "the ethics of the sermon on the mount are the absolute ethics of the Kingdom of God."[12]

Concentrating on the "exclamatory form of the qualities,"[13] and not the blessings given, here are the eight traits which Jesus tells us are blessed by God:

1. Poor in spirit
2. Mournful
3. Gentle or meek
4. Hungering and thirsting for righteousness
5. Merciful
6. Pure in heart
7. Peacemakers
8. Persecuted for righteousness, especially as a follow of Jesus.

By presenting these "blessed" forms of thinking and acting, Jesus confronted and informed his audience about what it actually meant to live under the reign and rule of God in their world and their time—as well as for us, in our world and our time. It is the way to "walk in a manner worthy of our calling" (Eph 4:1).

After introducing and illustrating the kingdom of God through the Beatitudes, Jesus continues his sermon with the famous depictions of believers as salt and light—sometimes called "the Similitudes." As he says in Matthew 5:13–15:

---

12. Augsburger, *Matthew*, 62.
13. Tasker, *Gospel according to St. Matthew*, 61.

The Freedom of the Kingdom

> You are the salt of the earth; but if the salt has become tasteless, how will it be made salty again? It is good for nothing any more, except to be thrown out and trampled under foot by men. You are the light of the world. A city set on a hill cannot be hidden. Nor do men light a lamp, and put it under the peck measure, but on the lamp stand, and it gives light to all who are in the house. Let your light shine before men in such a way that they may see your good works, and glorify your father who is in heaven.

With these metaphorical images Jesus points to the intended purposes or outcomes for the attitudes of heart depicted in the Beatitudes. First Jesus calls his followers "the salt of the earth" (v. 13). Salt preserves meat from decaying so that it can be stored away until needed. As Stott says,

> The world also manifests a constant tendency to deteriorate. The notion is not that the world is tasteless and that Christians can make it less insipid . . . but that it is putrefying. It cannot stop itself from going bad. Only salt introduced from outside can do this.[14]

Salt disinfects and changes the quality of the food. It "combats deterioration"[15] so that a better, more useful and more edible portion is preserved.

The followers of Jesus influence the world by pointing to the true value of fundamental things, such as personal relationships, empathy and understanding for those who suffer, and speaking honestly and truthfully in a world that, as one writer described it, has vandalized the "Shalom of God."[16] Most importantly, the Christian points to God as the One to whom all are accountable, for "it is He who has made us and not we ourselves" (Ps 100:3).

The believer not only disinfects the rottenness of the world and slows its decay, she also brings to light what is genuinely good. Jesus calls his followers "the light of the world" (vv. 14–16). Their lives must be seen and not hidden away under some kind of protective Christian shelter or subculture. The "good works" following from a heart centered on Jesus' life and love will illuminate the true character of our Lord and Savior, showing the world that he cares for the lives of people right now and wants them to know his salvation (John 8:12). Paul speaks of the Christian as a "luminary," a star that in the sky giving guidance to a "crooked and perverse generation" (Phil 2:15).

---

14. Stott, *Christian Counter-Culture*, 59.
15. Hendriksen, *Exposition of the Gospel according to Matthew*, 282.
16. Plantinga, *Not the Way It's Supposed to Be*, 7–27.

So the followers of Jesus are called to live lives that are visibly, lovingly different. The readers of Matthew's Gospel will understand that their Master calls them to impact their societies like the first believers in Israel and confront their culture with the radical truth and integrity of Christ. We are to perceive the world in a new way, seeing the world around us—our cities, neighborhoods, and streets—as places where Jesus Christ wants to enter in. We are to proclaim that something extraordinary has happened, a pure awesomeness that can change lives!

CONFRONTING THE VANDALISM OF SHALOM

Cornelius Plantinga, of Calvin Theological Seminary, offers a particularly helpful perspective on our calling as Christians living in the present world. His book *Not the Way It's Supposed to Be: A Breviary of Sin*, speaks to the devastating effects of sin both for individuals and for societies. The wreckage has altered every aspect of creation, from the physical environment of the universe to the hearts of human beings, generating mass confusion as well as mass cruelty. Sin and corruption have compromised humankind's relationship to any and all aspects of the world we inhabit. Where there should be peace, joy and harmony, we find instead treachery and discord.

Plantinga reminds us that God created the world as a place for his children to live in peace and a place where they may share that peace with one another. The word "peace" in Hebrew is *shalom*. It is a richly endowed word full of meaning and purpose. God's shalom is more than an inner quietude or an absence of conflict. As Plantinga explains,

> The webbing together of God, humans, and all creation in justice, fulfillment, and delight is what the Hebrew prophet's call *shalom*. We call it peace, but it means far more than mere peace of mind or a cease-fire between enemies. In the Bible, shalom means *universal flourishing, wholeness, and delight*—a rich state of affairs in which natural needs are satisfied and natural gifts fruitfully employed, a state of affairs that inspires joyful wonder as its Creator and Savior opens doors and welcomes the creatures in whom he delights. Shalom, in other words, is the way things ought to be.[17]

The kingdom of God is the Lord's restoration project, awakening the world to the way things would have been if the tragic events of the garden had not occurred. It explains why Jesus spoke as he did about the meanings

---

17. Ibid., 8, italics original.

of the exorcisms and healings he performed. Jesus was the personification of the kingdom. Where he walked, God's love abounded in overturning the results of sin and the power of Satan in this world (1 John 3:8) Jesus' healings, whether physical, emotional or spiritual were personal and practical manifestations of God's love for the sufferer. He showed the world what can happen when ordinary people freely respond to the presence of God.[18]

Through the ministry of the Holy Spirit, Jesus sent out his followers to spread the good news that "God so loved the world that He gave His only begotten Son, that whoever believes in Him should not perish but have eternal life" (John 3:16). Even today disciples of Jesus spread the kingdom by confronting the culture with the love that Jesus has shown them. His love challenges the "vandalism of shalom," the systems of the world that have rejected God. The Apostle John called these things "the lust of the flesh, the lust of the eyes, and the boastful pride of life," and said they are "not from the Father but from the world" (1 John 2:16).[19] In Dallas Willard's words, Christians do battle with the world by establishing

> beachheads of his person, word and power in the midst of a failing and futile humanity. They were to bring the presence of the kingdom and it's King into every corner of human life simply by fully living in the kingdom with him.[20]

THE SIN THAT SO EASILY ENTANGLES US

In the mystery of God's unfathomable love and concern, he provides a way for us to return to him. John explains this in his first epistle:

---

18. Ibid., 10.

19. The struggle against these temptations of the world becomes a major focus of the apostle's writings to the churches: John in 1 John 2:15–17; James in Jas 1:27; 4:4–5; Paul in Rom 12:2; Eph 2:17–20; Peter in 1 Pet 4:2–3. Also see the book of Proverbs, "Do not let your heart envy sinners, but live in the fear of the Lord all the time" (23:17; cf. 24:1, 19).

20. Willard, *Renovation of the Heart*, 15. Stanley Hauerwas and William Willimon state this in a different way in their book *Resident Aliens*, 51. They designate the church as a colony, "a beachhead, an outpost, an island of one culture in the middle of another" (12). They go on to describe God's work in this:
> Jesus Christ is the supreme act of divine intrusion into the world's settled arrangements. In Christ, God refuses to "stay in his place." The message that sustains the colony is not for itself but for the whole world—the colony having significance only as God's means for saving the whole world. The colony is God's means of a major offensive against the world, for the world.

Part I: The Norm of Christian Living

> By this the love of God was manifested in us that God has sent His only begotten son into the world so that we might live through Him. In this is love, not that we loved God, but that He loved us and sent His Son to be the propitiation for our sins. (4:9–10)

Simply stated, our sin has separated us from the presence of God. Every person who has ever lived knows that they have violated their own conscience through unloving, hurtful, and destructive acts, even with people they actually love. Every one of us has wished for the downfall of another and many times we have acted on those thoughts. Scripture says, "There is not a man who continually does good and who never sins" (Eccl 7:20), and, "Who can say, 'I have cleansed my heart, I am pure from my sin?'" (Prov 20:9).

That which is not done in love for another is sin (1 Cor 13:1–2). Purposely withholding goodness from another is sin (Jas 4:17). A fundamental attitude of selfishness, empty conceit, looking out for "number one" at the expense of others is sin (Phil 2:3; Rom 2:8).

Throughout their history the Scriptures have drawn our attention to this rebellious spirit in humanity. David says in Psalm 143:2, "For in thy sight no man living is righteous." Nearly a millennium later, Paul says to the Roman Christians, "For all have sinned and fall short of the glory of God" (3:23). John shares that if we believe that we never sin, "we lie and the truth is not in us" (1 John 1:10). It requires no effort to see the results of sin around us: selfish ambition, rejection of the good, and promotion of self-satisfaction above any other moral and spiritual concern. Our culture, thoroughly entrenched in "postmodern" thought and unreason, often seems to reduce life to the formula "whatever feels good is yours to explore and act upon, no matter what." If one is alive and has volition, why not? What else is there?

Descriptions of sinfulness often return to a lack of concern or love for others. In the Gospels, Jesus said that a time will come when "the love of many will grow cold" (Matt 24:12). He seemed to draw a distinction between the usual level of humankind's self-centeredness (see Rom 1:28–32) and this future time which Paul calls "the last days" (2 Tim 1:1–5). But this is also the time when people will see the kingdom of God being manifested by the love of Christ in his followers.

As a Christian and a practicing psychoanalyst, I have witnessed an increase in books written about the subject of narcissism in Western society, particularly in the United States.[21] We can define narcissism as an inordinate focus on oneself for one's personal advancement or enlargement. It is self-absorption with a clear sense of entitlement over whatever is sought or desired. It may be expressed in actions that are attention-getting, exciting, or grandiose, and under certain conditions may develop into a "Narcissistic Personality Disorder," to use the technical term.[22] But I am not concerned here with clinical syndromes; I am speaking of the populace and society at large, our neighbors and the people we meet in the street. Our culture as a whole as adopted a focused and unrelenting understanding of entitlement, an entirely self-oriented way of looking at life and one's place in it and what one deserves from the universe. This posture has become so natural that we no longer see it, even when it is celebrated in the cacophony of "award shows" and promoted as an inspiring message in more than a few "reality shows."

In 1979 Christopher Lasch, the late sociologist and cultural examiner, published *The Culture of Narcissism: American Life in an Age of Diminishing Expectations*.[23] The book describes many modern pressures, beliefs, circumstances, and cultural changes as potent antecedents to the country's downfall. Lasch followed this powerful critique of the ordinary person's place in the culture with *The Minimal Self: Psychic Survival in Troubled Times* in 1984. Here the author went beyond portraying individual self-absorption as a strategy for getting more of a diminishing pie. Now the stakes are much higher:

> The hope that political action will gradually humanize industrial society has given way to a determination to survive the general wreckage or, more modestly, to hold one's own life together in the face of mounting pressures. The danger of personal disintegration encourages a sense of selfhood neither "imperial" nor "narcissistic" but simply beleaguered.[24]

---

21. See Twenge and Campbell, *Narcissism Epidemic*; Pinsky and Young, *Mirror Effect*; Paris, *Psychotherapy in an Age of Narcissism*. For a Christian view, see King, *Overcoming the Spirit of Narcissism*. A further group of books confront these same issues but do not include the word "narcissism" in the title. See Bauerlein, *Dumbest Generation*, and Jackson, *Distracted*.

22. For a description of the full clinical syndrome, see the *Diagnostic and Statistical Manual of Mental Disorders DSM-IV-TR*, 4th ed., s.v., "Personality Disorders." Or the reader may refer to Kohut et al., *How Does Analysis Cure?*, for a more thorough explanation of the vicissitudes of narcissistic personality disorder and its treatment.

23. Lasch, *Culture of Narcissism*.

24. Lasch, *Minimal Self*, 16.

Part I: The Norm of Christian Living

On a societal level, the beleaguered sense of self suffered by so many people translates into the kinds of attitudes and behaviors that Lasch and others have profiled as the fallback position for personal survival. It is worth noting that in *The Minimal Self*, neither the table of contents nor the index cites a single topic related to God, faith, religion, church, Christ, etc. Undoubtedly Lasch is neither unaware of the influence of these concerns nor is he hostile to their possible meanings. But from the standpoint of his critique, he must have judged that they did not have sufficient social impact to require comment.

These changes in our culture have made it much harder to call a spade a spade; or specifically, to call a sin a sin! We don't worry much about who might be hurt by our actions, since the ends mostly justify the means and sometimes you just can't avoid collateral damage! The media and the whole community promotes and exalts in selfish, egotistical, self-seeking ways of living, pandering to the lowest common denominator and threatening to make the "jackass" the mascot of the twenty-first century. As Paul describes the culture that will become more pronounced in the latter days, people will be

> lovers of self, lovers of money, boastful, arrogant, . . . ungrateful, unholy, unloving, . . . without self-control, brutal, haters of good, treacherous, reckless, conceited, lovers of pleasure rather than lovers of God; holding to a form of godliness, although they have denied its power." (2 Tim 1–5)

David, praying to God, offers a cautionary response:

> For thou art not a God who takes pleasure in wickedness; No evil dwells with thee. The boastful shall not stand before Thine eyes; Thou dost hate all who do iniquity. Thou dost destroy those who speak falsehood; the Lord abhors the man of bloodshed and deceit. (Ps 5:4–6)

A Word from Paul and Peter

The Apostle Paul speaks of spiritual maturity as a central goal of his ministry. In Colossians 1:28 he says that he seeks to present every person "complete" in Christ,[25] using the Greek word *telos*. Various senses of the word

---

25. See also Eph 4:13; 1 Cor 2:6; Phil 1:6; 3:12, 15; cf. Heb 5:14; Jas 1:4. Rodney Reeves, in *Spirituality according to Paul*, 236, has written a summation of the Apostle

suggest maturity, full-growth, perfection, completion, or hitting the target dead on; in effect, scoring a bull's-eye.[26] Paul also speaks about the "renewing the mind" of the believer in order to better understand the ways of Christ in this world (Rom 12:1–2; Eph 4:23–24).[27] He describes character qualities that the Christian should practice with other members of the body of Christ, helping outsiders to "see" that same Jesus in the believers' lives (2 Cor 2:14–15; Col 3:12–15).

The apostle offers several lists in his depictions of the New Testament saint. They include virtues such as love, gentleness, patience, humility, compassion, kindness, forgiveness, generosity, longsuffering, integrity and more. They are qualities of life that followers of Christ should sincerely express to all those around them (Eph 4:1–2; Col 3:12–15; Gal 5:22–23).[28] They represent both the outworking of God's Spirit within our lives and the conscious choices of each Christian (Gal 5:22–23; Eph 4:23–24; Col 3:12–14; Rom 13:14).[29] Commenting on Colossians 3:12–17, N. T. Wright says,

> Sounds a bit like the Beatitudes, doesn't it? And, as with Jesus' own list of characteristics, you have to decide that you intend to put them on. You have to get them out of the closet. You have to learn how to put them on the right way, like someone learning how to do up a bow tie.[30]

Sounds a whole lot like the Beatitudes to this writer as well! Simply put, the ways we conduct ourselves in genuineness as followers of Christ

---

Paul's teaching about what the mature believer in Christ looks like. He states,

> In other words, Paul would expect us to walk in the Spirit by living the crucified life (not according to the law), by promoting the welfare of all people by edifying the church (we are the hope of the world in Christ Jesus) and by caring for all creation because the glory of Christ's resurrection invades every corner of the earth (the ultimate act of God's justice is resurrection). This is the timeless gospel of Jesus Christ according to Paul.

26. See Witherington, *Letters to Philemon, the Colossians, and the Ephesians*, 147–48, 292.

27. The renewing of one's mind is of paramount importance as suggested by Paul's exhortations in both Romans and Ephesians. This settled yet dynamic experience is meant to foster the kinds of moral, relational and characterological qualities noted in Rom 12:3–21 and Eph 4:25—5:21

28. Wright, *After You Believe*, 168–69.

29. Ibid., 142–48.

30. Ibid., 147.

should echo the life of Christ for anyone to hear and see. In Paul's words, we are to live out a "sincere faith" (1 Tim 1:5).[31]

The faith that allows us to "be steadfast, immovable, always abounding in the work of the Lord, knowing that your toil is not in vain in the Lord" (1 Cor 15:58) arises from the life and power of Jesus Christ within us (2 Cor 13:5; Rom 8:9; 1 Cor 15:10; Phil 2:13). It is the power flowing from salvation; it is sourced in the transformation of the new believer at his conversion. Peter tells us that God "has caused us to be born again to a living hope through the resurrection of Jesus Christ from the dead" (1 Pet 1:3). He further says,

> Seeing that His divine power has granted to us everything pertaining to life and godliness, through the true knowledge of Him who called us by His own glory and excellence. For by these He has granted to us His precious and magnificent promises, in order that by them you might become partakers of the divine nature, having escaped the corruption that is in the world by lust. (2 Pet 1:3–4)[32]

Like his fellow apostle Paul, Peter goes on to challenge believers to live out the gifts that the Holy Spirit has given to them. In 2 Peter 1:5 he exhorts, "Now for this very reason also, applying all diligence, in your faith supply," followed by an inventory of virtues that the follower of Christ should display: moral excellence, knowledge, self-control, perseverance, godliness, brotherly kindness, and love (v. 6). These qualities render the Christian "neither useless nor unfruitful in the true knowledge of our Lord Jesus Christ" (1 Pet 1:8).

The instructions given to us by the apostles of Christ are meant to be taken at face value. Their descriptions of the transformation in the life of the believer are not theological constructs to memorize and file away. They speak of an actuality, as real as that of physical birth or characteristics. You are 5 feet 8 inches tall, you are indwelt by the Spirit of Christ; you have black hair and brown eyes, you are an ambassador of Christ; you have been born into this world, you have been born again into a new sphere of existence. One realm is physical, one is of spirit. Each is as genuine and "real" as the

---

31. Wuest, *Word Studies*, 28.

32. The "living hope" of 1 Pet 1:3, Jesus Christ within us is the "divine power" spoken of in 2 Pet 1:3. This highlights once again the importance of our trust relationship with a Person. See Lenski, *Interpretation of the Epistles*, 255–57, for a discussion on the similarities of the opening statements of 1 and 2 Peter.

other though one is of sight and one of faith; each is to be lived out simultaneously in our everyday lives.[33]

In seminary Greek class we learned the difference between the indicative mood and the imperative mood of a statement. Briefly put, the indicative mood concerns itself with reality—that which is true and actual and experiential—while statements in the imperative are calls to action, either through commands, directions or demands.[34] Applying this understanding to the New Testament and the believer's life in Christ I saw that we are able to follow the *imperatives* of Scripture only if we believe and actually trust in the *indicatives*, i.e., the truth of what God has done for us and in us because we have received Christ as Savior and Lord. We cannot live the life unless we are able to embrace the capacities that God has bestowed on us and that we are to manifest through faith.

During Jesus' earthly ministry, people who received his grace responded with genuine expressions of gratitude and gratefulness and their lives were fundamentally altered and renewed.[35] When we, as believers, gain an experiential understanding of what God has done for us in salvation, our gratitude will likewise grow and deepen. It will manifest in how we respond to changes in our lives and especially in our relations with those around us.

How can this transformation develop within our self-experience; how do we actually *become* this? Knowing that faith is the necessary means, how do we internalize this understanding in such a fashion that it becomes both a spontaneous outworking of our lives and a steady reflective assurance of who we are? As psychotherapist Sandra Wilson warns us, without integration into lived experience the difference between "theological certainty and personal reality" may grow to be "light years apart."[36]

---

33. See Paul's description of the "outer man" and the "inner man" in 2 Cor 4:7–18, where the two spheres of existence are compared in their relationship to suffering and persecution.

34. See Dana and Mantey, *Manual Grammar of the Greek New Testament*, 165–69, 174–76.

35. See Bauckham, *Jesus and the Eyewitnesses*, 114–54, 290–318. In this well-researched work, Bauckham posits that the people named in the Gospels were identified for the purpose of historical attestation. As recipients of Jesus' grace, they are named because they were still alive and could confirm the stories in both the oral and now written traditions. Their lives really were changed by their encounter with the Lord and they became his witnesses as long as they lived.

36. Wilson, *Into Abba's Arms*, 40.

PART I: THE NORM OF CHRISTIAN LIVING

Enabling this kind of growth requires a deeper exploration of how the Christian may be motivated and empowered to live as one who loves the Lord—or as John Stott said, living "counter-culturally" for Jesus. We will begin that exploration in the next chapter.

CHAPTER TWO

The Boundless Affection of God

> He is jealous for me, love like a hurricane, I am a tree
> bending beneath the weight of His wind and mercy
> When all of a sudden, I am unaware of these
> afflictions eclipsed by glory and I realize just how
> beautiful You are and how great your affections are for me.
> And oh, how He loves us, oh. Oh how he loves us
> how He loves us all.
>
> "How He Loves"
> (John Mark McMillan, 2002)

Recently I heard Kim Walker sing "How He Loves," a song by John Mark McMillan about God's love for us, a song that touches me deeply. Walker sang with such passion and conviction that it took my breath away. His love is as powerful as a hurricane, full of spirit and mercy, eclipsing my afflictions with his glory and beauty! The singer and the song led me to a fresh experience of the very personal affection that God has for me.

Affection is a word wonderfully rich with sensation. Glancing in any thesaurus reveals a trove of synonyms such as fondness, delight, tender attachment, endearment, care, hankering, regard, and devotion. The Scriptures expand on the affection of God in passages such as Zephaniah 3:17,

Part I: The Norm of Christian Living

where the prophet says of God, "He will exult over you with joy, He will renew you in His love, He will rejoice over you with shouts of joy!" Psalm 149:4 says, "For the Lord takes pleasure in His people; He will beautify the afflicted ones with salvation" (cf. Ps 16:3).

To truly be built up in the faith, the Christian must gain an *affective* understanding of the dimensions of her salvation. When David says, "O taste and see that the Lord is good; how blessed is the man who takes refugee in Him," he speaks of a visceral sense of God's goodness (Ps 34:8). When he praises God by exclaiming, "In Thy presence is fullness of joy; in Thy right hand there are pleasures forever," we know that he experiences the relational presence of the Lord (Ps 16:11b). When the Bible speaks of the human heart responding to God's lovingkindness, it reaches beyond the cognitive, propositional part of the thinking brain and into the emotionally attuned nature of the believer. "Do not let kindness and truth leave you; bind them around your neck, write them on the tablet of your heart" (Prov 3:3). Blaise Pascal famously said, "The heart has reasons that reason cannot know."[1] Timothy Keller, in his book *The Prodigal God: Recovering the Heart of the Christian Faith*, elaborates on that same theme:

> The Bible insists on using sensory language about salvation. It calls us to "*taste and see*" that the Lord is good, not only to agree and believe it.
>
> Jesus' salvation is a *feast*, and therefore when we believe in and rest in his work for us, through the Holy Spirit he becomes real to our hearts. His love is like *honey*, or like *wine*. Rather than only believing that he is loving, we can come to sense the reality, the beauty, and the power of his love. His love can become more real to you than the love of anyone else. It can delight, galvanize, and console you. That will lift you up and free you from fear like nothing else.
>
> This makes all the difference. If you are filled with shame and guilt, you do not merely need to believe in the abstract concept of God's mercy. You must sense, on the *palate of the heart*, as it were, the *sweetness* of his mercy. Then you will know you are accepted. If you are filled with worry and anxiety, you do not only need to believe that God is in control of history. You must see, with *eyes of the heart*, his *dazzling majesty*. Then you will know he has things in hand.[2]

---

1. Pascal, *Pensées iv*, 34.
2. Keller, *Prodigal God*, 108–9, emphasis mine.

THE LOVE OF GOD IN JESUS CHRIST

We know Jesus felt deeply about his disciples—and not only the Twelve, but all those who responded to him (John 17:20–21). How many times did the Lord marvel at or respect the faith of believers who were not even Jews, such as the Roman Centurion (Matt 8:5–11, esp. 10) or the Canaanite women (Matt 15:21–28, esp. 28)? Jesus felt the same intense emotional pull for the five thousand people who had come out to hear him teach (Mark 6:34–44, esp. 34). They had probably been with him for many hours in a remote place and by the evening they were hungry but without food. So Jesus fed them bread and fish in a miraculous way! He did this not only for their physical nourishment but because he saw them as "sheep without a shepherd." Their plight moved him with tender affection.

As for his closest followers, those he would commission as apostles, Jesus loved them profoundly and completely (John 13:1). When he prayed for them in what has been called the High Priestly Prayer (John 17), He said that he had "kept" and "guarded" them so that they would not perish (17:12). That often-overlooked claim by Jesus should prompt reflection on the dangers faced by an itinerant band of young men traversing a countryside where events such as in the story of the "Good Samaritan" could occur (Luke 10:30–37)! We know that Christ intervened when the Twelve were in danger of capsizing on the Sea of Galilee during a particularly violent storm (Matt 8:23–7); and when Jesus was arrested by the Romans he said to this captors, "I told you that I Am He, if therefore you seek Me, let these go their way" (John 18:7–9). The same night all of the disciples (including Peter who actually drew his sword and physically defended Jesus) escaped from the professional soldiers of Rome and the elite of the temple guard! Clearly Jesus protected his friends from harm (John 15:5; cf. Rom 8:36). More than that he gave himself up for them; in that very hour his passion would begin, the supreme demonstration of his love for his own. Paul would say of Jesus, "who loved me and gave Himself up for me" (Gal 2:20; Eph 5:20), that to know the depth of his love is to be "filled up to all the fullness of God" (Eph 3:19).

Jesus' love mirrors the Father's love for us (Heb 1:3; Col 1:17; John 1:18; 14:9), giving us an image and a pattern for understanding our relationship with him. C. S. Lewis says that the Father's heartfelt love

> is not a senile benevolence that drowsily wishes you to be happy in your own way, not the cold philanthropy of a conscientious

magistrate, nor the care of a host who feels responsible for the comfort of his guests, but the consuming fire Himself, the love that made the worlds, persistent as the artist's love for his work and despotic as a man's love for a dog, provident and venerable as a father's love for a child, jealous, inexorable, exacting as love between the sexes.[3]

J. I. Packer, in his classic book *Knowing God*, continues Lewis's thought by saying,

> So the love of the God who is spirit is no fitful, fluctuating thing, as the love of man is, nor is it a mere impotent longing for things that may never be; it is, rather, a spontaneous determination of God's whole being in an attitude of benevolence and benefaction, an attitude freely chosen and firmly fixed. There are no inconstancies or vicissitudes in the love of the almighty God who is spirit. His love is "strong as death . . . many waters cannot quench it" (Song 8:6f.). Nothing can separate from it those whom it has once embraced (Rom 8:35–39).[4]

God loves us in order for us to make us capable of relating to him, to be in relationship with him. His love changes the one who receives it: humbling, disarming, assuring, informing, setting apart, cleansing, empowering, provoking, inspiring, and forgiving the receiver. The Apostle John sums it all by declaring that God's love enables us to become, and therefore to be called, "children of God" (1 John 3:1).

The essential point for our purposes is that God *initiates* toward us because he loves us. Theologian Kevin Vanhoozer comments on this:

> God's love for the world means that his concern passes into action, his compassion into passion—a self-communication and an identification that culminate in the incarnation and the cross.[5]

Vanhoozer's words are a commentary on John 3:16, likely the most beloved verse in the New Testament: "For God so loved the world that He gave His only begotten Son, that whoever believes in Him should not perish but have eternal life." God's love is not passive or inert; it is not "drowsy," as Lewis put it. God's love for his people and for his creation is passionate and proactive; it does what needs to be done; it is personal and relevant to

---

3. Lewis, *Problem of Pain*, 35; quoted in Hall, *God & Human Suffering*, 160.
4. Packer, *Knowing God*, 110.
5. Vanhoozer, "Love of God," 17.

those who receive it. Diogenes Allen simply says, "Divine love is active: it creates, redeems and elevates. If divine love is known and received, we come to share in this activity."[6]

THE AFFECTS OF SALVATION

In the preceding chapter I touched on some spiritual implications of the moods of verbs, particularly the indicative (events that actually occurred) and the imperative (orders or commands). Significantly, New Testament verbs relating to the believer's justification, redemption, regeneration and reconciliation are in the indicative mood; they are not commands but actual accomplished facts, settled truths about the Christian's identity. Only by deeply comprehending these truths, these changes enacted in us through the loving salvific efforts of Almighty God, can we be enabled to follow the apostolic commands in the New Testament. The empowering of the Christian's life by the Holy Spirit is unleashed by our faith in what he has done for us. The indicative *empowers* the imperative: knowing *who we are* sanctions and enables what we can *do* (1 Cor 15:10; Col 1:29).

THE GRACE OF JUSTIFICATION

For many theologians, *justification* is the fundamental descriptor for the believer's "state change" in salvation:

> In Christian theology justification is that act of God by which the sinner, who is responsible for his guilt and is under condemnation but believes in Christ, is pronounced just and righteous or acquitted, by God the Judge (Rom 3:28; 4:25; 5:16, 18; 8:28–34).[7]

Simply put, justification is God's forensic proclamation that the believer is forgiven and declared righteous before his eyes (Rom 3:24–28; 5:16–18). The theological definition continues:

> It is this declarative act of the God of grace by which He declares sinners free from the guilt and consequences of their sin through faith in the atonement of Christ.[8]

---

6. Allen, *Traces of God*, 9.
7. Petersen, "Justification," in Tenny, *Zondervan Pictorial Encyclopedia*, 3:764.
8. Ibid.

The reference to the atonement of Christ points to his substitutionary death on the cross. As the Apostle Peter said, "He Himself bore our sins in His body on the cross that we might die to sins and live to righteousness" (1 Pet 2:24; cf. 2 Cor 5:21; Col 2:14; 1 John 4:9–10). Justification occurs when God imputes our sin onto Christ; it is the greatest trade-off in history![9]

In a classic illustration of justification, a judge in a courtroom sets a guilty defendant free because the penalty for the offense was taken up by another. It is not enough to imagine a good person committing a crime and being freed simply through the good graces of the judge. Even the grace shown to the thief Jean Valjean by the bishop in *Les Miserables*, or stories of rich benefactors rescuing people deep in debt fall short as parables for this truth. It may be that Christ's substitutionary death and self-sacrificial love have more power and impact than any story can suggest.

THE WONDER OF REDEMPTION

Romans 4:24 tells us we have been "justified as a gift by His grace through the redemption which is in Christ Jesus." Whereas justification uses the law court as a primary metaphoric image for salvation, redemption turns to the slave market. Biblical scholar R. D. Knudsen says that "in its biblical usage, redemption is intimately associated with the idea of ransom and substitution"[10]—including the purchase of human beings. Knudsen continues,

---

9. This assertion about God's imputing our sin onto Christ relates to the current controversy about penal substitutionary atonement, i.e., that Christ took the penalty of God's wrath upon himself in place of the person dead in his sin and deserving of God's punishment. With the preponderance of evidence supporting the sacrificial aspect of Christ's death—e.g., the alignment with the cultic system of the temple, Christ as "the Lamb of God who takes away the sin of the world" (John 1:29, cf. 1 Cor 5:7), and our own status as redeemed "with the precious blood, as of a lamb unblemished and spotless, the blood of Christ" (1 Pet 1:19; cf. Heb 9:12–14)—my own view aligns with penal substitution and propitiation. The cup that Jesus was to drink was not only that of tremendous suffering, but of God's wrath (Matt 20:22; Ps 75:8; Rev 14:10).

For a viewpoint that rejects penal substitution/propitiation and argues for an expiational, scapegoating metaphor for the atonement, see Green and Baker, *Recovering the Scandal of the Cross*.

For arguments counter to that position, see I. Howard Marshall, *Aspects of the Atonement*. See esp. 53–54, where the author responds to the primary arguments of Green and Baker.

10. Knudsen, "Redemption," in Tenney, *Zondervan Pictorial Encyclopedia*, 5:49.

> The heart of the biblical message of redemption is the deliverance of the people of God from the bondage of sin by the perfect substitutionary sacrifice of Jesus Christ and their consequent restoration to God and his heavenly kingdom.[11]

In Scripture God is the purchaser, using his Son's death on the cross—symbolically represented by the shedding of his blood—to make the exchange for our lives. As Peter tells us,

> Knowing that you were not redeemed with perishable things like silver or gold from your futile way of life inherited from your forefathers, but with precious blood, as of a lamb unblemished and spotless, the blood of Christ. (1 Pet 1:18–19)

When the apostle speaks of our deliverance from a "futile way of life," we understand that we have been rescued from a horrendous situation, the "bondage of sin." Paul calls it the "domain" or authority of darkness (Col 1:13–14) and says that we have been placed (transferred) to a new home, the "kingdom of the Son of His love." Paul, like Peter, tells us we have been redeemed "through His blood, the forgiveness of our trespasses according to the riches of His glory" (Eph 1:7).

THE GLORY OF REGENERATION

The third gift from the riches of salvation is regeneration. The specific Greek word for regeneration, *paliggenesia*, can be found only in Matthew 19:28 and Titus 3:5, where Paul says,

> He saved us not on the basis of deeds which we have done in righteousness but according to His mercy, by the washing of regeneration and renewing by the Holy Spirit, whom He poured out upon us richly through Jesus Christ our Savior, that being justified by His grace we might be made heirs according to the hope of eternal life. (Tit 3:5–7)

The phrase "washing of regeneration" signifies a fundamental change. We *become* again, or more precisely, we are *born* again since that is *paliggenesia's* literal meaning.[12] New Testament scholar Kenneth Wuest says, "It is the new-birth of the believing sinner to which Paul refers. Our Lord spoke

---

11. Ibid.
12. Wuest, *Word Studies*, 199–200.

Part I: The Norm of Christian Living

of it in John 3:3–7."[13] Indeed, in one of the most famous conversations in Scripture, Jesus tells the pharisee Nicodemus that in order to enter into the kingdom of God he must be born again. This second birth must be from above; not a physical rebirth but a spiritual one; a rebirthing in and through the Holy Spirit. One theologian says of this,

> The source of the new birth, as Jesus' reference to the inscrutable activity of the wind shows, lies beyond the range of our earthly experience (John 3:8). It is not enough, therefore, to call this a "new birth": it is a birth "from above," by the agency of the creative activity of the Spirit of God. The ideas of "newness," "regeneration," and the supernatural origin in the activity of the Spirit are all joined together.[14]

Though the word *regeneration* is used only once in the New Testament for the activity of God's Spirit in the believer, the concept of being made alive or being born anew appears in many other places. Peter refers to the new birth in 1 Peter 1:23. Paul alludes to the idea by calling the Christian a "new creation" (2 Cor 5:17; Gal 6:15). John speaks of believers many times as being "born of God" (1 John 2:9; 3:9; 4:7; 5:1, 4, 18). He even tells us that believers are children of God because his "seed" (*sperma*) remains in them (1 John 3:9). Some commentators read this as a reference to the word of God indwelling the believer, as in 1 John 1:10 and 2:5.[15] But it is quite possible to take John's words more directly as a metaphor, seeing the spiritual seed of the Holy Spirit as the causative agent of the new birth.

We should not be surprised to find organic language used for this regenerative activity since salvation is so fundamental and transformative. Humankind has become dead in trespasses and sins (Eph 2:1; Col 2:13). We cannot understand the deep things of God and we don't even want to, because we have a different focus and therefore a different master (1 Cor 2:14; Eph 2:1–3; 1 John 5:19). No matter the external trappings of a life that rejects Christ as Savior and Lord, the person is spiritually dead.

> The one who believes in the Son of God has the witness in himself; the one who does not believe God has made Him a liar, because he has not believed in the witness that God has borne concerning His Son. And the witness is this that God has given us eternal life, and

---

13. Ibid.
14. Knudsen, "Regeneration," in Tenney, *Zondervan Pictorial Encyclopedia*, 5:53.
15. Lenski, *Interpretation of the Epistles*, 462–63.

this life is in His Son. He who has the Son has the life; he who does not have the Son of God does not have the life. (1 John 5:10–12)

There are two kinds of people living in the world, those alive by the Spirit of God and those alive only through their temporary biological endowment. In effect, Scripture tells us that the world is filled with the walking dead.

At the risk of irreverence, one wonders whether an instinctive, uneasy awareness of this spiritual truth may underlie the themes and imagery of the "undead" that have become deeply ingrained in popular culture. The films, graphic novels, television shows and video games portray a world that, for whatever reasons, has been overwhelmed by people who act as if they are alive but are actually dead. The stories depict great battles, moral dilemmas, much suffering and gruesome deaths, yet the public continues to "devour" them and the genre keeps on growing. Perhaps this cultural obsession hides (or indirectly expresses) a longing for a fuller kind of life, a regeneration from the living death that results from our separation from spiritual truths and ultimately from God.

THE JOY OF RECONCILIATION

Regarding reconciliation, the Apostle Paul says:

> Now all these things are from God, who reconciled us to Himself through Christ, and gave us the ministry of reconciliation, namely, that God was in Christ reconciling the world to Himself, not counting their trespasses against them, and He committed to us the word of reconciliation. (2 Cor 5:18–19)

> For if while we were enemies, we were reconciled to God through the death of His Son, much more, having been reconciled, we shall be saved by His life. (Rom 5:10)

> And through Him to reconcile all things to Himself, having made peace through the blood of His cross; through Him, I say, whether things on earth or things in heaven . . . yet He has now reconciled you in His fleshly body through death, in order to present you before Him holy and blameless and beyond reproach. (Col 2:20, 22)

Here we see one of the grand unifying themes in Paul's teaching: the finished work of Christ has achieved the rapprochement between God and

Part I: The Norm of Christian Living

the people of the earth. The estrangement of our minds and our subsequent sinfulness and impiety had alienated us from God; we had been living without hope. But now we are reconciled to God because our sins have been forgiven and replaced by Christ's righteousness.[16] The atonement once again comes to the forefront. Christ on the cross has eliminated the enmity between God and humankind (Col 2:14). We have been restored through "the blood of His cross" (Col 2:20) and the "death of His Son" (Rom 5:10) because "God was in Christ reconciling the world to Himself" (2 Cor 5:19). Paul minces no words in telling us that outside of salvation we were "enemies" to God: legally guilty as lawbreakers, functionally enslaved to the selfishness of sin, and actually dead to the life of God which is the basis for all creation.

Theologian Ralph Martin expounds on the importance of grasping the depths of this truth:

> Reconciliation, the present author believes, can be presented as an interpretative key to Paul's theology and if we are pressed to suggest a simple term that summarizes his message, the word reconciliation will be the chief theme or femur of his missionary and pastoral thought and practice.[17]

Strictly speaking, the justification, redemption, and regeneration of the believer all serve to enable and support the believer's relationship to God.[18] The theological terms are dynamic: they describe actual changes in the essential being (ontology) of the person. God's work of salvation ushers in the kind of relatedness that God had in mind when he created humankind (to borrow a phrase from my longtime pastor, the Rev. Lloyd Ogilvie). The believer can experience God's kindness, gentleness, encouragement, correction, forgiveness, and especially his steadfast love because Christ has effected the reconciliation.[19]

As Timothy Keller says, salvation is "experiential." Stories, illustrations, and parables about these great transcendent themes can captivate and inspire us, provoking us into a deeper and more meaningful love for God while enlarging our reflection of his presence. In the same vein, theologian and prolific author Peter Kreeft speaks powerfully about this love:

---

16. Knudsen, "Reconciliation," in *Zondervan Pictorial Encyclopedia of the Bible*, 5:45.
17. Martin, *Reconciliation*, 5.
18. Ibid., 5–6.
19. Martin, "Reconciliation in Romans 5:1–11," 47–48.

To whom do we entrust our heart? That is, whom do we love? Love determines faith. Faith is not an intellectual opinion arrived at by abstract reasoning. It is a lived relationship of trust with a person arrived at by love and will, choice and freedom.[20]

IDENTITY AND ACTION

David Needham of Multnomah Bible College sees the believer's identity in Christ as the driver for living meaningfully and responsively as a Christian. As he puts it, "Is there a biblical relationship between awareness of personal identity, and finding meaning in life? Indeed there is!"[21]

In his book *Birthright*, Needham explores the ways the New Testament writers present the settled reality of salvation as a challenge to live a life worthy of Christ's calling. Salvation is the inheritance, indeed the birthright, of every person in Christ, and from this "equipping" comes works of righteousness that exemplify the Spirit-led life. In other words, our comprehension of our identity in Christ—as people who have been justified, redeemed, regenerated, and reconciled, and are being sanctified in partnership with the Holy Spirit—defends us against the pressures of living in this fallen world. The believer has become a "little Christ" because the Spirit of Christ dwells in her (John 14:16–18; 15:26–7; 16:7–14; Rom 8:14–17 for starters). Our trust in who we are in Christ (our identity) produces righteous and godly living (a meaningful life). Needham demonstrates this connection in Scripture by quoting a sampling of indicative/imperative couplings:

> But you are a chosen people, a royal priesthood, a holy nation, a people belonging to God [that's identity] that you may declare the praises of him who called you out of darkness into his wonderful light [that's meaning]. Once you were not a people, but now you are the people of God; once you had not received mercy, but now you have received mercy. Dear friends, I urge you, as aliens and strangers in the world [that's identity], to abstain from sinful desires, which war against your soul. Live such good lives among the pagans that, though they accuse you of doing wrong they may see your good deed and glorify God on the day he visits us [that's meaning] (1 Pet 2:9–12).

---

20. Kreeft, *God Who Loves You*, 166.
21. Needham, *Birthright*, 71.

Part I: The Norm of Christian Living

> Since, then, you have been raised with Christ [that's identity], set your hearts on the things above, where Christ is seated at the right hand of God [that's meaning] ... therefore as God's chosen people, holy and dearly loved [that's identity], clothe yourselves with compassion, kindness, humility, gentleness and patience [that's meaning] (Col 3:1, 12).
>
> For we are God's workmanship, created in Christ Jesus [that's identity] to do good works, which God prepared in advance for us to do [that's meaning] (Eph 2:10).
>
> For you were once darkness, but now you are light in the Lord [that's identity]. Live as children of light (for the fruit of the light consists in all goodness, righteousness, and truth) and find out what pleases the Lord [that's meaning] (Eph 5:8).[22]

The imperatives in these passages would not make sense and could not be obeyed unless the new realities described by the apostles have actually taken place and have been internalized by faith. In her transformed state the believer is not compelled to live a life of sin anymore; she is no longer a slave, she has a choice. This is the great arena of willful choice and living life under the grace of God.

The working out of the believer's identity, living meaningfully through the indicative/imperative progression, results in *sanctification*. This marvelous word-concept speaks to the process of being sanctified or made holy, the progressive experience of living more like Jesus Christ in the world.[23] As Paul explains in his letter to Titus:

> For the grace of God has appeared bringing salvation to all men, instructing us to deny ungodliness and worldly desires and to live sensibly, righteously and godly in the present age, looking for the blessed hope and appearing of the glory of our great God and Savior, Christ Jesus; who gave Himself for us, that He might redeem us from every lawless deed and purify for Himself a people for His own possession, zealous for good deeds. (Tit 2:11–14)

---

22. Ibid., 69–70.
23. Turner, "Sanctification," in Tenny, *Zondervan Pictorial Encyclopedia*, 5:264–65.

The Boundless Affection of God
"More Than the Concrete Christ"

The lyrical phrase above is a reference to "Christ the Redeemer," the colossal statue mounted on a peak above Rio de Janeiro, Brazil. This ninety-eight-foot concrete structure has long stood as a symbol of Christ's presence in its host city, and indeed in all the world; it reminds all who see that "God so loved the world. . . . " Yet despite the great "weight" of that artwork and that message, we each need something more in our lives than an intellectual understanding of John 3:16. In the first verse of his first letter John tells us that he and his fellow disciples saw, heard, beheld, and touched the "Word of Life":

> And the life was manifested and we have seen and bear witness and proclaim to you the eternal life, which was with the Father and was manifested to us—what we have seen and heard we proclaim to you also, that you also may have fellowship with us; and indeed our fellowship is with the Father and with His Son Jesus Christ. And these things we write, so that our joy may be made complete. (1 John 1:2–4)

When John or any other New Testament author speaks of fellowship and joy with Jesus Christ, we know that they mean so much more than adherence to an abstract truth. It's the contrast between "cognitively believing in God and emotionally connecting, trusting and walking with Him everyday."[24] Christians too often compartmentalize their relationship with God, reducing it to a belief system, a rule-based morality, or a propositional statement. This simply will not do. As eighteenth-century preacher Jonathan Edwards once said,

> There is a difference between believing that God is holy and gracious, and having a new sense on the heart of the loveliness and beauty of that holiness and grace. The difference between believing that God is gracious and tasting that God is gracious is as different as having a rational belief that honey is sweet and having the actual sense of its sweetness.[25]

This "sense of [His] sweetness," this aroma, this taste, internalized as our identity in Christ, draws us to the path where we "walk in love, just as Christ also loved us and gave Himself up for us, an offering and a sacrifice

---

24. Clinton and Straub, *God Attachment*, 29.

25. Kimnach et al., *Sermons of Jonathan Edwards*, 127–28; quoted in Keller, *Prodigal God*, 108.

to God as a fragrant aroma" (Eph 5:2). Embracing the love of Jesus spreads an aroma of Christ to all around us (2 Cor 2:14). People will come to desire the love of God for his children because they see this love incarnated in us![26] If instead they see a faith that lacks "aroma," a faith devoid of any passion, our words to them about the Savior may not make any sense. And what will become of a person who is deeply loved, appreciated and enjoyed by another, but is unable to experience the reality of that love?

The gracious, virtuous, obliging, agreeable, profitable, gentle, and *kind* disposition of God invites and beckons us to enter into salvation in all of its wonders. Our direct relationship with God is of such magnitude that all else depends on this. We connect every day with the living God, we are loved by the One who is Personhood, who is far more than the sum total of our propositional descriptions.

To live genuinely as a Christian, few things are more important than this true, direct knowledge of the ways of our God and his loving work for us and in us. What then can we make of Paul's assertion that a Christian cannot know in ways that he ought to know? From a biblical perspective, how can we really *know* that we have the true knowledge that is so essential to our lives? To seek practical answers to these questions we must turn to another subject: the various ways that human beings actually learn relational truth.

---

26. The words of the late Brennan Manning in *Abba's Child*, 140, are poignant:
   > The Christian commitment is not an abstraction. It is a concrete, visible, courageous, and formidable way of being in the world forged by daily choices consistent with inner truth. A commitment that is not visible in humble service, suffering discipleship, and creative love is an illusion.

PART II

Oh, You Got to Carry That Weight

CHAPTER THREE

Knowing, Being, Doing

> This child is so small its mind is not fully developed
> to deal with the world in rational intellectual terms
> and so it makes contact with the world in other ways:
> in sucking in touching and being touched...
>
> "Our Craving"
> (Ulrich Schaffer, 1980)[1]

THE EFFECTS OF AFFECTS

The past thirty years have seen increasing interest in the role played by affects in the development of our self-understanding and our understanding of the world. Webster defines "affect" in two forms: as a verb ("to have an effect on; influence; produce a change in; implies the producing of an effect strong enough to evoke a reaction") and as a noun ("an emotion or feeling attached to an idea, a stimulus arousing an emotion, feeling, or mood").[2]

---

1. Schaffer, *For the Love of Children*, 5.
2. *Webster's New World Dictionary of the American Language*, s.v. "affect."

Part II: Oh, You Got to Carry That Weight

Psychoanalysts tend to use the word in its nominative sense. It indicates a clear reactive emotional experience, an experience that produces an effect in the person's state of mind and possibly their circumstances. Michael Lewis describes affects as "all states that are not cognitive by nature. Thus such bodily sensations as hunger, fatigue, and pain are affects."[3] Psychoanalyst Joseph Jones quotes a definition from Laplanche and Pontalis:

> It connotes any affective state, whether painful or pleasant, whether vague or well defined, and whether it is manifested in the form of a massive discharge or in the form of a general mood.[4]

Jones goes on to say,

> Within the framework of psychoanalytic theory, diverse emotions such as love, hate, and fear; bodily sensations such as hunger, thirst, and physical pain; and moods such as mania and depression are usually lumped together as affects. . . . The apparent preference for the more scientific-sounding term "affect" is sometimes justified on the ground that the terms of our everyday vocabulary—words such as feelings and emotions—are too difficult to define.[5]

One can see that "affects" may take on the composite meanings of words such as emotions, feelings, sensations, dispositions, and moods. In this book I use the term to reference all types of "gut level," integral, emotional felt-experiences. They may be expressed at various levels of awareness but they inevitably impact a person's subjective state of mind.

Relationally speaking, affects govern each person's attitudes toward the other. The particular affective experience of the other is based on several factors. It can be (and typically will be to some extent) highly influenced by previous experiences of persons similar to the person one is relating to in the present moment. It may be shaped by conjecture, inference, or even faulty knowledge of the other person. It can be impacted by a person's fantasies of positive or negative relatedness drawn from outside cultural sources such as the media or traditions. It could also be generated from an honest encounter with the other person where mutual respect is communicated in the dyad; a relational matrix where dialogue is practiced as the touchstone for communications. I define true dialogue as a mutual expressing: it is just as important for me to hear and understand what you

---

3. Lewis, *Shame*, 13.
4. Jones, *Affects as Process*, 39.
5. Ibid.

are expressing as it is for me to experience this from you.[6] True dialogue naturally leads to better understanding between two people. In this kind of relationship each person is free to express what they are feeling and are not chastised for spontaneous displays of emotion. Affectively speaking, there is freedom from the fear that one may be rejected because of how one expresses their gut-level feelings.

The capacity for knowing that you are loved and accepted comes from experiences on an affective level. You are touched in loving ways; you are told with caring words, paralinguistically congruent with their meanings (use of a soft voice, smooth spacing, and slow delivery); you can see converging physical expressions in the other person's appearance, the look, body posture, and actions. Together the experiences provide a consistent manifestation of love that you feel deeply. You receive it as a profound showing of respect.

In this explanation, love is as love does. It is meant to be felt by the other person; to be received with joy. Diogenes Allen says of this receiving,

> To receive from another requires profound respect. In fact, it takes exactly the same kind of respect to receive as it does to give. Unless another human being is respected as a reality independent of oneself, the act of giving becomes patronizing and insulting. Agape is not to be characterized as always giving and never receiving, or as freedom from even the desire to receive. Rather, agape is the profound respect for the reality of others, a respect which makes it compatible both with giving and receiving. When agape is present as an ingredient in friendship and romantic love, these relations in which we give and receive can be unselfish.[7]

"Respect for the reality of others" understands that they live a life centered in their own experience and volition. This truth must be acknowledged and embraced with one's own subjectivity. The recognition of this separateness and its partial overcoming in the desire to know and be aware of the other makes "meeting" the other deeply rewarding. Martin Buber describes this meeting of persons profoundly in his philosophy of existential encounter:

> Human life and humanity come into being in genuine meetings. There man learns not merely that he is limited by man, cast upon is own finitude, partialness, need of completion, but his own

6. Friedman, *Martin Buber*, 98–113.

7. Allen, *Love*, 26.

relation to truth is heightened by the other's different relation to the same truth—different in accordance with his individuation, and destined to take seed and grow differently. Men needed and it is granted to them, to confirm one another in their individual being by means of genuine meetings. But beyond this they need and it is granted to them, to see the truth, which the soul gains by its struggle, light up to others, the brothers, in a different way, and even so be confirmed.[8]

THE KNOWLEDGE OF BEING LOVED

The reader may wonder what all this talk of affects, love, and existential encounter has to do with really knowing what we have knowledge of. It seems simple enough to say that a person knows something if he can remember the facts, follow the directions, pass a test, recite important information. Or perhaps a person knows something if she can intellectually teach it with accuracy or use other corresponding data to explain it better. Indeed, in those cases we can agree that the person knows the subject with some acumen, at least on a cognitive level (which given the subject matter may be all that is necessary).

What about relational knowing? What about knowing that someone genuinely loves you or forgives you? How does a person gain assurance that this knowledge is really the "truth" so that it affects what she thinks or feels about herself, or that it changes the way he behaves? Is it the same as knowing that you are your father's son, or that you love soccer, or that you love ice cream? When do we really trust the words "I love you" when they are spoken to us by parents or by a romantic partner, or even by a spouse?

We all recognize that knowledge about facts, dates, places, incidents, and other hard data is of a different kind than knowing that we are loved or forgiven. Perhaps we can differentiate the two by designating the knowledge of facts, etc., as astuteness, or intelligence, or comprehension. The second kind of knowing we could describe as a realizing or an appreciation, or even a grasping of the essence of this knowledge. Obviously these are two very different experiences, two kinds of learning, two ways of knowing. My concern in this chapter is the second way of knowing: the encounter or experience of what it means to be loved and forgiven.

---

8. Buber, *Knowledge of Man*, 59.

I would contend that this is the true knowledge of God's love for us in Jesus Christ. Paul's prayer in Ephesians 3:14–21 is very instructive here. In vv. 18–19 he asks that believers "may be able to comprehend with all the saints what is the breath and length and height and depth, and to know the love of Christ that *surpasses knowledge*, that you may be filled up to all the fullness of God" (emphasis mine).

How amazing to think that one can know something that surpasses knowledge. "Knowing" how personally and how deeply one is loved by Jesus is the experience of utter acceptance from God! Paul even seems to support the two kinds of knowing described above. In Ephesians 3:18 the apostle first says that the believer should comprehend (*katalabesthai*) something; "to come to a decided conclusion from facts vividly presented to the attention."[9] He wishes us to recognize and be aware of the immensity of God's love for us as demonstrated by the cross of Christ (Eph 1:7), by his rich mercy toward us (Eph 2:4), and by the promise of his gracious kindness for evermore (Eph 2:7)! Along with other Christians we can celebrate the efficacy of God's love in thoroughly meeting our need of reconciliation. We are to talk about this whenever we are together (Phil 2:1–3).

Paul then simply prays that the believer would "know the love of Christ that surpasses knowledge." The phrase is intentionally oxymoronic: it combines two contradictory terms to convey a special meaning. How can a person know something beyond knowledge? Or as Ben Witherington says, to "know the unknowable" or "perceive the imperceptible"?[10] John Eadie in 1883 offered this description of Christ's love:

> It led from Divine immortality to human agonies and dissolution, for the victim was bound to the cross not by the nails of the military executioner, but by the "cords of love." It loved repulsive unloveliness, and unnourished by reciprocated attachment, its ardor was unquenched, nay is unquenchable, for it is changeless as the bosom in which it dwells. Thus it may be known, while yet it "passeth knowledge"; thus it may be experimentally known while still in its origin and glory it surpasses comprehension, and presents new and newer phases to the loving and inquiring spirit. For one may drink of the spring and be refreshed, and his eye may take in at one view its extent and circuit, while he may be able neither

---

9. Eadie, *Commentary on Ephesians*, 251.
10. Witherington, *Letters to Philemon, the Colossians, and the Ephesians*, 276.

to fathom the depth nor mete out the volume of the ocean whence it has it origin.[11]

Eadie puts forth that while this tremendous love of Christ "passeth knowledge" it can be known on another level or in a different manner. It can be known *experimentally*—that is, through experience or by means of repeatable encounters. You can experience Christ's love in such a way as to appreciate its impact on you. Eadie describes the encounter as drinking from a spring of water and being refreshed by it. This "knowing" is an experimentally refreshing experience which opens the eyes of the believer to the personal reality of the love of God.

To reinforce the experimental nature of knowing Christ's love for us, Paul uses a similar phrase about peace in Philippians 4:7. After urging the Philippians to not be anxious about the things of life, but to pray, letting their needs be known to God, he says: "And the peace of God which surpasses all comprehension (*nous*) shall guard your hearts and minds in Christ Jesus." The experience of peace from one's prayerful bond with Christ is said to be beyond what the mind can rationally comprehend.[12] Yet

---

11. Eadie, *Commentary on Ephesians*, 258. See also Hendriksen, *Exposition of Ephesians*, 173. Hendriksen adds to Eadie quite commendably:

> The *Lofty Ideal* is to get to know *thoroughly* Christ's deep affection, self-sacrificing tenderness, passionate sympathy, and marvelous outgoingness. All of these are included in love but do not exhaust it. Paul prays that the addressed may appropriate and know this *love* in all its breadth and length and height and depth! . . . What is meant is simple this: Paul prays that the Ephesians (and all believers down through the centuries) may be so earnest and zealous in the pursuit of their objective that they will never get to the point where they will say, "We have arrived. *Now* we know all there is to know about the love of Christ" . . . so also the apostle prays that the addressed may concentrate so intensely and exhaustively on the immensity and glory of Christ's love that they will come to understand *that this love ever surpasses knowledge*. The finite heart and mind can never fully grasp or know *infinite* love. Even in the life hereafter God will never say to his redeemed, "Now I have told you all there is to be told about this love. I close the book, for the last page has been read." There will always be more and more and still more to tell. And that will be the blessedness of the heavenly life. (italics original)

12. Eadie, *Commentary on Philippians*, 251. Eadie says of this peace,

> The noun *nous* is here used of mind in its power of grasp or conception. . . . The mind cannot rightly estimate this peace, or rise to an adequate comprehension of it. It is so rich, so pure so noble, so fraught with bliss, that you cannot imagine its magnitude.

the reception of this grace protects both our feelings (our heart) and our thinking (our mind) from debilitating fear.

In short, there is an experience of God's love and peace that cannot be understood reasonably but it is still *known*. It is known with a sensitive, intuitive awareness that its receiver can trust as real. One feels this gift from God; one tastes it (Ps 34:8)!

"TO KNOW, KNOW, KNOW YOU IS TO LOVE, LOVE, LOVE YOU"

This deepened understanding of what it means to know someone (or something about them) is supported by the much-celebrated use of the Hebrew verb *yada* ("know") for sexual intercourse. In speaking of sexual relations between Adam and Eve, Genesis 4:1 says literally, "Now the man knew his wife Eve and she conceived and gave birth to Cain." A few verses later in 4:17 the Scripture says, "And Cain knew his wife and she conceived." The multiple aspects of the word *Yada* may include:

> To perceive, to be sensible of by sight, by touch; but chiefly in the mind; hence to understand, observe; to consider; to mark and observe with a purpose. To come to the knowledge of by seeing, by hearing, and by experience.... In Hebrew words of knowledge imply also the exercise of the affections.[13]

The word is used of sexual intercourse because it connotes a knowing by touch, by experience, and by "the exercise of the affections." We may safely assume that Genesis 4:1 is not saying that Adam knew Eve by some abstract intellectual reasoning! The knowledge he received of his wife came straight through the experience of his senses and his awareness of the encounter. Paul Jewett, in his book *Who We Are: Our Dignity as Human: A Neo-Evangelical Theology*, says,

> The "oneness of mind and heart" that describes the marriage bond is, in our judgment, entailed in the biblical expression "to know" as used of sexual intercourse. ("Adam knew [*yada*] Eve his wife, and she conceived" [Gen 4:1].) Such an expression is no mere euphemism. To know another person, that person must disclose him or herself to the other. While it is true that husband and wife come to know each other through the fellowship of married life generally,

---

13. Wilson, *Old Testament Word Studies*, 240.

the physical intimacy of coitus in the larger context of married love is an apt symbol of such disclosure. The verb "to know" describes what happens in intercourse with a depth of meaning that goes far beyond the physical act itself as a biological mechanism for procreation.[14]

FROM ATHENS TO JERUSALEM

The various uses of the Hebrew word *yada* illustrate the different means by which knowledge can be taken in and can be said to be known. In a general way the two distinct ways of knowing were also exemplified by the two dominant cultures of the ancient Mediterranean world, the Greek and the Hebrew.

A generation ago the Norwegian theologian and linguist Thorleif Bomen wrote an influential book addressing this topic, under the simple title *Hebrew Thought Compared with the Greek*. In it he speaks to the differences between the two cultures' views of life and living. He states for instance,

> There are two ways to approach reality and its appearances intellectually and to grasp them: we call these two ways logical thinking and psychological understanding. When we think logically we place ourselves objectively and impersonally outside the matter and ask what is the strict truth about it; when we would understand a matter psychologically, we familiarize ourselves with it and through sympathetic pursuit of its development we try to grasp it as a necessity . . .
>
> When we speak hereinafter of psychological understanding and logical thinking, we mean the two different ways of thinking by means of which the reflecting man is able mentally to appropriate reality; formally speaking they are mutually exclusive, but speaking materially they are complementary.
>
> It is hardly necessary to demonstrate that Greek thinking is of the logical sort. . . . It is considerably more necessary to penetrate the peculiarity of Israelite thinking, first because the psychological kind of thing is, in general, more foreign to us than the logical.[15]

The "peculiarity of Israelite thinking" concerns that which is grasped and understood through experience. To a Jew in conversation, it is the

---

14. Jewett with Shuster, *Who We Are*, 226.
15. Boman, *Hebrew Thought Compared with Greek*, 193, 195.

dialogue that discerns the truth before the grand statement. One knows in her being that a fact or pronouncement is true; it matters in her actual life to know it. Bomen continues,

> In short, the Hebrews really do not ask what is true in the objective sense, but what is subjectively certain, what is faithful in the existential sense; therefore , it is not what is in agreement with impersonal objective being that interests them, but what is in agreement with the facts that are meaningful for them. This shows that Hebrew thought is directed toward events, living, and history in which the question of truth is of another sort than in natural science. In such matters the truth is the completely certain, sure, steady, faithful.[16]

When compared to the Hebrew, the Greek understanding of truth can be characterized as static, i.e., "harmonious, prudent, moderate and peaceful. This means as coming to conclusion, to be at rest with it."[17] In speaking about God, the essence of the Supreme Being for Plato would be his complete power, a static attribute. For the Hebrew, "the prodigious dynamic of God is eternal, real and therefore *is*. The distinction lies . . . in the antithesis between rest and movement."[18] Greeks seek for clarity, for evidence that they got it right; objective truth is seen as genuine truth; it is seen with the objectifying eye. In contrast, "Hebrews seek personal certainty about the laws of life, of history, and morals."[19]

For the Hebrew, to know someone (or something) relationally is of more importance than to only know it through abstraction. Relational knowledge is practical, personal, affective and effective. If knowledge is only theoretical or conceptual it cannot be as valuable or meaningful—that is, as useful or helpful for one's life. The Hebrew and therefore the Judeo-Christian reception of truth is compromised if it is only approached or applied in an intellectual fashion. Psychiatrist Curt Thompson gives an example of this when he says,

> Many of us hold steadfastly to our theological and scriptural mandates. We may find that what we are told to believe does not match our intuitive experience and often lacks relevance in our daily lives. Our Christian faith seems to be mostly a cognitive assent

---

16. Ibid., 202.
17. Ibid., 27.
18. Ibid., 54–55, italics original.
19. Ibid., 9.

to a series of rational beliefs that don't seem to help us resolve our family conflicts, our struggles with sexuality, our sense of isolation, or our ongoing burden of shame and guilt....

We keep hoping for God's magic wand to sweep over and transform us—but his incantation never seems to arrive.[20]

For too many of us, the great themes touched on in this book—such as understanding the reality of redemption, or reconciliation, or being able to grasp with one's heart the profundity of God's love and forgiveness—end up filed away in the scholastic drawer in our minds. Modern academic circles typically emphasize informational learning or quantitative learning with measurable outcomes, an approach certainly appropriate for subjects like the physical sciences. However, the social sciences (including the "queen of the sciences," theology) do not lend themselves to informational learning for measurable outcomes!

We can see the influence of the cognitive-oriented way of learning in practices such as Bible memorization in conservative churches. Of course this practice is valuable for a believer's spiritual growth; a good Jew in the first century would not even give it a second thought, since in a primarily oral culture memorization was a basic requirement for sharing and disseminating texts. However the Bible's primary concern is "meditating" on the Word of the Lord (Ps 1:1–3). We must not only know what the text says, but what it is trying to communicate to us about our lives. We must allow the word to impact how we live for Jesus and care for others (Rom 15:1–7; 2 Tim 3:16–17). Over the years, especially in the public square, we have seen too many Christians attempt to speak God's word about ethics, relationships, and public policy while not living out that word to the very people they were speaking to.

David said, "Thy word have I treasured in my heart that I might not sin against Thee" (Ps 119:11). In that psalm, David uses a plethora of words to describe his immersion into God's Word (or law, commandments, precepts, testimonies). He says that he delights in, meditates on, loves, longs for, observes, keeps, cleaves to, and learns the Word of God. "Thy Word is a lamp to my feet and a light to my path.... I have inherited Thy testimonies forever, for they are the joy of my life" (Ps 119:105, 111). If meditating on the significance and personal application of God's word becomes the joy of our lives, we have gone somewhere far beyond only a cognitive comprehension!

---

20. Thompson, *Anatomy of the Soul*, 15.

DOES THE LEFT KNOW WHAT THE RIGHT IS DOING?

In recent years we've seen much discussion about the left and right hemispheres of the brain and their contrasting roles in learning and appropriating ideas and experiences. The field of neuroscience has been very helpful in exploring the actions of the brain in our mental and emotional processes.

In Curt Thompson's book, he explains that the two sides of the brain are "connected by a strip of tissue known as the corpus callosum. It is through this tissue that the two hemispheres have the opportunity to 'talk' with each other through the neurons synapsing with each other."[21] Since each of these hemispheres carries out differing duties with different foci, the central communication plays a crucial role.

The right hemisphere comes "on line" earlier in our development and its primary focus is a person's subjective state. Situational spatial realities, bodily experience, awareness of nonverbal communicational cues of different kinds, holistic consciousness of environmental contexts, nuanced attentiveness to social surrounds, and emotional levels of communication are all associated with right brain processing.[22]

The left hemisphere develops more fully during the end of the second year of life, right around toddlerhood. Its primary foci are "language, linear, logical, and lateral processing—the four L's."[23] One can see that left brain processing provides a more defined or cohesive understanding of a given event. The development of language allows for experience to "make sense," be thoughtfully reflected on, or repeated in one's thinking. In relationships, left hemisphere functions create meanings from the data of interactions. That data can begin as right-brain oriented items such as nonverbal cues or paralinguistic signals (tone of voice, intensity of voice, pauses, etc.). The same interaction will be processed by the left hemisphere through the use of words, checking to see whether the situation made sense or the meanings were confused. Thompson provides illustrations for this kind of encounter:

> For example, if a child feels ashamed when his father uses an overly harsh and demeaning tone of voice with him, the child's left hemisphere will try to make sense of why he feels so bad. If his father does not repair that emotional injury by apologizing and owning responsibility for his own actions, the boy will likely conclude that

---

21. Ibid., 33.
22. Ibid., 33–34.
23. Ibid., 34–35.

he did something to provoke his father. He will not likely figure out that his father is responsible for creating the shame he feels. The child will probably feel responsible and will try not to upset is father so that he won't experience the same feelings of shame again.[24]

If the child is taught that giving the right answer or not questioning adult authority are critical priorities, he will consciously develop his left brain skills of logical evaluative thought to protect himself from future hurt. He will likely deny any deep emotions of fear or disappointment or anger since expressing them would only invite more rejection. Psychiatrist Iain McGilchrist says of left hemispheric responses,

> The values of clarity and fixity are added by the processing of the left hemisphere which is what makes it possible to control, manipulate and use the world . . . the implicit is unpacked; language becomes the instrument of serial analysis; things are categorized and become familiar. Affect is set aside, and superseded by cognitive abstraction; the conscious mind is brought to bear on the situation thoughts are sent to the left hemisphere for expression in words and the metaphors are temporarily lost or suspended.[25]

Appreciating how the brain processes experience into different modes of understanding becomes especially important when we consider that the development of both hemispheres is impacted by life events. The plasticity of the brain has been a hot topic for some time now. UCLA psychiatrist Daniel Siegel stated in 1999 that "research has provided no data as yet to answer the question of, can poor or missed development of right brain functioning be repaired by new experience?"[26] By the year 2010 Siegel, in his book *The Mindful Therapist: A Clinician's Guide to Mindsight and Neural Integration*, described psychotherapeutic interventions that can foster changes in the brain's neural pathways:

> As clinicians we can feel the pulse of integration and when chaos or rigidity are present we can then strategically place a spotlight of attention on the various domains that are blocking the linkage of differentiated aspects of a person's life. Neuroplasticity—the process of change in the structural connections in the brain in

---

24. Ibid., 35.
25. McGilchrist, *Master and His Emissary*, 195.
26. Siegel, *Developing Mind*, 194.

response to experience—is promoted with such focused awareness and serves to activate specific neural groups simultaneously.[27]

Right brain functioning embraces the significance of particular experiences on an intuitive level. It "hears" the meanings in the affects that are provoked by human relatedness. The integration of left brain factual analysis can be helpful if one's affects have not been guided into meanings that contradict the words being spoken. Right hemisphere development can be powerfully affected by trauma or abuse, especially by significant others in childhood.[28] The cumulative effect of parental misattunement and disregard for core aspects of the self of the child also can distort right brain development.[29]

The ability to feel satisfied or pleased with oneself, let alone fair with oneself, becomes truncated by the need to judge according to the abstract standards that harsh or insensitive words provoke in us. We will explore this question of misattunement or "parental disregard" in depth in chapter 5, "Train Up a Child." The issue is not about simple disagreements or situational disputes such as eating too much candy, staying up too late, or whether a teenager can borrow the car. Rather it is a fundamental clash over what Proverbs 22:6 calls the child's "way." As I have mentioned, that "way" represents some fundamental aspect or aspects of the young person's life (temperaments, aptitudes, abilities, proclivities, physical capabilities, energy levels, etc.) that are prevented from developing or even actively rebuffed. The child experiences this kind of conflict as a deeply personal form of rejection.

When children are young, such as preschool age, they are inclined to strictly adhere to parental demands. The integrity of their attachment must be protected at all costs. I will explore the importance of the developing of a secure attachments in chapter 6, "Help from 'The Study of the Soul.'" In this regard, Thompson associated the impact of *connected* parental relationships with well-developed neurobiological *connections*. He deserves being quoted at length.

> Parents who are mindful of their children's needs and flexible in their interactions with them are literally assisting the neural wiring process in their children's brains. This enables their children to be open and receptive to the image of God who is interested

27. Siegel, *Mindful Therapist*, xxiv.
28. See Schore, *Science and Art of Psychotherapy*, 52–117, 259–320.
29. Ibid.

and delighted in them, compassionate and full of grace when they stumble, yet willing to discipline them without simultaneously shaming. As they grow older, when life feels less integrated, more disconnected ... they will still retain *in their neural circuitry* the imprint of a God who is *there*. A God of bone and blood. A God of strength, mercy, and mystery. A God of history, acting in their lives, the proof being in what they feel in a manner that is undeniable, rooted in their very bodies. And they do not simply have an awareness of this being "true" as a *fact* (an explicit encoded, dominantly left hemisphere function), but rather as an existential, emotional, remembered experienced *as a recalled autobiographical memory* (one that requires the integration of the left and right, as well as lower and higher regions of the brain).[30]

I would caution the reader not to give ascendance or precedence to the right hemisphere of the brain with its intuitive, affect-oriented self-awareness. God created humankind with complementary aspects that are designed to work together. It is, however, reasonable to regret that our society has elevated cognitive mastery above all else and that the church has for the most part has followed suit. It is no new idea that the natural sciences have fixed the agendas of the social sciences to their detriment. Iain McGilchrist's book *The Master and His Emissary: The Divided Brain and the Making of the Modern World* speaks about the dominance of left hemisphere thinking in our society today. As summarized on the back cover:

> The left and right hemispheres have differing insights, values and priorities. Each as a distinct "take" on the world ... the right hemisphere sees itself as connected to the world, whereas the left hemisphere stands aloof from it ...
> We need both hemispheres, but, McGilchrist argues, the left hemisphere has become so far dominant that we're in danger of forgetting everything that makes us human ... he traces how the left hemisphere has grabbed more than its fair share of power, resulting in a society where a rigid and bureaucratic obsession with structure, narrow self-interest and a mechanistic view of the world hold sway, at an enormous cost to human happiness and the world around us.[31]

I would contend that much of the evangelical church has favored the kinds of "knowing" that writers like McGilchrist, Siegel, and Thompson

---

30. Thompson, *Anatomy of the Soul*, 120, italics original.
31. McGilchrist, *Master and His Emissary*, back cover.

Knowing, Being, Doing

have described as essentially left-brained.[32] In other words, the church has favored the Greek approach to reality over the Hebraic. The cognitive, analytically informed investigation of life is of course necessary, but it cannot stand by itself as a complete knowledge of the subject.[33] The different approaches to knowing need each other because each "knows, embraces, or welcomes" aspects that the other does not.[34] However we must be clear that

> [it is] the right hemisphere that is in direct contact with the embodied lived world: the left hemisphere world is by comparison, a virtual, bloodless affair. In this sense, the left hemisphere is

---

32. In no way do I wish to disparage books that have been written during the last twenty years about how the church has become anti-intellectual regarding the factual or apologetic aspects of the faith. Your mind matters! (As John Stott said over forty years ago in his book by the same name.) My conflict is with the sometimes misunderstood and therefore misleading mentality that Christianity is first and foremost a set of dogmas that are to be understood and then believed in (a predominantly left-brain function). Obviously this leaves out the fundamental reality that we receive Jesus Christ through faith (all that he is, and also him personally). Relational experience takes the data and blends it with our trust in our emotional responses to being loved and accepted (a predominantly right-brain function). Words such as joy, peace, kindness, forgiveness, and most of all love, are to be taken in affectively as a result of knowing their historical/ theological facts and motivations. When Scripture talks about loving your neighbor, some in the church spend more time defining what love means on paper and less time on being that love to other people. Sometimes it is hard to discern when a "mind-writer" is speaking to the weak state of Christian thinking as it confronts the world, or to a personal belief of the ascendency of intellectual understanding over intuitive or affective understanding. For further reading in this area I recommend Moreland, *Love Your God with All Your Mind*; Blamires, *Christian Mind*; and Stott, *Your Mind Matters*.

33. See Taylor, *Myth of Certainty*, 126–37. Addressing skepticism and the ways that the church can get caught up in the intellectual "doubting games" of the secular world when it comes to determining truth (134), he says,

> The church also plays this game to a great extent. The mystery of the gospel, the paradox of the incarnation, the wondrous enigma of grace are freeze-dried into a highly rationalized and/or authoritarian system of theologies, codes, rules, prescriptions, orders of service, and forms of church government. Everything is written down, everything is organized, so that all can be certain and those in error detected.
>
> I am not advocating irrationalism, obscurantism, sloppy thinking, or sappy emotionalism. I am merely suggesting that among the things one should be skeptical about in our skeptical age is the unchallenged primacy of this way of ascertaining truth. *It must be balanced by other ways of knowing* which employ faculties at least as powerful as reason and which encourage risk and adventure. (emphasis mine)

34. McGilchrist, *Master and His Emissary*, 199.

"parasitic" on the right. It does not itself have life: its life comes from the right hemisphere.[35]

Right hemisphere / left hemisphere; Hebraic thought / Greek thought; heart / mind. The pairing can be viewed as dynamic opposites, but to see either as standing against the other is to miss the essence of their relationship. Each informs the other in dialectical fashion. Each member of the dyad contributes to a complete entity: right and left hemispheres make a total brain; Hebraic and Greek thought make an enriched mind; heart and mind make a complete inner life.

TELL ME THE OLD, OLD STORY OF JESUS AND HIS LOVE

Bringing this perspective to the growth and maturation of the Christian, we can see the crucial need for taking a holistic approach to understanding the Word of God. Certainly the Scriptures are to be studied and their ideas and structures recognized with our intelligence (2 Tim 2:15; 3:16; Acts 17:11; Rom 15:4). But we must also meditate on them, taking in and contemplating the descriptions of people and events, pondering both sympathetically and empathetically the situations in which the people of God found themselves (Ps 1:2–3; Ps 119; Matt 22:29). We are to teach ourselves, teach each other, and be taught by the Holy Spirit. We are to appreciate the actions of God toward his people both critically and personally; we are simultaneously observers and participants though the use of our imagination. We see, hear, and feel the love of God toward those he has dealt with (Rom 15:4; 1 Cor 10:11).

When Jesus taught he used abstract theological reasoning as well as illustrative stories called parables. He also used figures of speech such as metaphors and similes to assist his listeners' understanding.[36] Jesus was a storyteller, taking his material from the common experiences of the people, putting flesh and bones on complex theological truths.[37] How much does God love his wayward children? Consider the father of the prodigal son

---

35. McGilchrist, *Master and His Emissary*, 199–200.
36. An example of each of the ways that Jesus' thought:
"Abstract theological reasoning's"—John 5:19–47
Parables—Matt 13:1–52
Metaphors—John 6:35; 10:14
Similes—Matt 5:15–16.
37. See Witherington, *Christology of Jesus*, 207–15.

(Luke 15:11–24). How far should we go in loving our neighbor as we love ourselves (and the corollary, who is my neighbor)? As far as using all the resources at our command when in the presence of real need, as did the Good Samaritan (Luke 10:25–39). Why does the message of the gospel not change everyone who hears it? Because all people are free to receive it or not receive it, and will respond to it in their lives as they see fit, as in the Parable of the Soils (Matt 13:1–23).[38]

As we saw in the previous chapter, the major aspects of salvation can be approached both through logically reasoned argument and through stories. Justification, redemption, regeneration and reconciliation can all be illustrated by powerful popular narratives and stories that have influenced many. John Eldredge describes the importance of this primary right hemisphere modality by saying,

> Stories nourish us. They provide a kind of food that the soul craves.... Stories shed light on our lives.... Every story, great and small, shares the same essential structure because every story we tell borrows its power from a Larger Story, a Story woven into the fabric of our being.
>
> All of these stories borrow from *the* Story. From Reality. We hear echoes of it through our lives. Some things written on our hearts. A great battle to fight, and someone to fight for us. An adventure, something that requires everything we have, something to be shared with those we love and need.
>
> There is a Story written on the human heart. As Ecclesiastes has it, "He has planted eternity in the human heart" (3:11 NLT).[39]

---

38. Lloyd Ogilvie, *Autobiography of God*, 51–65. Psychologically sensitive devotional work (54) by the long time senior pastor of First Presbyterian Church of Hollywood and chaplain of the United States Senate:

> Jesus is compassionately concerned about the hearing capacity of our hearts. He knows all about us; what life has done to us and what we've done to ourselves to impair the delicate listening ability we have been given. As we catch His eye, He gives us a knowing look. He understands the grids we have placed over our hearts and how little can get through. Does He know about our set ideas and inflexible presuppositions? Is He aware of our prejudices, our wardrobe of excuses, or resistance to truth? Yes! In His gaze we can't seem to hide our hurts which have made us unfeeling. He knows how out of touch we are with our feelings about ourselves and others. Most of all, He is aware of beliefs and convictions which have been put into concrete actions of obedience. Jesus understands what's happened to our hearing hearts. When He directs our attention to the sower, we know He's talking about Himself and our hearing impediment.

39. Eldredge, *Epic*, 5, 12–13, italics original.

Part II: Oh, You Got to Carry That Weight

Fundamentally, the gospel is the true story of God's gracious love, the great work he performed in bringing his children back into relationship with himself. He gave them life, real life as it was meant to be lived. As has been said, it is "the greatest story ever told!"

We learn the truth of this story and its profound relevancy to our desperate state of need by understanding the words conceptually and applying them to ourselves humbly. Humility is a Hebrew virtue; it was of little use in the brutal world of the Roman Empire. It is a right-brain affective realization of our entire self. Our humility is rooted in our capacity to see ourselves honestly and clearly. It is the opposite of defensive pride, a self-absorbed attitude that begins with the sad discovery that I can more easily protect myself through aggrandizement than through truthful evaluations. Aggrandizement certainly has power: it influences people, it intimidates them. In developing children or young people, it is often a reaction to constant parental disregard of what the young person deems as important for his life. It creates a false sense of self-protection; or worse (the opposite response), a caving in of one's self-image, a self-doubting loss of cohesiveness and integrity. When one's intrinsic bent(s) are neglected, marginalized, or downright rejected, the self has to perform some kind of salvaging operation in order to use that which feels good to her. This rescue does not come without a cost. The uncertainty of the enterprise leaves her with continuous miscalculations of her true abilities and mistaken methods for acting them out. All kinds of self-aggrandizements may arise from this. If the child cannot muster up the courage to continue believing that she can hold on to her "way" and gives up any external manifestations of it, she may slide into a crashing loss of self with all of its accompanying depression and anxiety. This last state of affective being may have the appearance of humility but is actually a self-aberration. It has a profound effect on the Christian's relationship with God.[40]

---

40. See Thompson, *Anatomy of the Soul*, 140. Profoundly stated by a professional who has brought cutting edge research in the neurosciences into the service of biblical truth:

> How is it that despite our "belief" in God's love for us, we don't experience that love transforming our inner lives or our relationships with friends, parents, children, spouses, or neighbors? We assent to the idea of the Holy Spirit's capacity to transform us as theological dogma imbedded in the neural networks of our semantic memory. But often we don't sense God's transforming power comprehensively with our mind's right mode of being. In fact, our right mode is often overcome by our left mode's systematic tendency, so that when we're asked how God views us, we automatically respond with words like *sinful*, *depraved*, and *wicked*. And we can refer to

The importance of comprehending just how crucial our parents are to us from a spiritual, developmental, and biblical perspective has not been addressed clearly enough by the church, despite the discussions in myriads of psychotherapy or family relations books written by professionals who are Christians. In particular, the topic has not been addressed in nearly enough depth from a theological, exegetical perspective.[41] What do the Scriptures tell us about our earthly parents in comparison or in contrast with God's relationship with us? We will explore this subject in the next chapter.

---

particular passages of Scripture to prove it. We're really good at that. But *that* is not always good for *us*. (italics original)

41. One wonderful exception, where theological and psychological foci are both integrated in a user-friendly way, is the work of Ray Anderson and Dennis Guernsey, both formally of Fuller Theological Seminary. Their *On Being Family* would be a good place to start.

CHAPTER FOUR

(The) Father Knows Best

> Be a good boy, try a little harder
> You've got to measure up
> And make me prouder
>
> Be a good girl, you got to try a little harder
> That simply wasn't good enough
> To make us proud
>
> Be a good boy, push a little farther now
> That wasn't fast enough to make us happy
> We'll love you just the way you are
> If you're perfect
>
> "Perfect"
> (Alanis Morissette, 1995)

Alanis Morissette's song "Perfect" imagines a father speaking to his son and daughter and imposing certain standards. We see that he is not a very good father; in fact, he is selfish, rigid and demanding. He uses his children for his own aggrandizement and grows angry when they respond with hurt feelings. In the end he insists that they be nothing less than perfect. The heart of the song reveals his motivations:

(The) Father Knows Best

> I live through you; I'll make you what I never was
> If you're the best then maybe so am I
> Compared to him compared to her
> I'm doing this for your own damn good
> You make up for what I blew
> What's the problem, why are you crying?[1]

It hardly needs stating that children need parents who are caring and understanding and are available to them. Human infants begin life in a nearly helpless state with little more than a capacity to signal their dependency to others.[2] The child's needs for food, shelter, physical warmth, and relatedness are of the same kind as an adolescent or an adult though different in degree.

Most parents have the maturity to put their children's physical needs before their own—though the literature offers many examples of mothers and fathers who have difficulty even with this primary level of care.[3] Better parents make it a priority to know, accept and respond to their child's emotional needs as well. Woolfolk and Perry provide some perspective:

> Infants and toddlers in all cultures have emotional needs for safety, a sense of security, affection, support in regulating intense negative emotions, reciprocal interactions, language interactions, and beneficial social experiences. They need positive emotional and social experiences to build a sense of self-worth and efficacy—a sense that they have some control that makes a difference in their lives and the lives of others. Or as Bronfenbrenner stated, "All children need someone who is just crazy about them."[4]

We are reminded of the Apostle Paul description of a nursing mother, one who "tenderly cares for her own children" (1 Thess 2:7) and cherishes

---

1. "Perfect," by Alanis Morissette and Glen Ballard (1995).

2. See Stern, *Present Moment in Psychotherapy*, 83–89. Stern uses terminology that has become quite familiar in contemporary psychoanalytic thought to describe this signaling capacity between baby and mother: intersubjective matrix, correspondence, intermodality, and my favorite, the infant's "innate contingency detection analyzers."

3. I am not referring to parents who have been diagnosed with significant psychiatric illnesses such as psychotic disorders, serious personality disorders or major affective disorders. It is not my purpose to unfairly criticize any person suffering from a mental/emotional condition.

4. Woolfolk and Perry, *Child and Adolescent Development*, 118.

them with a gentleness that supplies what they need from her.[5] The early relationship between child and mother (and father)[6] proves all important:

> Relationships have an effect on relationships. This concept means that what infants learn in their first relationships is how to be in relationships. If the initial relationships are satisfying and enjoyable, then young children learn to trust, communicate, negotiate, show empathy, and cooperate with parents, peers, and others they meet—the building blocks of satisfying relationships. How they are cared for in these first relationships influences their sense of self-worth and whether they view themselves as lovable. . . . When relationships are comfortable, stable, and constant rather than anxiety producing, confusing or frightening, then babies have the emotional energy and feelings of safety to focus on exploring and investigating—important aspects of learning.[7]

These initial freedoms gained by the infant/toddler must be continued and expanded as the child grows. Parents should naturally adjust their nurturing in age-appropriate ways as children mature; the nurturing itself should not to be abated.

CHILDREN AS GIFT AND POSSESSION

The Psalms tell us that "children are a gift from the Lord" (Ps 127:1). In Israel the heritage of family, clan and tribe was considered a great blessing. In my own family, with its strong Italian-American legacy, the birth of a child has always been a show stopper! Every generation has seen children as God's gift to their parents and extended family alike. The Scriptures say that children naturally bless their mothers and that sons (and daughters) honor their fathers (Prov 31:28; Mal 1:6; Prov 17:6b). The fifth commandment explicitly instructs children to "honor your mother and your father" (Exod 20:12a). Paul points out that this is the first commandment with a built-in promise: "that it may go well with you and that you may live long on the earth" (Eph 6:3b; Exod 12b; cf. Prov 23:22). The book of Proverbs speaks harshly of the consequences for offspring who castigate their parents: "He who curses his father or his mother, his lamp will go out in time of darkness" (Prov 20:20). Without a lamp to guide the way, one would

---

5. Hiebert, *Call to Readiness*, 94–95.
6. Pruett, *Fatherneed*, 17–58.
7. Wittner and Petersen, *Infant and Toddler Development*, 10.

surely lose oneself in the darkened evenings of ancient Palestine! Likewise a mind-set or attitude that would curse father or mother would not serve a person well when life becomes difficult (cf. Prov 19:26; 30:11ff.).[8]

The Apostle Paul, believing that family relationships were of great importance, wrote "household codes" for Christians in the epistles to both the Ephesians and Colossians. Paul had good reasons to address these areas of concern, considering how family relationships were understood in the Roman Empire. The culture was awash in Roman injunctions about husbands, wives, parents, children, masters, and slaves, well-known Greek teachings and even some rabbinical instructions from Israel. However for Paul, being "in Christ" meant that the Holy Spirit brought a new reality into household life, a center and a source very different than the surrounding culture.

Crucially, the apostle's teachings about the believer's responsibilities to others in the church, and to unbelievers or people in authority, and to those who are weak or suffering, were not to be set aside when the focus turned to family relations. For perspective we should briefly consider the meaning of childhood in first century Rome. How were children treated by parents; how did adults view their value or identity; what were the consequences of their disobedience? Did the pagan world see their offspring as "gifts from the Lord" (Ps 127:3)? We have evidence that this may not have been the case:

> In the ancient world children were very much under the domination of their parents. The supreme example of that was the Roman *Patria Potestas*, the law of the father's power. Under it a parent could do anything he liked with his child. He could even sell him into slavery; he could make him work like a laborer on his farm; he had even the legal right to condemn his child to death, and to carry out the execution. Once again all the privileges and rights belonged to the parent, and all the duties to the child.[9]

Maxie Dunnam, commenting on Ephesians 6:4 ("And, you fathers, do not provoke your children to wrath") says,

> To a world in which father had absolute power over a child, in which that power was regularly expressed in casting female babies away and drowning sickly or deformed children; to a world in

---

8. Needless to say, how many problems are suffered by adult sons or daughters with extreme and unresolved issues with their parents? Guilt, shame, depression and basic emotional immaturity are sadly commonplace in these people.

9. Barclay, *Letters to the Philippians, Colossians, and Thessalonians*, 193.

which children were property, chattel to be held, used, or disposed of according to the wishes of the father—to this world Paul spoke a revolutionary word about the infinite value of all persons, and the respect parents should have for their children.[10]

In short, the Roman culture into which Paul spoke his "revolutionary word" was an exclusively adult world. Children were often treated as indentured servants, or at best, extensions of their parents' aspirations. Undoubtedly many households operated with affection and care, but both practically and philosophically children were treated in accordance with their utility for easing their father's burdens.[11]

Classical fathers simply had immense power. As Witherington says, "Indeed in the Greco-Roman world a child was under the control of his father until he died (a Greek Custom), or until he was sixty (the Roman custom)."[12] It is true that Seneca, the much admired Stoic philosopher, said that "the proper philosophy will instruct fathers how to best rule in family contexts."[13] But even he did not envision a two-way relationship. Fathers were to use their reason to help guide them, but the overall rationale for family structure remained strictly patriarchal. Males as heads of households exercised ultimate authority over wives and children, even as they did over their slaves.

PAUL'S INTERVENTION

This was the world in which Paul spoke his "revolutionary word," in Dunnam's vivid phrase. "Fathers, do not provoke your children to anger but bring them up in the discipline and instruction of the Lord" (Eph 6:4). "Fathers, do not exasperate your children that they may not lose heart" (Col 3:21). In his role as apostle, Paul has the audacity to tell fathers what *not* to do with *their own children*—a radical transgression against the dominant culture.

In a similar vein Paul introduced his "household codes" to guide the functioning of the Christian family. In many places the apostle describes how believers should be self-giving and sacrificially loving with others,

10. Dunnam, *Galatians, Ephesians, Philippians, Colossians, Philemon*, 235.

11. Meeks, *Origins of Christian Morality*, 38–39. Meeks rightly points out that children of the higher classes fared much better. Education was a prime focus for these parents.

12. Witherington, *Letters to Philemon, the Colossians, and the Ephesians*, 336.

13. Ibid., 184n40.

even with unbelievers (Phil 2:3–4; Rom 12:10; 15:10; Gal 6:2, 9–10), echoing Jesus' injunction that "the greatest among you shall be your servant" (Matt 23:11; cf. Matt 20:26–28). Since the father exercised the power and authority in the household, could Paul be suggesting that the father be a servant to his family?[14] Why shouldn't the teachings of the apostles regarding relationships in general be applied to the familial?

A great many sermons or adult education series have focused on Paul's direct instructions to married couples: "wives, be subject to your husbands" (Eph 5:22; Col 3:19), and "husbands, love your wives" (Eph 5:25; Col 3:19). Much could be said about these imperatives, particularly in the Ephesians passage (6:21–33). However, few studies have illuminated the larger context in which these familial directives are imbedded.

The shorter "household" passage, in Colossians 3:18—4:2, depicts what these relationships look like now that the Christian has "put on the new self who is being renewed to a true knowledge according to the image of the One who created him" (Col 3:10). This new person lives out the image of Christ in the everyday world. The demeanor of this life is animated by

> a heart of compassion, kindness, humility, gentleness and patience; bearing with one another, and forgiving each other, whoever has a complaint against any one; just as the Lord forgave you, so also should you. And beyond all these things put on love, which is the perfect bond of unity. (Col 3:12–14)

A heartfelt attitude of Christ-like living informs the more specific teaching of marital relationships, as Witherington explains:

> The household code must not be abstracted from its present context and analyzed on its own, as is often done.... When what comes immediately before the code is taken into account, it becomes clear that Paul expects all household members to behave in ways that are in accord with Christian virtues and not continue or go back to old patterns of behavior in their family relationships. The general ethic enunciated in 3:5–17 prepares for and undergirds the advice given in 3:18—4:1. If love, peace, forgiveness, respect, and a recognition that in Christ even social relationships like slave and master or husband and wife have been relativized and transformed (3:11) are the ruling principles guiding conduct, then a reforming and refashioning of the household relationships is not only possible

---

14. Ibid., 337.

but required. Paul is not offering up suggestions in the household code but exhorting by means of imperatives. And each exhortation is tied to the person in question's relationship with the Lord. Even the household ethic and its living-out are christocentric.[15]

Paul clearly set himself against powerful cultural mores. They were as entrenched as those of Dr. Benjamin Spock or Emily Post in the twentieth century! Again Ben Witherington provides a relevant perspective:

> To the contrary, when one compares this material to either the ancient discussions on household management in Aristotle and other sources or to Stoic or other Greco-Roman codes, one is profoundly struck by not just the Christian elements but also the social engineering that is being undertaken here to limit the abuse of power by the head of the household, using Christian rationales to equalize and personalize as well as Christianize the relationship between the head and the rest of the family. We do not find the exhortation to heads of household to love their wives, not to break the spirit of their children, or to treat their slaves with some equity and justice in most of the parallel literature.
>
> What we see throughout this household code is a deliberate modification of the existing patriarchal household structure, an attempt, that is, to rein in the authority and behavior of the head of the house-hold, making it more nearly Christian in character.[16]

Being "more nearly Christian in character" applies quite directly to the exhortations given to fathers/parents. Parents are to treat their children with compassion, kindness, humility, gentleness, etc. They are also to instruct, discipline, and encourage them all under the rubric of love. Paul desires that his primarily Gentile readers treat their children as if they really believed that they were gifts from God!

Particularly meaningful is Paul's admonitions to fathers to "bring [children] up in the discipline and instruction of the Lord" (Eph 6:4). In Eugene Peterson's translation the verse reads, "Take them by the hand and lead them in the way of the Master."[17] The phrase "take them by the hand" is Peterson's rendering of the Greek word *ektrepsete* (the word *trepho* plus the intensifier, *ek*.[18]) *Trepho* typically means to thicken, nourish, feed, support, cherish, or provide for (Matt 6:26; 25:37). Adding the preposition

---

15. Ibid., 185–86.
16. Ibid., 184, 193.
17. Peterson, *The New Testament*, p. 412.
18. *Analytic Greek Lexicon*, 408.

ek bolsters and enhances the action: the word now means to nourish, to promote health and strength, to bring up and educate.[19] Therefore the rendering in the New American Standard Bible ("bring them up in the . . . ") is both too anemic and too generic. Peterson's "take them by the hand and lead them in . . . " cuts closer to the truth, pointing to an engaged and gentler leading of the child.

In short, Paul wants to tell fathers to lead their children with a wise and tender hand into an understanding of God's grace for them. His admonitions are in concert with the great themes of the book of Ephesians: the incredible grace of God in the work of Jesus Christ to establish a new people of God (Eph 2:11–22). Paul's mind "dwells on the theme of Christ and the church resulting in an exalted Christology and a high appraisal of the privileges of believers in Christ."[20] As members of the "new people" with great privileges, it is no longer appropriate for fathers to act as provoking, domineering authority figures. Hendriksen explains this new role:

> Paul places the positive over against the negative by continuing: *but rear them tenderly*. Fathers—mothers too—must provide their children with food, not only physical but also mental and spiritual. They must nourish them, *rear them tenderly*. "Let them be fondly cherished" (Calvin). However, this does not exclude *firmness: in the discipline and admonition of the Lord.*[21]

Hendriksen explains the concepts further in a footnote:

> Since *ektrepsete* is used here as the antonym of *provoke to anger*, full justice should be done to its prefix; hence, love must replace anger. The children should be reared *tenderly*.[22]

---

19. Ibid.
20. Guthrie, *New Testament Introduction*, 515.
21. Hendriksen, *Exposition of Ephesians*, 262, emphasis original.
22. Ibid., 262n164, italics original. See also Lincoln, *Ephesians*, 406, cited in Witherington, *Letters to Philemon, the Colossians, and the Ephesians*, 338.

> Fathers are made responsible for ensuring that they do not provoke anger in their children. This involves avoiding attitudes, words, and actions which would drive a child to angry exasperation or resentment and thus rules out excessively severe discipline, unreasonably harsh demands abuse of authority, arbitrariness, unfairness, constant nagging and condemnation, subjecting a child to humiliation, and forms of gross insensitivity to a child's needs and sensibilities.

Part II: Oh, You Got to Carry That Weight

Children should be reared tenderly so that they can be nourished by the truth of God's discipline and instruction. The late Ray Anderson, theologian par excellence, wrote impressively about this:

> Religious education can never replace, nor seldom compensate for the failure of parenting to affirm the child in its humanity by placing its sense of openness and wonder in touch with the reality of God. And God is love, and whoever abides in love abides in God. (1 John 4:16)[23]

FATHERS: EARTHLY AND HEAVENLY

Paul was certainly not the first to offer the image of the nurturing father as an analog for the love of God; he was inspired by themes and imagery found throughout Scripture. Out of that great wealth we will consider three examples from the Psalms, the Gospels, and the book of Hebrews.[24]

Psalm 103, a magnificent ode of praise to God, is perhaps the most powerful continuous statement of the Lord's gracious and efficacious love for believers in the Old Testament.[25] In its verses David expresses his deep gratitude for the Lord who had so captured his heart (Acts 13:22). God had truly met his people in their need as he sought to bring Israel, his children, back to him.

---

23. Anderson and Guernsey, *On Being Family*, 68.

24. See ibid., 61, where the authors offer a theological understanding of this analogical use of earthly fathers:

> Human parents stand in relation to their children in a way analogous to the way in which God is related to his people, as father. The seniority of parents over their children is relative, not absolute. Also both parents, the mother and father, equally bear the responsibility of fulfilling, by analogy, that which is represented by the Fatherhood of God. . . . God's fatherhood includes all of the nuances of parenting represented by analogy in human parents. For example, both nurture and discipline, both compassion and chastisement are exemplified by the fatherhood of God, as generally portrayed in the Old Testament.

25. See M'Caw and Motyer, "Psalms," 515, where they describe Ps 103 by saying,

> The Psalm is an expression of praise evoked first by the psalmist's own experience (note the singular pronouns in vv. 1–5). But it is tremendously strengthened by the evidences of the Lord's amazing compassion and mercy toward men in general; His forgiveness and solicitude for . . . men must lead to universal adoration.

Admonishing us to "forget none of His benefits" (v. 2), David tells us that the Lord pardons, heals, redeems, crowns, satisfies, renews, performs, and makes known "His acts to the sons of Israel" (v. 7b), capping it all by quoting the words of Exodus 34:6: "The Lord is compassionate and gracious, slow to anger and abounding in lovingkindness." The psalmist then presents an extraordinary image or metaphor of God's wondrous compassion for his people:

> Just as a father has compassion on His children, so the Lord has compassion on those who fear Him. For He Himself knows our frame. He is mindful that we are dust.

With his tremendous portrayal of the Lord's profound love for his children as the background, David offers up parental love as an analog. An earthly father/parent knows what his children are made of; after all, the father was once a child and has been near to his children since they were born. He knows their vulnerabilities and has been present to meet those needs. In the same way, God's understanding of his children's limitations is expressed in his knowledge of their frame: he knows that we are but dust because he formed (framed) the first human from the dust of the earth (Gen 2:7).[26] He knows where we come from because he shaped us; he is filled with compassion because he knows who we are.

Jesus himself draws from the experience of children with their fathers in order to illuminate God's giving nature:

> Now suppose one of you fathers is asked by his son for a fish; he will not give him a snake instead of a fish, will he? Or if he is asked for an egg, he will not give him a scorpion, will he? If you then being evil know how to give good gifts to your children how much more shall your Heavenly Father give the Holy Spirit to them who ask Him? (Luke 11:11–13)

> Or what man is there among you, when his son shall ask him for a loaf, will give him a stone? Or if he shall ask for a fish, he will not give him a snake, will he? If you then, being evil, know how to give good gifts to your children, how much more shall your Father who is in heaven give what is good to those who ask Him! (Matt 7:7–9)

In both accounts the illustrations of the earthly father exemplify the "ask, seek, knock" exhortations of the preceding verse. They operate for

---

26. Jamieson et al., "Jeremiah–Malachi," 322.

Jesus as an argument from the lower to the higher, using parental actions to appeal to the crowd's reasonable experience.[27]

Somewhat shockingly Jesus tells his hearers that they are "evil," or as Tasker describes, "unkind or ungenerous."[28] But their fallen selfishness is mitigated by the natural care and commitment they give to their children: even in their "evil" state they that know real fathers give good gifts rather than committing base deception.[29] If earthly fathers can act with compassion and grace, how much more will our Heavenly Father give us what is good and what we really need?

The third example of earthly and heavenly parenting comes from the book of Hebrews:

> Furthermore we had earthly fathers to discipline us and we respected them; shall we not much rather be subject to the Father of spirits, and live? For they disciplined us for a short time as seemed best to them; but He disciplines us for our good; that we may share His holiness.

The writer tells us that we can see the goodness of God in the actions he takes to discipline the believer. Discipline in the book of Hebrews "is a process of learning or schooling"[30] with the aim of achieving concrete results in the life of a child of God. The Greek word for "discipline" here is *paideia* from the word *paideuo*, or "little children" as John uses it in 1 John 2:18.[31] The Father's corrections are experiential, aiming to exorcise

---

27. See Augsburger, *Matthew*, 98:
   > A father whose son has asked him for bread will not respond with a stone, nor when asked for fish will instead give him a serpent or an eel—something unclean and forbidden in his diet. This is to say, with these illustrations, that a father won't mock a son in his requests. He concludes with, "*How much more will your father who is in heaven give good things!*" (italics original)

   John Stott in *Christian Counter-Culture*, 188–89, adds an interesting and important wrinkle:
   > We have already heard Jesus say that human parents would never give a stone or snake to their children who ask for bread or fish. But what if the children (through ignorance or folly) were actually to ask for a stone or a snake? What then? Doubtless an extremely irresponsible parent might grant the child's request, but the great majority of parents would be too wise and loving.

28. Tasker, *Gospel according to St. Matthew*, 81.
29. See Hendriksen, *Exposition of the Gospel according to Matthew*, 36.
30. Hughes, *Commentary on the Epistle to the Hebrews*, 529.
31. Ben Witherington, in *Letters and Homilies for Jewish Christians*, 330, says,

draining encumbrances or sinful actions. They guide the Christian into living more righteously and sharing in God's holiness by reflecting Christ's endurance (Heb 12:9–10). The "Father of Spirits" (v. 9), the God who "deals with you as with sons" (and daughters) will do his work of reproof—even to the point of a spiritual "scourging!"—as a natural outworking of his great love.

In the middle of this exposition of God's vigorous but loving discipline we find reference to earthly fathers/parents. Much as in Psalm 103, the writer offers human fatherhood as an existential analog to clarify the teachings.

We have all had "earthly fathers to discipline us, and we respected them" (v. 9). Why did we do that? Because we understand that our fathers did what "seemed best to them" (v. 10); they tried to do what was needed by their child.[32] In the same manner our Heavenly Father commits himself to draw out those things that can tear us down or distract us from Christ as our sustainer. Our Lord will find a way to get us back in the race; he will restore us when we make wrong choices or get caught up with things that would damage us. Like the Father of the prodigal son, he will let nothing stand in the way of bringing us back into his household.[33]

THE PROVOKING OF CHILDREN

If images of the good father inform our understanding of the love of God, they also raise questions in our contemporary experience. When a father is *not* good, what then? What about abusive fathers or parents who do not even recognize the essential needs of their children, continually inciting them to insecurity and anger? How does the experience of a "provoking

---

> The function of such *paideia* is correction; it is not punitive in character. This becomes especially clear in Hebrews 12:8 when our author says that all God's children have shared in God's *paideia*, he surely does not mean that all the challenges they face were punishments. The outcome of this discipline is not repentance but rather a larger capacity for endurance. (italics original)

32. Raymond Brown, in *Christ Above All*, 234, says of this,

> A father who really loves his children is anxious that they should realize their potential and come to maturity. Without his discipline they will remain immature, childish and undeveloped. Furthermore, these verses make it clear that the father equips his children. Fathers who love their children do not merely issue orders; they encourage our response by the quality of their love and do all within their power to help.

33. See Keller, *Prodigal God*, xv.

parent" affect a child's ability to progress from the lesser to the greater, from the earthly to the heavenly in the development of trust?

The household codes in Paul's letters address this phenomenon, which we may refer to simply as "parental disregard." Ephesians 6:4 tells us: "And fathers do not provoke your children to anger; but bring them up in the discipline and instruction of the Lord." The latter part of the verse uses the same word for discipline, *paideia*, as the passage in Hebrews 12. We have already seen how important it is that God "*paideias*" his children; he does this in parallel with the practices of good earthly fathers. But Paul's primary concern here is to tell parents what they should *not* do: provoke their children to anger instead of "tenderly rearing them" in the Lord.

Parents need to hold themselves accountable to Paul's admonition. The word he uses for "provoke" (*parorgizete*) means to instigate, anger, irritate, or outrage another person; its root is *orge*, meaning anger, annoyance or resentment. The word does not simply connote displeasure—it is a harsh word and a strong emotion that impacts all in close proximity. The Scottish commentator John Eadie says that *parorgizete*

> signifies to irritate—to throw into passion. . . . The paternal reign is not to be one of terror and stern authority, but of love. The rod may be employed, but in reason and moderation, and never from momentary impulse and anger. Children are not to be moved to "wrath" by harsh and unreasonable treatment, or by undue partiality and favoritism.[34]

Eadie lived at a time when accepted forms of parental discipline were far more rigorous than what would be considered reasonable and healthy today. Even so he uses terms such as passion, terror, sternness, wrath, harshness and unreasonableness to portray the damage caused by the provoking father/parent.[35]

Writing to the church at Colossae, Paul uses a slightly different word (*erethizo*, in Col 3:21) than the one used in the Ephesians passage. Commentaries suggest that the term both supplements and enlarges the prohibition Paul sent to fathers at Ephesus. R. C. Lucas says of Colossians 3:21, "It is problem fathers [that are] the cause of problem children. What is evil here is the destructive nature of such provocations as endless criticism and harsh punishments."[36] Charles Erdman describes the provocations as "un-

---

34. Eadie, *Commentary on Ephesians*, 444.
35. Ibid.
36. Lucas, *Message of Colossians & Philemon*, 163.

just and severe treatment and continual faultfinding."³⁷ John Eadie, in one of the most disparaging passages I have ever read on this subject, says:

> In the discharge of this duty, and in every step of their proceedings, [Paul] directs them to beware, as parents, of provoking their children to anger; that is to say as the original term evidently implies, of exercising their own authority with irritating unkindness, with needless and vexatious severity; of harassing their children by capricious commands and restrictions; of showing groundless dissatisfaction, and scattering unmerited reproof.³⁸

The NASB translates *erethizo* as "exasperate," a word that connotes much more than simple annoyance. People who are targets of *erethizo* become enraged, driven into a fight or flight response. The word suggests such intensity that Homer used it to describe the Greek call to battle during the Trojan War.³⁹ When parents "exasperate" their children through extreme and continuous criticisms and demands, Paul warns that the children can "lose heart" (Col 3:21). They lose the ability to be passionate or inspired in heartfelt ways, becoming downcast, dejected, listless and deeply discouraged.

The word translated as "lose heart," *athumos*, literally means without passion or strong emotion.⁴⁰ It indicates a loss of desire, and possibly an inability to understand one's own emotions. The psychoanalytic concept of a loss of "affect regulation" offers a close parallel: individuals who are unable to control or modulate their own feeling states, continually moving from one agitated state to another without self-control. They can neither self-soothe nor adjust from gaining new information (an aspect of self regulation).⁴¹ In Dunnam's sorrowful rendering, their spirits are simply broken.⁴²

---

37. Erdman, *Epistles of Paul*, 104.
38. Eadie, *Commentary on Colossians*, 257.
39. Moule, *Studies in Colossians & Philemon*, 132.
40. *Analytic Greek Lexicon*, 8.
41. Maroda, *Psychodynamic Techniques*, 163–64.
For a description of a more "extreme" variation of dysregulated affect, see Cohen and Sherwood, *Becoming a Constant Object*, 123–30.

42. Dunnam, *Galatians, Ephesians, Philippians, Colossians, Philemon*, 235. See also Erdman, *Epistles of Paul*, 104, "Making a child lose heart and become sullen and listless and *depressed.*" Again see Lucas, *Message of Colossians & Philemon*, 163–64:

> The result of the irritable parent is to produce discouraged children in the sense that they are fearful and timid, shy and lacking in normal

Part II: Oh, You Got to Carry That Weight

Once again John Eadie captures the passion in Paul's message:

> What the apostle guards against has been often witnessed, with its deplorable consequences . . . the young spirit is to be carefully and tenderly developed, and not crushed by harsh and ungenerous treatment. Too much is neither to be demanded nor expected. The twig is to be bent with caution, not broke in the efforts of a rude and hasty zeal. Approbation is as necessary to the child as counsel, and promise as indispensable as warning and reproof.[43]

MEMBERS OF A CLUB

This type of familial dysfunction—parental disregard for children's healthy self-expression—has often been explored in popular motion pictures. We can think of the caustic, humiliating conversations between Colonel "Bull" Meechin and his oldest son, Ben, in the *Great Santini*, or the conflicts between Allie Fox and his son, Charlie, in *The Mosquito Coast*. These may be considered extreme examples of parental despotism since even difficult parents rarely approach those levels of verbal and emotional abuse.

A more relevant offering may be *The Breakfast Club*, a film that portrays five middle-class high school students opening up about the disconnects within their families during a Saturday detention session at their school.[44] In the adolescents called "the criminal" (played by Judd Nelson) and "the basket case" (Ally Sheedy), we can easily see the emotional damage caused by the "provoking to intense anger" they experienced from their parents. Less obvious but equally compelling are the effects of parental misattunement in the characters we might consider more "normal." The emotional anguish expressed by "the brain" (Anthony Michael Hall), "the princess" (Molly Ringwald), and particularly "the athlete" (Emilio Estevez), achieves an unexpected intensity that gives the film much of its impact.

---

self-confidence. It is no use such a father bemoaning the inability of his children to be strong and self-reliant like himself, since he has used his strength to *crush and undermine them*. (emphasis mine)

My reason for citing numerous commentators about Paul's concerns is to highlight the critical nature of parental disregard. The authors write as theologians, not psychologists, when they talk about the severe consequences of "exasperation" and "losing heart."

43. Eadie, *Commentary on Colossians*, 256.

44. *The Breakfast Club*, written and directed by John Hughes (A&M Films, Universal Pictures, 1985).

I suggest that these last three characters carry burdens that the more obviously discontented students do not share. The criminal and the basket case express their loss of heart in the ways they present themselves to others: they do not attempt to hide their inner wounds. But the brain, the princess, and the athlete are each hiding behind what Donald Winnicott calls a "false self."[45] They have adopted reactive and accommodative ways of presenting themselves in the world, aiming to maintain some kind of attachment to their caretakers (parents), who gave them impingement and disregard in place of direction and encouragement. By some measure the three have been successful: significant people in their lives value them because they sold out to what their parents expected of them. They performed as others demanded that they should. But their success came at the price of extreme internal dislocation: their hearts are lost but they are not even granted permission to show that reality to the world.

NOT JUST IN THE MOVIES

For children in Christian families, the experiences of "provoking to anger" followed by "loss of heart" have significant consequences for the development of an affect-rich trust in a loving Father God. Eadie speaks of the outcome when parents do not heed Paul's injunctions:

> To act thus, the apostle declares, would be so far from advancing the religious improvement of children, that it would discourage them. It would not only deaden their affections towards their parents, but would dispirit their exertions, and check their desires after holiness."[46]

All healthy parents want their children to grow up, mature, and flourish. Christian parents want them to "grow strong in the Lord and the strength of his might" (Eph 6:10). The apostle Paul certainly wanted this also. Eadie warns us that parental actions and attitudes may directly influence children's ability to desire "after holiness" toward God; severe deficits in parenting may even leave children "discouraged" in their faith. We will explore the roots of these insights in the next chapter.

I can do no better than conclude with Maxine Dunnam's comments:

---

45. Winnicott, "Concept of a Healthy Individual," 33–34, and "Concept of a False Self," 65–70, both in *Home Is Where We Start From*.

46. Eadie, *Commentary on Colossians*, 257.

Part II: Oh, You Got to Carry That Weight

Parents' relationships with children shape their personalities and specially influence how they relate to themselves and others. Paul was far ahead of his time in his concern about children. He knew that children could be robbed of their self-esteem, have their spirits broken early in life, and have to pay painfully, sometimes for a life-time, for being emotionally crippled as a child.

When the family is a place for persons, it becomes a center of caring. Where Christ's love is communicated through parent's love, children are affirmed. In that caring context of love, children obey. A persistent style of disobedience on the part of children is usually a lack, or a distortion, or a perversion of love.[47]

---

47. Dunnam, *Galatians, Ephesians, Philippians, Colossians, Philemon*, 395.

PART III

All in the Family

CHAPTER FIVE
───────────

Training Up Your Child

> From the moment I could talk
> I was ordered to listen... if they
> were right, I'd agree—but it's them
> they know, not me.
>
> "Father and Son"
> (Cat Stevens, 1970)

In the song "Father and Son," Cat Stevens brilliantly develops two vocal personas and lays bare the roots of their conflict. The father makes an attempt to instruct his son about life and about settling down. The son, in anger, rejects his father's counsel because he feels that he has never been seen, never been known; that from the beginning of his life his parents did not genuinely want to hear him. One can imagine that the parents had their own agenda for their son's life and that agenda has driven the son to leave home in what seems like less than optimal timing. His was a life of obeying the *shoulds* of his parents—the actions and directions they had chosen for him without actually seeking out his own concerns.

In the terminology of Proverbs 22:6 (or more accurately, the common interpretation and application of the Proverb), one could say that this son had been trained *according to the way he should go* but had rejected it. He had been raised according to the path that his parents thought he should follow, yet he refused it.

As I suggested earlier, this proverb about bringing up one's child lies at the crux of my argument about developmental woundedness. It has most often been translated and applied in the manner described above. All of the most-used English editions of Scripture (KJV, NIV, RSV, NKJV, ESV, and NASB) present it in this way. The New American Standard Bible, uniquely, includes a note stating that the first part of the couplet in verse six can be literally read as, "according to his own way." Why does the NASB provide this phrase as a literal translation? Simply because this construction best conveys the meaning of the proverb in the original Hebrew.

According to Gleason Archer, the proverb refers to "the general custom of, the nature of, the way of acting, the behavior pattern of a person."[1] He discusses this in context by saying,

> There can be little doubt that "his way" here implies "his proper way" in the light of the goals and standards set forth in verse 4 and tragically neglected by the "perverse" in verse 5. Yet there may also be a connotation that each child is to be reared and trained for God's service according to the child's own personal and peculiar needs and traits.[2]

Albert Barnes, in his much-used *Barnes Notes on the Old & New Testaments*, says concerning Proverbs 22:6a that "according to the tenor of his way" is the proper translation. He elaborates by rendering it as

> the path specially belonging to, specially fitted for, the individual's character. The proverb enjoins the closest possible study of each child's temperament and the adaptation of "his way of life" to that.[3]

In addressing more fully the misguided rendering of this scripture, Guy Woods says:

> The phrase, "*In the way he should go,*" is often misapplied. The *assumption* is that it means "*in the way of righteousness and the true religion,*"—a course which all, both young and old, ought to follow—but this is not what Solomon meant here.
>
> The Hebrew phrase from which the words "*in the way he should go,*" means "*according to the tenor of his way,*" that is, in

---

1. Archer, "Proverbs 22:6," 274.
2. Ibid.
3. Barnes et al., *Proverbs to Ezekiel*, 62.

harmony with his *disposition*, his natural *talents*, and his individual *character*.

Taught here is the obligation of parents to study the *nature* and *disposition* of their children and to train them accordingly. This is in harmony with Paul's instructions to the Ephesians and Colossians (Eph 6:4; Col 3:21). Instead of giving all the emphasis to a rigorous standard to be applied *"indiscriminately,"* each child's *"temperament"* is to be *closely considered* and the teaching is to be done so as to achieve the *greatest* possible adaptation to the child's need.[4]

Even with the emphasis on God's concerns and priorities in the instruction of the child, one writer asserts:

> What is the "way"? It could mean the way that the child ought to go according to God's law: the proper way in light of God's revelation. It could also mean the way best fitting the child's own personality and particular traits.
>
> Which is correct? There is no doubt that the first presents the highest standard and more traditional meaning. However, it has the least support from the Hebrew idiom and seems to be a cryptic way of stating what other proverbial expressions would have done much more explicitly.
>
> Therefore we conclude that this enigmatic phrase means that instruction ought to be conformed to the nature of the youth. It ought to regulate itself according to the stage of life; evidence of God's unique calling of the child and the manner of life for which God is singling out that child. This does not give the child carte blanche to pick and choose what he or she wishes to learn. It does, however, recognize that the training children receive must be as unique as the number of children God has given to us.[5]

---

4. Woods, *Questions and Answers*, 192, emphasis original.

5. Quote taken from "Troy" in the Talk Jesus Forum (www.talkjesus.com/parents28829-proverbs-22-6-train-child.html). The anonymity of the author may be a problem for some. It seems that the "Talk Jesus" people do not reveal the full names of their contributors. However, I found "Troy's" comments to be such an effective summary of the perspectives of most commentaries and other works that I studied that I felt it instructive enough to include.

Part III: All in the Family

DESCRIPTIONS OF TRAINING "ACCORDING TO THE WAY HE SHOULD GO"

The contrast (or struggle) between these competing translations of Scripture has been reflected in the daily practices of child-rearing. I would argue that the misunderstanding of *the way that he should go* has spawned or supported an array of domineering and even repressive styles of parenting. They proceed from the assumption that, since a child does not know "the way," his parents are responsible for identifying the "shoulds" and inculcating them into their offspring, regardless of the child's "bent" or temperament (e.g., docile, even-tempered, or strong willed).

Essentially, child-rearing is reduced to the parent *against* the child: two opposing wills, two conflicting approaches to the world. It is unarguably true that children, because of their youth and inexperience, should be protected from dangers that their ignorance of the world could lead them into. Likewise, every parent knows that children are capable of doing hurtful things to others and to themselves and therefore need clear boundaries for acceptable behavior. But when parenting is reduced to opposition and conflict, the child is left isolated in regulating his emotions when the interactions create limits that are both confusing and frustrating to him.[6]

The real problem arises when a parent comes to believe that the child is *never* a good judge of what he needs. That when an infant attempts to communicate by emotional cues what he would find soothing or exhilarating at that moment,[7] the parent cannot trust him. When a preschooler expresses his desires verbally, the parent is predisposed to believe that the

---

6. See Eigen, *Toxic Nourishment*, 74. He provides a clear example of this from one of his patients:
> He had learned early on that emotional aliveness was destructive or irrelevant. Mother could not take much of it. Optimally, a child's aliveness makes the mother more alive—a virtuous circle. Aliveness stimulates aliveness. Larry's mother could not be bothered. She tended to turn off when he was expressive, as if too much feeling threatened her.

7. See Stern, *Interpersonal World of the Infant*, 100–123, and Beebe et al., *Forms of Intersubjectivity*, 55–88. See Gerhardt, *Why Love Matters*, 197–98.
> This is also what babies need to develop a strong sense of self. In fact, this recognition of the baby's states is what brings the "self" fully into being. Parents can learn to be more contingently responsive to their babies by following the baby's lead, taking their cue from the baby, observing their baby's moods and desires, and *thinking about what it is like for the baby*. This can be a fast track back to harmony with their baby and to the unfolding of much more satisfying relationship through childhood. (emphasis mine)

child should not have what he wants simply because he wants it so much, and that his desire must therefore be wrong. Clarence Lewis supports this line of thought:

> God's word says in Proverbs 22:6, "Train up a child in the way he should go; and when he is old, he will not depart from it" (KJV). Now notice what God did not say. God did not say to train up a child in the way the child wants to go. *"God said to train up a child in the way he should go."* Now if God said to train up a child in the way he should go then it must be possible to train up a child in the way the child wants to go too, and that is the wrong way to train up a child and the parents will pay a negative price for it later on in life.[8]

Therefore the wrong way to parent is to let the child do what he wants; this is presented as a fundamental principle, not an evaluation of individuals or situations. Children are incapable of knowing what is best for them in any and all circumstances regardless of their own understanding or experience.

Perhaps the clearest prescriptions for "going against" a child's spontaneous personal expressions can be found in popular pedagogical manuals from the eighteenth and nineteenth centuries. Psychoanalyst Alice Miller, a prolific writer on abusive child-rearing methods and their consequences, cites numerous European and American parenting handbooks which instruct parents to effectively "break the will of their child."[9] An example from J. Sulzer in 1748:

> As far as willfulness is concerned, this expresses itself as a natural recourse in tenderest childhood as soon as children are able to make their desire for something known by means of gestures. They see something they want but cannot have; they become angry, cry, and flail about. Or they are given something that does not please them; they fling it aside and begin to cry. These are dangerous faults that hinder their entire education and encourage undesirable qualities in children. If willfulness and wickedness are not driven out, it is impossible to give a child a good education. The moment these flaws appear in a child, it is high time to resist this evil so that it does not become ingrained through habit and the children do not become thoroughly *depraved*.[10]

---

8. Lewis, *Death and Life*, 30, italics original.
9. Miller, *For Your Own Good*, 43.
10. Ibid., 10–11, emphasis added. Miller is quoting Sulzer, "Essay on the Education

Part III: All in the Family

The author claims that a preverbal child should be restricted whenever she shows that she *wants* something. The very act of wanting is seen as "willfulness" and must not be tolerated, since children must be trained to simply obey. Sulzer goes on to offer instructions to the parent:

> Therefore, I advise all those whose concern is the education of children to make it their main occupation to drive out willfulness and wickedness and to persist until they have reached their goal. As I have remarked above, it is impossible to reason with young children; thus willfulness must be driven out in a methodical manner and there is no other recourse for this purpose than to show children one is serious.[11]

In a manual by J. G. Kruger, also in the eighteenth century:

> It is my view that one should never strike children for offenses they commit out of weakness. The only vice deserving of blows is obstinacy.... If your son does not want to learn because it is your will, if he cries with the intent of defying you, if he does harm in order to offend you, in short, if he insists on having his own way
> *Then whip him well till he cries so:*
> Oh no, Papa, oh no!
> Such disobedience amounts in a declaration of war against you. Your son is trying to usurp your authority, and you are justified in answering force with force in order to insure his respect, without which you will be unable to train him. The blows you administer should not be merely playful ones but should convince him that you are his master.[12]

This author recommends that parents demonstrate their mastery over their children by administering blows upon them in serious fashion. The child's difficulty in "wanting" to do his studies or other tasks is seen as outright defiance of his father. If he cries, it's a sign that he is escalating his defiance. No other possible interpretation is offered.

In the present day, it is not difficult to find Christian authors who recommend corporal punishment methods similar to those cited in Miller's book, even for toddlers and preschoolers. Some of these authors mitigate their advice with admonitions about the father's anger level when he is

---

and Instruction of Children," as quoted by Rutschky, *Black Pedagogy*.

11. Miller, *For Your Own Good*, 11.

12. Ibid., 14–15. Miller is quoting Kruger, "Some Thoughts on the Education of Children" (1752), as quoted by Rutschky, *Black Pedagogy*.

punishing his child and reminders that children are young and their understanding is limited. Some use terms such as *tenderness* and *understanding* in relation to corporal punishment. Unfortunately, these are too often paired with descriptions of the punishments as beating, whippings, and administering blows.[13] The authors do not account for children's emotional terror at being battered by an authority figure who should be loving them and ensuring the safety of their environment. Parents are simply advised to make the child cry and scream in order to come to "repentance" for desiring things that the parents have proscribed, or for not wanting to do what the parents wish him to do. The dissenting will of the child must be forced out of him through the infliction of physical pain, and the pain will lead him to submit to his father's commands. Typically there is no mention of methods to help the child understand his father's wishes in age-appropriate ways. In short, the reasoning and prescriptions of these authors closely parallel the examples cited from the "Poisonous Pedagogy" chapter of Alice Miller's book. Miller herself states,

> Those concerned with raising children have always had great trouble dealing with obstinacy, willfulness, defiance, and the exuberant character of children's emotions. They are repeatedly reminded that they cannot begin to teach obedience too soon.[14]

The ultimate goal of this military-type submission by the child justifies the means parents use to obtain it. Miller continues:

> But it is perfectly normal to speak of the necessity of striking and humiliating children and robbing them of their autonomy, at the same time using such high-sounding words as *chastising, upbringing* and *guiding onto the right path*.[15]

A section of Miller's book (provocatively titled *Building Grounds for Hatred: Guides to Child-Rearing from Two Centuries*) provides further examples and descriptions of "poisonous pedagogy." Here again children's inclinations are seen as fundamentally detrimental to their well-being. Their innate desires, rooted as they are in a "willful spirit," are inimical to their moral, relational, and spiritual development. K. A. Schmid, writing in 1887, quotes Proverbs 23:14 to support this contention: "Thou shalt beat him [the

---

13. Ibid., 8–62. This is clearly seen in this section of popular pedagogic manuals covering over a period of one hundred and fifty years (1749–1902).
14. Ibid., 10.
15. Ibid., 16, italics original.

child] with the rod, and shalt deliver his soul from hell."[16] As problematic as this scripture has been, with various interpretations of the word "beat" and the principle of discipline versus punishment, etc., we may safely conclude that it does not recommend the physical torture of one's child. Yet that verse, along with a few others, has been employed by some authors to support forms of discipline applied with a parental zeal that reasonable persons could describe as sadistic.

Though we might wish to treat this approach to parenting as a relic of an ill-advised past, in my own psychoanalytic practice I have regularly worked with adults coping with the damage it caused them in their childhoods. Their experience was not always physically harsh or punitive; often it could be more accurately described as unrelenting parental intrusiveness.

One of these patients was Andy, a man in his mid-forties. As a preschooler he displayed a high level of energy typical of most young boys, constantly desiring to run and play outdoors and very inquisitive about his surroundings. His mother, however, believed that little boys should be as calm and peaceful as most little girls—or at least as his big sister was at his age. Her anxiety about his behavior led her to impose severe limitations on Andy's activities. He was forced to spend long hours of "inside play" with his action figures, coloring books, and the television (of course), rather than exerting himself in imaginative outdoor play. Andy developed a state of agitation and anxiety because his natural "get-up-and-go" had become "get up and gone!" This led to other forms of acting out which were also punished by his mother, imposing further restrictions on his activities.

Since Andy "could never stay still" his mother was convinced that something must be wrong with him. Medical examinations produced no evidence that he was hyperactive, overactive, or suffering from excessive adrenalin, yet his mother's belief did not waver. His situation began to improve only at ten years old when his father took him away to play Little League baseball. When he reached high school Andy became an accomplished basketball player and sprinter on the track team. He finally found positive outlets for expressing his energy.

Even so, Andy came to me for treatment as a middle-aged adult because he felt it was wrong to exert himself in anything that required "exhausting" physical energy. In relational assertiveness, work or play that demanded bodily exertion, and sexual vitality, he would feel guilty to the point of circumventing the activity. His original "training" taught him to

16. Ibid., 29.

stifle his inner propensity to move, take action, and feel the strength of his own physicality. His natural sense of himself was disregarded by a mother who saw it as problematic, even unsafe. The "should" of this training arose entirely from the mother's own fears about the world. She never seriously considered what the desire for action meant for her son; her distress about it proved it was unacceptable and must be crushed.

Another of my patients, Larry, experienced a high level of parental intrusion during his growth years. His mother, apparently believing that left-handedness was an undesirable trait, taught him to use his right hand for writing, eating, etc. She enforced this training by rapping Larry's hands with a ruler whenever he put a pencil or a fork in his left hand. It was only at eight years old that Larry's father discovered he was left-handed when they began playing catch with a baseball. The father had not been aware until then that his wife had taught their son otherwise. The impacts for Larry included horrendous difficulties with handwriting and conceptual confusion when using hand tools, forcing him to take twice as long to complete ordinary tasks. As a younger man this "clumsiness" was a source of shame and embarrassment: he did not want to learn how to fix cars or work on the house plumbing because he did not feel comfortable or confident manipulating the tools. All of this because his mother thought that left-handers were sloppy and uncoordinated, and might even have sexual problems!

In our time together Larry was able to explore and work through the guilt, fear, and anger that accompanied the discoveries of persistent parental intrusion into his development. Beyond the actual changing of his handedness, the induced awkwardness and sheer inability to do things that felt uncomfortable had driven so many doubts into Larry's life. Fundamentally he had been hobbled by the awareness that his parents (in this case his mother) did not know him very well, and that aspects that felt natural to him seemed to be unnatural to them. His early experiences had set up a basic mistrust for his parents.

Controversial pedagogical author Michael Pearl even exceeds Larry's mother in his comments on Proverbs 22:6:

> Parents should not wait until their child's behavior becomes unacceptable before they commence training—which would be discipline. . . . Training is the conditioning of the child's mind before the crisis arises. It is preparation for future, instant, unquestioning obedience.[17]

---

17. Pearl and Pearl, *To Train Up a Child*, 4.

Pearl would have the "shoulds" firmly established in the parents' minds even before they could discover how their child might wish to express himself.

This application of Proverbs 22:6 follows naturally from the common English interpretation of the verse's conditional clause. Steve Sherbondy, though correctly conveying the importance of submitting to authority, misuses the scripture in this manner when he says,

> When kids don't learn the value of submitting to authority, they are severely handicapped. As they get older the consequences will get more serious. Childhood is the perfect time to teach children valuable lessons.... "Teach your children to choose the right path, and when they are old they will remain upon it."[18]

Teaching (or training) your children to "choose the right path" connotes a much different approach than "train up a child according to his own way." If the training should be "according to the way he should go" or "according to the right path," the standard must be entirely external to the child. The child can only learn by fundamentally looking away from himself to the (supposedly) objective demonstration by his parents. The "way" becomes a kind of pattern for the preschooler to mimic, or at best "learn" through a form of classical conditioning.[19] For the slightly older child the "way" can be conveyed as a body of knowledge such as the Ten Commandments, or a list of behaviors from the latest child-development book.

DESCRIPTIONS OF TRAINING "ACCORDING TO HIS WAY"

When we understand that Scripture asks us to train up a child "according to his way," we can truly look at a child and discern what is unique about her personhood. We can bear in mind the myriad of elements that distinguish each child, from biological endowments to birth order, from nuances of temperament to experiences of previous caretaking. Charles Swindoll clearly expresses this understanding of v. 6a:

> The popular translation of, "train up a child in the way that he should go," fails to appreciate the rich practical childrearing advice

---

18. Sherbondy, *Changing Your Child's Heart*, 39.

19. See Pearl and Pearl, *To Train Up a Child*, 10–11, for the use of the conditioning of a cat and a dog as examples compared to human children. Pearl has stated publicly that children are to be trained (conditioned) as animals are.

the verse contains. It doesn't mean that parents dictate the correct way, but rather that they observe the child in order to discover his or her unique *abilities, temperaments and interests*. Then parents should adapt their training to help the child know and become his or hers unique self.[20]

Swindoll draws out the essence of "according to his own way" by challenging parents to pay attention to their children's "abilities, temperaments and interests," i.e., their God-given aptitudes and emotional makeup and their natural joy in discovering and acting on them. In Andy's example above, Swindoll would have advised his parents to recognize Andy's physical energy and his desire for movement and activity. Parental strategies that gave Andy the freedom (and safety) to "roam about" would demonstrate to him that he was known and appreciated by his parents.

Writing this chapter during the 2012 Summer Olympics, I was pleasantly startled by a television commercial. It described the background of a member of the United States gymnastics team, saying that "when he was a child he climbed to the ceiling of a department store!" His parents did not reprimand or punish him—instead they signed him up for gymnastics lessons. Clearly the parents recognized their son's exceptional physical abilities and found an environment that would both set limits for him and allow him to grow. They made certain that his natural strength, balance, and perseverance could be properly expressed and fulfilled—and the Olympic audience was grateful for it. The commercial closed by saying "It is amazing how far you can go with a little help along the way."[21]

Training a child "according to his own way" does not mean parenting in any manner contrary to the general teaching of the book of Proverbs. The book continually reinforces the themes of living with integrity in the community, aligning parental instruction with the precepts of God-given wisdom, and obeying the commands of YHWH. These precepts are applied first in the family and the community of Israel and then to the stranger and the sojourner. Underlying it all is the fundamental truth that "the fear of the Lord is the beginning of wisdom" (1:7, 9:10). As Old Testament scholar

---

20. Swindoll, *Parenting*, 5–6, italics mine.

21. The gymnast is Jonathan Horton and the story can be found at "TD Ameritrade TV Commercial for Support featuring Jonathan Horton," https://www.ispot.tv/ad/7kwj/td-ameritrade-support-featuring-jonathan-horton.

Part III: All in the Family

George Parsons said, "Proverbs is designed to teach people how to steer their lives properly (cf. 1:5) under the command of Yahweh."[22]

Proverbs 22:6 falls at the end of a section popularly called "the proverbs of Solomon: first collection"[23] (or "first book,"[24] or "miscellaneous proverbs of Solomon"[25]) which begins at verse 10:1 and continues through 22:16. It collects general statements concerning the life of wisdom, in contrast to the initial and more intense section of Proverbs, a lengthy instruction concerning wisdom's attributes and purposes (1:7 to 9:18). William Brown says of this first section,

> It is important to note that Prov. 1–9 was intended to provide a unifying focus to the book as a whole, serving . . . as its introduction particular themes that delineate the chief virtues presented by the characters of parent and wisdom. In other words, these initial instructions and profiles provide an organizing paradigm designed to guide the reader in the act of reading, listening, and appropriating the myriad of proverbial sayings that begin in ch. 10.[26]

Our passage contextually speaks to supporting the child's character and attitude with the aim of developing a good name or reputation in the community (vv. 1–2), developing an awareness of evil and knowing how to shun it (v. 3), and living a life of knowledgeable humility toward others, remembering his reliance on the Lord (vv. 4–5).

My contention is that a parent's disregard for their child's particular and individual sensibilities instills anxiety and confusion in the child, a woundedness exacerbated by ongoing criticisms and rejections rooted in the parent's initial disregard. The result, in terms of Colossians 3:21, is an embittered, exasperated son or daughter who has "lost heart" (that is, their fundamental self-acceptance; the internal sense of security about who they are; the confidence that they can live a healthy life by being themselves).

In the outworking of this damage, the young person or adult instinctively focuses his life around methods for filling the emotional holes left by his self-rejection. It's a pain that just seems to be there; it always seems to have been there. Christians are not exempt from trying to find peace of

---

22. Parsons, "Guidelines for Understanding," 15.
23. Helmbold, "Book of Proverbs," in Tenny, *Zondervan Pictorial Encyclopedia*, 919.
24. Wells, "Proverbs," 550.
25. Bullock, "Book of Proverbs," 26.
26. Brown, *Character in Crisis*, 45.

mind in actions or "acting out" that are inimical to living humbly in the fear of the Lord.

So training up a child "according to his way" is in truth training him according to God's way. It is not primarily about the morality of the chosen path, such as a child growing up to be either a bank worker or a bank robber; obviously the wisdom of Proverbs abhors those who steal. Rather it is about becoming an accountant or a statistician or a surveyor or a math teacher, if you have a natural enjoyment and proclivity for numbers and calculations. It means walking your own path with integrity and self-discipline and being of service to those around you. In the historical context of Israel, it means doing your work honestly, being upright in the community and before YHWH.

In the modern context, if children were raised "according to their way," middle schoolers who love math and working with numbers would not be belittled because they are poor at batting a baseball or have no interest in getting tackled. Young women would not be ostracized if they had no desire to be a homemaker, or likewise if they did not want to work at an office job as their mother did for thirty years. Nor should one be ignored because they like to sing, read, or spend most of their time in nature or inside studying the computer. (With the possible exception of playing foolish and violent video games for hours on end—there are limits, after all!) If your father has a PhD in biology and teaches at a local college but you are obsessed with automobiles—so be it, continue in your love for the internal combustion engine! If your parent is a suspicious and cautious person when it comes to working with others but you play at creating teams and quests with dolls or action figures, then keep that entrepreneurial spirit alive; just prepare yourself to be honest and caring for those who will work for you.

I learned firsthand the ups and downs and other dimensions of recognizing and promoting a child's particular "way" through my eldest son, Paul. By way of background: I have served in the church as an ordained minister, earned four graduate degrees, and worked as a psychotherapist/psychoanalyst for the past thirty years. I read constantly and instinctively explore the nuances of situations (or as my wife describes it, "You enjoy thinking about what you are thinking about"). I love most kinds of sporting events and most kinds of music. Paul, by contrast, did not quite follow my "way." As a child he loved action figures and especially the professional wrestlers. He devised day-long tournaments with complicated rules and formulas about who would win and how the stories would play out. Though very bright, he asked to drop out of high school and take his GED—and with much fear and trepidation his mother and I agreed. At nineteen he developed a full-fledged wrestling organization. His enterprise entailed working with men many years his senior, some of whom had performed on television; procuring standard wrestling equipment, including a competition-sized ring; finding appropriate venues; obtaining liability insurance; handling complicated monetary transactions; and developing an infrastructure that could manage the two hundred–plus people who would attend his shows. All this before his twentieth birthday! Later, at twenty-two, Paul fulfilled his dream of becoming a police officer. He has continued in this career for many years now, winning several awards for community service along the way.

Paul was an active, confident, boundary-testing little boy. In contrast to his father he did not read very many books and does not spend much time in philosophic thought, though he has the intelligence to do it. He has become a good man, a fair-minded manager of people who cares for those who are downtrodden. He has not departed from the love and acceptance he received as a kid, even after clashes over limits and suffering the consequences of overly-dominating his younger sister and brother. He is a wild and crazy Christian who would startle a lot of believers who define the faith in less vital ways. What a mistake it would have been if my wife and I had tried to mold him into thinking and behaving as I did at his age, or to conform to the particular Christian "subculture" we identified with at the time (the early 1980s evangelical crowd).

Speaking of Proverbs 22:6, James Keil relates that "this common mistake of viewing our children through adult eyes is the way we often try to approach the task of leading our children . . . try to get our children to fit into our world, instead of adapting our worlds to them."[27] How many patients in my psychotherapy practice over the years have fervently lamented their incapacity for following their inclinations just to be themselves and do the things that bring them joy? Keil concludes his thoughts on this:

> What the writer is getting at in this highly touted verse is that each child has his own unique personality traits. Some may be more inclined to be a carpenter and build things. Others may be gifted musically. Still others may have a knack for numbers. Get to know your child's uniqueness, because Proverbs 22:6 literally says, train your child according to his own uniqueness, and you will make

---

27. Keil, *Leading Your Family to Water*, 76–77.

the world you are trying so desperately to communicate to them, more palatable.[28]

Let's remind ourselves again that the unique way(s) of the child are necessarily guided by the instruction and tutelage of the Lord. The way of every man or woman is to live godly in the community, serving in a manner that promotes justice and compassion for its members. The book of Proverbs places enormous responsibilities on parents for their offspring, engaging mothers and fathers in a special partnership with YHWH to distill and practice wisdom, first in the family and then for the betterment of the populace.[29]

Theologian Ted Hildebrandt views the commands of Proverbs in much this manner. His distinctive exegesis of 22:6 sees the focus of the training directed to an older child, actually a late adolescent, with the purpose of fulfilling the teenager's desire to become a "squire" for the benefit of the community. As he says,

> "According to his way" meant according to the standard and status of what would be demanded of the (child/adolescent) in that culture. Thus the squire's status is to be recognized and his experience, training, and subsequent responsibilities are to reflect that high stature.[30]

One could say that Hildebrandt is speaking of a "squire way" for the training of young men.[31] The boy is to be "recognized, encouraged and supported in this pursuit." He must not be discarded as one who is making trouble. The community should initiate him with "an appropriate level of dignity, respect and responsibility" so that he will not become discouraged.[32] Hildebrandt, though rejecting the common interpretation of the word "child" and viewing the person as a teenager, still sees the verse as focused on his aspirations and yearnings. Parents play a powerfully important role in this context along with the rest of the community. The aspiring squire

---

28. Ibid., 77.

29. See Brown, *Character in Crisis*, 31–32. Describing the difference in the relationship between a father's instruction and that of wisdom's, Brown says, "While the father warns his son, wisdom indicts those who have rejected her counsel (1:25)" (32).

30. Hildebrandt, "Proverbs 22:6A," 291.

31. See ibid., 287. "He is a royal squire who is in the process of being apprenticed in wisdom for taking on royal responsibilities consistent with his status as an adolescent."

32. Ibid., 291.

> should be given experience, training, status and responsibilities correspondent to his role in the kingdom of God. An adolescent should be initiated into the adult world with celebrations. His status as a redeemed image bearer should demand parental involvement in terms of opening horizons, patient instruction, and loving discipline. It is his dominion, destiny, and status that the parent must keep in mind. The parent must not violate the adolescent's personhood by authoritarian domination, permissive allowance of immaturity, or overprotection from the consequences of his actions.
>
> This verse also teaches that when someone engages in an activity for the first time, a celebration of the event would encourage him in the correct path. . . . . Thus a word or deed of encouragement (recognition and celebration) that bestows respect and responsibility commensurate with status is one of the most powerful aspects of parental involvement in the life of an adolescent.[33]

This "powerful aspect of parental involvement in the life of an adolescent" applies with equal force in the lives of much younger children. The teenager's ambition or quest to become the kind of adult who can serve with responsibility, equity, and wisdom in the societal structures of Israel would have begun at a younger age, in his formative years.

Allen Ross, a scholar who disagrees with the "*according* to his own way" interpretation, sees the scripture promoting "a standard of life to which one should go."[34] This standard, similar to Hildebrandt's view, prepares the child for living life in the theocracy of Israel. Ross asserts,

> Training in accordance with the child's natural bent may be a practical and useful idea, but it is not likely what this proverb has in mind.
>
> In the book of Proverbs there are only two "ways" a child can go: the way of the wise and the righteous, or the way of the fool or wicked. Moreover, it is difficult to explain why a natural bent needs training.[35]

It is unarguably true that Proverbs speaks first of all to the people of Israel and to the necessity of living in wisdom, righteously before the Lord (Prov 2:1–13). However, despite Ross's assertions, the focus of the "training" is the individual life of the child in the various dimensions we have

---

33. Ibid., 291–92.
34. Ross, *Proverbs–Isaiah*, 88–89.
35. Ibid., 189.

explored. Ross even concedes this by citing two authors who explicitly state it.[36] One of them, "Saadia," writing over a thousand years ago, said that the training of the child should be "in accordance with his ability and potential. This wise parent will discern the natural bent of the individual child and train it accordingly."[37] Ross then cites Old Testament scholar Derek Kidner, who "acknowledges that the wording implies respect for the child's individuality but not his self will: he reminds us that the emphasis is still on the parental duty of training."[38]

In the end, my contention is simply that the wisdom and admonition of Proverbs 22:6 requires a parent to know the particularity of their child. The requirement is explicit for a child growing up as a Jew in Palestine and implicit for parenting everywhere.

The point may have been best expressed by the well-loved Bible expositor G. Campbell Morgan. A parent must seek to be "in harmony with the child's own disposition, mentality, character, natural talents, abilities, temperament. You must discover what the child is if you would train the child."[39]

ILLUSTRATIONS FROM THE MOVIES

The theme of parental intrusion into a child's fundamental longings, as generated by his own psychological/emotional/physical makeup, has longstanding currency in Hollywood. Two of my favorite films address the issue quite poignantly, though with very different outcomes.

Good Will Hunting[40] was released in 1997. The central character, Will Hunting (played by Matt Damon), works as a janitor at the Massachusetts Institute of Technology. Hunting has a brilliant mind for mathematics, including the highest and most complex issues in advanced algebra and calculus. He demonstrates this by anonymously solving problems that a math

---

36. Ibid.

37. Ibid.

38. Ibid.; see also Kidner, *Proverbs*, 147. Ross also quotes C. H. Toy about the phrase "according to his way," describing it as "but in accordance with the manner of life to which he is destined." Ross continues, "The implication being that the manner of life will not be morally bad." See Toy, *Proverbs*, 415.

39. Quoted in Lambert, "Proverbs 22:6," 97.

40. *Good Will Hunting*, written by Matt Damon and Ben Affleck, directed by Gus Van Sant (1997).

Part III: All in the Family

professor leaves on a chalkboard each night in a building where Hunting washes the floors. No one knows he is doing this and he does not seem to care if anyone finds out. The accuracy and creativity of the work amazes the professor when he starts his classes each morning. Through cinematic circumstances Hunting's secret is exposed and he is given a choice to either go to jail or enter into therapy. Responding to his resistance, the math professor sends Hunting to his colleague and good friend, a psychology professor played by Robin Williams.

Through their contentious interactions we learn that Hunting was physically and mentally abused by his working-class father and several foster parents, who denied him any opportunity to use his gifts or even imagine that his abilities had value. With the psychotherapeutic help of Williams, Hunting comes to realize that acting on his mathematical expertise is good and right (or really, exploring almost any academic subject since Hunting is clearly a genius). He finds the freedom and internal permission to leave his low-level job and neighborhood for a career more commensurate with his capabilities. Watching this change process unfold, we understand that the radical experience of parental humiliation along with the accompanying parental injunctions had derailed young Hunting. He had to uncover and reject the damage done by others in order to clearly see who he was and what he could accomplish. It was not a change he could accomplish alone; he needed another to assist him in affectively experiencing the wrongs done to him and discerning the truth about himself, "that it wasn't his fault."

The setting and outcomes are quite different in the second film: *Dead Poets Society*,[41] released in 1989. Neil Perry (played by Robert Sean Leonard) is a high school–age adolescent from a well-to-do two-parent family in New England. He attends a prestigious all-male college prep school along with the cream of the academic crop. Neil loves Shakespeare and the stage and harbors a secret ambition to become an actor. His father (Kurtwood Smith) clearly desires his son to focus on his studies in order to get into medical school and become a doctor. The balance of their relationship is upended by a creative and innovative English teacher at the school, John Keating (Robin Williams again!), a former student of the academy. He exhorts his students "to make their lives extraordinary" and realize their potential; "*carpe diem*—seize the day" is his battle cry. He encourages Neil to audition for a local production of Shakespeare's *A Midsummer Night's*

---

41. *Dead Poets Society*, written by Tom Schulman, directed by Peter Weir (1989).

Dream. Neil lands the role of Puck and portrays the character with great success, receiving a resounding standing ovation that affects him deeply.

Neil's father and mother attend the performance at his invitation, but afterward the irate father tells Neil that he is switching him from the academy to a military school and will seek John Keating's dismissal because of his wild and subversive ideas about life. Neil's dreams of acting are crushed and his father condemns him to a school that seems a death camp for his aspirations. The next night the young man shoots himself with his father's handgun, orchestrating his death in a manner that both accommodates his parents' wishes (i.e., that he not perform anymore) and liberates him from a life directed solely by his father.

The resolution of *Dead Poets Society* is one of the most poignant I have ever seen. Mr. Perry simply did not understand his son. He did not see the gentle, kindhearted side that John Keating and Neil's friends at school had experienced firsthand. He saw him only as a tool for realizing his own designs. The conversations that Neil held with his friends (in their club, the Dead Poets Society) showed us that Neil's father never sought to know him and always demanded absolute obedience to the plan he had laid out for him.

The tragic irony of the film is that Neil's suicide occurs in a family context that many people, including many Christians, would view as healthy and correct. Clearly the father only wanted, from his perspective, the best possible training for his son in order to live a successful life. He pursued this according to his own understanding and not his son's—and that's the rub, that he lacked even an inkling of awareness regarding how his son functioned and how he viewed his life. Most tragically, Neil's father did not recognize his son's temperament and did not see that rejecting Neil's artistic abilities and desires was tantamount to rejecting Neil himself. It never would have entered his mind that Neil might kill himself; after all, his son was *his* son.[42]

EXTERNAL BEHAVIORS, INTERNAL MOTIVATIONS

My personal study and research regarding the translating and expositing of Proverbs 22:6 have yielded interesting results. Though the sampling is

---

42. My purpose for saying this is that, counterintuitively, my practice (like many others) includes more men who come from an experience of rejection like that of Neil Perry's rather than from more dramatic situations like Will Hunting.

admittedly anecdotal and not extensive enough for scientific purposes, commentaries that exegete this verse and books that describe its application seem to fall invariably into two camps, based on their prescriptions for parents.

Those commentaries and books that translate Proverbs 22:6 as "according to his way" focus on the child's inherent qualities, her temperament, nature or disposition. Some would describe this focus as knowing the child's "spirit." As G. Campbell Morgan stated, "the child's own disposition, mentality, character, natural talents, abilities, temperaments" should be known and lovingly recognized.[43] The child's essential nature—who the child *is*—becomes the basis for evaluating and understanding what the child is doing and why. Like the other camp, this group of expositors translates the word *train* as *discipline*. However, to tease out what kind of discipline should be considered and how it should be actualized, the authors use terms such as instructing, nurturing, dedicating, initiating, encouraging, and even celebrating.[44] Gleason Archer writes that the idea of training in this verse is to "dedicate the child to God, prepare the child for future responsibilities, exercise or train the child for adulthood."[45]

The works that translate 22:6 as "according to the way he should go" center on the child's misbehaviors, rebelliousness, indiscipline, and rowdiness, even describing the fundamental motivations of the child (whether infant, toddler, preschooler, school-age child, or older) as malevolent, greedy and selfish toward her parents. The authors make repeated references to the propensity of the child to act out "sinfully" toward others. They see the "training" of 22:6 as correcting, commanding, ordering, chastising, disciplining and punishing; an array of words that limit or stop the free expression of the child's life.

This authoritarian approach toward the child's "way" naturally has practical impacts for the parents' methods of discipline. Michael Pearl, in his book *To Train up a Child*, suggests that parents must begin molding their children from the earliest possible age. He argues that a child's spontaneous behavior will always demonstrate a willfulness that is destructive to its parents, so the child's motivations can only be considered malevolent. He describes a one-year-old who throws his bottle on the floor as he and his mother sit in a church meeting. In Pearl's view, the child was "determined

---

43. Lambert, "Proverbs 22:6," 97.
44. See Hildebrandt, "Proverbs 22:6A," 279–83, 291–92.
45. Archer, "Proverbs 22:6," 273–74.

to make [his mother's] life as miserable as possible—and to destroy her reputation in the process."[46] One hardly needs to say that ascribing this kind of motivation to a one-year-old is ludicrous. The key point, however, is the identification of this infant as a *malevolent child*. Pearl says that as this child grew, his life "was one of unlimited, unrestrained self-indulgence," and that his parents "helplessly watched while selfishness and meanness of spirit took root in a void of understanding."[47] The author also states that a one-year-old will manipulate his parents by his "whining and crying," and will continue his demands as "he connives, calculates, and resorts to angry tantrums."[48] Ordinary infant behaviors that parents may have difficulty understanding are recast as malicious with spiteful intentionality.

To support his arguments, Pearl refers to Psalm 58:3b (KJV) which describes the wicked as those who "go astray as soon as they are born, speaking lies." A closer look reveals that the subject of the verse and of the entire psalm is the wicked in Israel; more precisely, evil judges who use their authority unrighteously. It is they who are "estranged from the womb. These who speak lies go astray from the womb" (Ps 58:3). The psalm describes the wicked judges as "the venom of a serpent, deaf cobras, young lions, headless shafts, water that runs off, snails that secrete slime and the miscarriages of women" (vv. 4, 6, 7, 8). God will "shatter their teeth in their mouths" (v. 6) and the righteous (in counter-distinction) will "wash their feet in the blood of the wicked" (v. 10).

Clearly the psalmist is not offering a doctrinal statement regarding the nature of children, saying that they are inherently estranged from the womb or invariably lie and go astray from birth. He is saying that the wickedness of the evil man begins very early and/or extends and projects throughout his life. Pearl does attempt to rectify the faulty exegesis a few pages later by saying,

> Parents do not deal with the small child's "selfishness" as sin, but they must be aware that it will soon move in that direction. Drives which are not in themselves evil, nonetheless, form the occasion to sin. As parents train the young child, they must take into consideration the evil that a self-willed spirit will eventually bring.[49]

---

46. Pearl and Pearl, *To Train Up a Child*, 13.
47. Ibid.
48. Ibid., 15.
49. Ibid., 17.

I would contend that the "drives" Pearl warns about arise at least in part from the particular bent or unique nature of the child, along with the outworking of behaviors that are its manifestations. A preschooler who wants to bounce a ball against the wall despite his parents' wishes may be doing it because of an inner compulsion to exercise his natural coordination rather than an obstinate attempt to get his own way and disrupt his parents. The parents may find it necessary to stop the child's actions and even take the ball away from him. However, it is not reasonable for them to view him as evil simply for desiring to bounce the ball or for responding negatively to harsh or unfair reprimands. As we've seen, when children are prevented or forbidden from being themselves in their temperaments and their actions, they may assimilate that self-rejection into their subjective experience. This is especially true when the parents' boundaries do not take into account the child's intrinsic motivations for the thing that is being done.

CONCLUSION

When a parent views his two- to seven-year-old child's behavior as abhorrent because it is simply something that bothers him, he may give himself permission to discipline radically with the aim of bringing the child into right relationship to God. For support, parents and parenting authorities have looked to Proverbs 22:6, reading it as a conditional clause: "Train up a child in the way he should go." That common interpretation has seemingly given some parents the freedom and even the obligation to determine the smallest details of how their child will act and be present in the world. The parents concern themselves not only with behavior, the simplest expression to regulate, but also with the more internal aspects of personhood. The child's spontaneity, aptitudes, emotional expressions, even his own experience of his physical energy are seen as obstinate, even rebellious if they run counter to the fervent wishes of the adult.

Opposing this mentality is the alternate reading of the verse: "Train up a child according to his own way." Parents who act on this understanding pay attention to the children's actual motivations, often discovering that their actions are rooted in something other than defiance or disrespect. More conversation is required; more empathy and perspective must be developed. Parents must still curb behavior that is truly obstinate and brazenly insubordinate, disciplining the child with limit-setting interventions. I do not advocate giving children the freedom to do anything they wish or to refuse to hear the instructions and commands of their parents. I am familiar with the current debates about spanking, with their political, psychological, and spiritual aspects. My concern is for the all-too-common abuse of children in the name of training them for adulthood. Naturally as a psychotherapist, I see many patients who as children were ill-treated to the point of physical abuse and severe emotional damage by parents who could not manage their own anger. I would be grateful, and my work would be simpler, if all parents sought to train their child "according to his own way," with the aim that no child ends up essentially at war with himself in what he does, how he expresses himself, or how he relates to his parents.

A child brought up with the idea that he is bad and needs to be broken, or that showing willfulness and wanting certain things is evidence of his "wickedness," naturally develops a mistrust toward those who say they love him. He cannot grasp or reconcile the contradictory messages that he is valued as a beloved son or daughter while at the same time devalued as a rebellious troublemaker. The relational outworking of this confusion leads to a range of conflicts, and since so much of the impact occurs in roughly the first six years of life, most of it cannot be recalled in depth or detail. It takes root as an amorphous or even inchoate negative sense of self. It becomes a root of bitterness (Heb 12:15).

With this mistrust ingrained into the mind (heart) of the child, she inevitably encounters serious struggles as she grows into adolescence. Here I have posited that the painful consequences for fathers and their children, warned about by the Apostle Paul in Colossians 3:21 and Ephesians 6:4a, come to fruition. The embitterment, provocation, and intense anger in these relationships seriously hinder the children from reaching a felt experience of trust in the Heavenly Father.

To explore the development of the "exasperated, embittered" child from a psychologically relational perspective, I turn to three renowned master theoreticians of contemporary psychoanalytic thinking, clinicians with deep experience working with those who have grown up with a continuous and intense sense of parental disregard.

CHAPTER SIX

Help from "The Study of the Soul"

> These parents don't really care about their children
> and the harm they can come to.
> They are more concerned about the impression they will make
> And about what their neighbors will think and say
> If they forget some of the precautions
>
> They are Christians and do not want their name soiled
> they want to be exemplary...
>
> "Living for Someone Else"
> (Ulrich Schaffer, 1980)[1]

Abusive homes are not the only places where children experience parental disregard. The problems may just as easily occur in what seems the best of environments. The "disregarding" can happen when parents follow a rigid plan or philosophy of child-rearing that advocates a "one size fits all" approach. It can occur where the parent's unresolved anxieties lead them to limit their children's activities or when their insecurities make them feel that they fall short compared with other families. Guilt over a child's "failure" to meet familial or societal standards can likewise motivate

---

1. Schaffer, *For the Love of Children*, 74.

Help from "The Study of the Soul"

parents to label the child's actions as counterproductive, selfish, or even rebellious.

When parents do not take the time to understand their children's drives to express themselves or be involved in particular activities, their lack of interest can become distressing. Bruno Bettelheim, in his book *A Good Enough Parent*, gives sage advice in this regard:

> This is why a good enough parent is one whose actions and reactions, whose approvals as well as his criticisms (both equally important and necessary in raising one's child), are tempered by thoughtful regard for his child's perceptions. Good enough parents endeavor to evaluate and respond to matters both from their adult perspective and from the quite different one of the child, and to base their actions on a reasonable integration of the two, while accepting that the child, because of his immaturity, can understand matters only from his point of view.[2]

A parent who genuinely seeks to understand his child's desires and aspirations will inevitably spend more time evaluating him. I am not talking about hunger for sweets or obsessive activities like video games or overly aggressive behavior that may violate the freedom of others or dangerous activities stemming from the child's ignorance. As Bettelheim suggests, immaturity should be protected with limitations. However, the child's desire to express himself in deeply self-satisfying ways should draw close attention. Parents should learn how to perceive and respond to these kinds of activities or forms of play in their own children.

Several years ago I treated a woman, Donna, who struggled with compulsive overeating. When she came to me her weight was nearly three times the American Medical Association's recommendations for her height. Donna was a "big girl" by the time she was ten years old—not seriously overweight, but still larger than most of the boys in her class at school. She wanted to play park league football and was strong and fast enough to compete. But girls at that time were discouraged from competing with boys in any sport, particularly contact sports like football. Donna valued her physical abilities and wanted to use her size and strength athletically but her parents absolutely refused to let her participate in any organized league in which she would play against boys. They also did not encourage her to join sports leagues that were girls-only.

---

2. Bettelheim, *Good Enough Parent*, 48.

Part III: All in the Family

Donna experienced her parents' attitudes (her mother's in particular) not only as a rejection of her athletic interests but of her body, her physical self. Since at this time she was only marginally overweight the demands of any organized sport would have been extremely valuable for her overall health. Instead, as a defense of her selfhood and an expression of her anger, she started to gain weight in earnest.

Donna rejected her mother's expectations and embraced the external trappings of a large body that gave her status and identity in the eyes of her peers. She continued to gain weight and increase in size as years passed; in her own words, she learned to "really throw her weight around."

Parental failure to understand children's needs for freedom of expression can generate a range of problems, especially when they involve issues of basic aptitude, temperament, or natural ability (i.e., the child's "way"). Certainly in Donna's case other factors contributed to her dilemma, but its origin lay within a classic pattern of pathological accommodation.

Adults can be very persuasive in opposing their children's aspirations. When my son Paul demonstrated his desire to pursue wrestling as a career, as a parent I held all the cards: authority, knowledge, financial means, even the physical strength (at the time) to deny his participation. As I described earlier, I could have said "no" to his interests at any stage, from watching televised wrestling events and playing with his wrestling action figures to joining the "junior" professional entertainment circuit and then creating his own wrestling federation.

My wife and I sometimes struggled with our choices as we watched to see how Paul's energy would manifest itself, and whether his enthusiasm was taking him in a positive direction. Some of our Christian friends pressured us to curtail his interest in theatrical wrestling. However, this was obviously not what Paul wanted and we knew it was not what he needed. Bettelheim describes the impact of unreasonable expectations of parental authority:

> An adult can easily outreason a child without even realizing that he is doing it, the parent's reasoning power being much greater than that of the child, who is unable to marshal his arguments in a convincing way. But the grown-up's superior ability to argue and his greater command of relevant facts—so convincing to the parent—can be experienced by the child as simply the beating down of his opinion....
>
> So the child feels outreasoned, and to be outreasoned is a frustrating and debilitating experience. It is a far cry from being

convinced—it usually makes us shut up, but we hold on even more stubbornly to our own opinion. The child falls silent, and the parent believes he has won his point. When he asks, the child usually agrees that the parent is right, in order to stop arguments, and all too often the parent *confuses compliance with conviction*.³

The error of confusing "compliance with conviction" is quite important. Children will nearly always comply with the pressure from a parent, whether it is brought from a threatening father or an exhausted mother. They will also submit to parents' wishes in reaction to criticism that seems to jeopardize the attachment tie in some way.⁴ A child's worst fear is abandonment and children accommodate swiftly to avoid that outcome. Psychiatrist and author M. Scott Peck says of this,

> All children are terrified of abandonment and with good reason. The fear of abandonment begins around the age of six months, as soon as the child is able to perceive itself to be an individual, separate from its parents. For with this perception of itself as an individual comes the realization that as an individual it is quite helpless, totally dependent and totally at the mercy of its parents for all forms of sustenance and means of survival. To the child, abandonment by its parents is the equivalent of death.⁵

Abandonment experiences don't usually entail the actual physical desertion of the child, but parents have sometimes used extended periods of isolation as a form of punishment. Patients have told me that they were put into closets, or outside on the back porch at night, or in the garage, as well as into closed rooms with the lights turned off. Speaking about children who do not undergo an actual abandonment but are left in other ways, Peck continues:

---

3. Ibid., 49, emphasis mine.
4. See Beebe et al., *Forms of Intersubjectivity*, 220–21.
    The attachment process is a learning experience that generates predictions. A child learns what will happen if, for example the child smiles, becomes distressed, becomes separated, needs attention, becomes self-focused, or purses his own curiosity. What will the parent do: smile, shout, sigh, look anxious, or ignore him? Children learn to predict how to best engage the parent in responding to their needs, and what they need to do, for example, *to keep connected, be soothed, or avoid being overstimulated*. (emphasis mine)
5. Peck, *Road Less Traveled*, 25.

Others, while not abandoned in fact, fail to receive from their parents the reassurance that they will not be abandoned. There are some parents, for instance, who in their desire to enforce discipline as easily and quickly as possible, will actually use the threat of abandonment, overly or subtly, to achieve this end. The message they give to their children is: "If you don't do exactly what I want you to do I won't love you any more, and you can figure out for yourself what that might mean." It means, of course, abandonment and death. These parents sacrifice love in their need for control and domination over their children, and their reward is children who are excessively fearful of the future. So it is that these children abandoned either psychologically or in actuality, enter adulthood lacking any deep sense that the world is a safe and protective place.[6]

Peck's words are sobering enough even if most parents never intend to follow through on their threats. The threatened child will experience various levels of emotional withdrawal from the disapproving adult. The estrangement he feels when his sense of attachment is endangered brings a kind of dread: "where is my mommy or daddy, do they still love me and want to protect me?" To a child whose "disobedience" has invoked this reaction from his their parents, accommodation is the only safe response.

Children naturally need guidance in learning about acceptable behaviors for different contexts and with different types of people. They need to be taught, by constant repetition, family norms about conversations, debates, complaints, boundaries, limits, and consequences as well as the emotional flexibility and restrictions of each parent. When a child does not yet understand these norms she will find it very difficult to "argue" her case to her parents passionately yet respectfully. She will also struggle to find modes of expression that convey the importance of her particular desire.

THE IMPORTANCE OF ATTACHMENT

Psychoanalysts and other behavioral scientists have focused on the quality of the attachment between parent and child as an indicator for the emotional health of the child (and also of the parent). They have been particularly concerned with how the child experiences her parents' understanding and responsiveness to her needs. Psychologist Robert Karen, in his book

---

6. Ibid., 26.

Help from "The Study of the Soul"

Becoming Attached: First Relationships and How They Shape Our Capacity to Love, describes the concept of attachment:

> It encompasses both the quality and strength of the parent-child bond, the ways in which it forms and develops, how it can be damaged and repaired, and the long-term impact of separations, losses, wounds, and deprivations. Beyond that it is a theory of love and its central place in human life.[7]

The magnitude and value of a healthy attachment is hard to overstate. So much of the psychological and relational development of a child takes place within the safety of that bond. John Bowlby, the founder of modern attachment theory, describes it by saying:

> Attachment theory regards the propensity to make intimate emotional bonds to particular individual as a basic component of human nature, already present in germinal form in the neonate and continuing through adult life into old age. During infancy and childhood bonds are with parents (or parent substitutes) who are looked to for protection, comfort, and support. During healthy adolescence and adult life these bonds persist, but are complemented by new bonds, commonly of a heterosexual nature ... the relationship exists in its own right and has a key survival function of its own, namely protection. Initially the only means of communication between infant and mother is through emotional expression and its accompanying behaviour. Although supplemented later by speech, emotionally mediated communication nonetheless persists as a principal feature of intimate relationships throughout life.[8]

Bowlby also describes the associated behaviors:

> Attachment behaviour is any form of behaviour that results in a person attaining or maintaining proximity to some other clearly identified individual who is conceived as better able to cope with the world. It is most obvious whenever the person is frightened, fatigued, or sick, and is assuaged by comforting and care giving. ... Nevertheless for the person to know that an attachment figure is available and responsive gives him strong and pervasive feeling of security, and so encourages him to value and continue the relationship. Whilst attachment behaviour is at its most obvious in early childhood, it can be observed throughout the life cycle,

---

7. Karen, *Becoming Attached*, 3.
8. Bowlby, *Secure Base*, 120–21.

especially in emergencies . . . it is regarded as an integral part of human nature. . . . The biological function attributed to it is that of protection. To remain within easy access of a familiar individual known to be ready and willing to come to our aid in an emergency is clearly a good insurance policy—whatever our age.[9]

When a young child feels safe in his environment he can creatively explore it. With encouragement he can develop feelings of competency, a nascent sense of self-confidence. Mary Ainsworth, a colleague of Bowlby's, says that parents should set a primary goal of creating a "secure base" for their children, proposing the concept of "maternal sensitivity" as a means of developing that secure base.[10] Many modern parents may find these ideas unexceptional or even self-evident. But in the professional world of child development or psychiatry fifty-plus years ago, when Bowlby, Ainsworth, and other champions of attachment theory first proposed them, they incited no little controversy.[11]

The Ainsworth describes group "maternal sensitivity" as follows:

1. The mother must be able to attune to her infant's signals with attentiveness. Hesitation in her ability to attune may result from external or internal preoccupation with her own needs and well-being.

2. She must appropriately interpret the signals from the perspective of the infant. For example, she must decipher the meaning of the child's crying (from hunger, illness, pain, boredom). There is a danger that the infant's signals may be distorted or incorrectly interpreted as a result of her own needs, or by projection of these needs onto the child.

3. She must respond appropriately to the signals. For example, she must ascertain the correct amount of nourishment, soothe the child, if possible, or offer play stimuli without burdening the mother-child interaction either by overstimulation or under-stimulation.

---

9. Ibid., 26–27. See also Brisch, *Treating Attachment Disorders*, 15.

    Sensitive behavior by an attachment figure requires the ability to attune to the child's signals (e.g., crying), interpret them correctly (e.g., as proximity- and contact-seeking), and satisfy them promptly and appropriately. Ideally this "sensitive behavior" occurs countless times in the interactions of daily life. . . . An infant is likely to develop a secure attachment to an attachment figure whose sensitive care giving behavior satisfies his needs in the manner described above.

10. Brisch, *Treating Attachment Disorders*, 20.
11. See Karen, *Becoming Attached*, 26–46.

4. Her reaction must be prompt, taking place within a time period that does not cause intolerable frustration for the child. The time period during which an infant can wait to be nursed is very short during the first weeks of life but becomes longer over the course of the first year.[12]

The mother seeks to understand and respond to her child's genuine needs; she gains knowledge of his rhythms and his particular expressions of his subjective state. The mother looks to her child to help her in caring for him, learning from his signals and cues. It's a way of mothering that leads naturally to the true understanding of Proverbs 22:6, "Train up a child *according to his way* and when he is old he will not depart from it." The parent becomes a student of the child's biology and psychology in all of its nuances.

This contrasts rather starkly with parenting philosophies that imply a "one size fits all" approach,[13] suggesting that infants, preschoolers, school age children and adolescents should be "taught" to conform to the parents' schedules, particular lifestyles, or approach to parenting no matter their circumstances or actual needs. Nothing is more important than compliance, submission, and accommodation to the needs of the parents. The situation may become even more extreme if parents perceive the "internal

---

12. Ainsworth et al., "Infant-Mother Attachment," 99–135; quoted in Brisch, *Treating Attachment Disorders*, 2.

13. See Gerhardt, *Why Love Matters*, 197, in addressing the parent's responsiveness to her baby's needs:

> What is more, the best responsiveness for babies is the 'contingent' kind. This means that the parent needs to respond to the actual needs of their particular baby, not to their own idea of what a baby might need. A timid baby needs a different response from an outgoing baby, and a tired baby needs something different from a bored one. Each baby needs a tailor-made response, not an off-the-shelf-kind, however benign. If the baby is distressed, he needs holding and rocking. If he's bored, he needs a distraction. If he's hungry, he needs food. If he has caught his foot in a blanket, it needs releasing. Each situation requires its own appropriate, contingent response, suitable for the personality of this particular baby. Clearly, it isn't much use being given a rattle when you are hungry, nor being rocked in your basket if your foot is uncomfortably stuck.

Gerhardt says that this "may sound too simple" (198), meaning that any parent would do this, but unfortunately this is not the case. In my years as a clinician, both with my patients and from colleagues, I have observed and heard numerous instances of parents who would not meet a basic need of an infant/toddler only because they are following a certain parenting philosophy. In social settings, even in my own home, I have observed this practice *in vivo*.

motivations" of the child, no matter how young, as intentionally rebellious or even malicious.[14]

> 14. A particularly impactful example of this is the significance that some Christian authors assign to a child's "sin nature." Children of any age are defined as fundamentally depraved, even evil. Parents of this persuasion will view most of the child's behavior as coming from some egotistical sinful place even as a toddler, or (even more bizarre) an infant. I do not deny the doctrine of original sin or that children often act from a selfish mind-set. But the disciplinary measures recommended by these authors are entirely driven by the parents' abstract perceptions of events without exploring their child's experience. When the child is in a needy or deprivational state the parents see it only as a selfish or "proud" place. All this is exacerbated by the parent's desire to curb their child's sin nature at the age of two, or even before! Applying a blanket rule about sinfulness relieves the parents of any responsibility for investigating their own child's internal experiences. Here are some examples of this mentality:
>
>> Children are not born morally and ethically neutral. The Bible teaches that the heart is "deceitful and desperately wicked" (Jeremiah 17:9 KJV). The child's problem is not an information deficit. His problem is that he is a sinner. There are things within the heart of a sweetest little baby that, allowed to blossom and grow to fruition, will bring about eventual destruction....
>>
>> Proverbs 22:15 says, "Folly is bound up in the heart of a child, but the rod of discipline will drive it far from him." God says there is something wrong in the child's heart. Folly or foolishness is bound up in his heart. This folly must be removed, for it places the child at risk....
>>
>> This is the natural state of your children. It may be subtly hidden beneath a tuft of rumpled hair. It may be imperceptible in the smile of a baby. In their natural state, however, our children have hearts of folly. Therefore, they resist correction. They protest against your attempts to rule them. Watch a baby struggle against a diaper change or wearing a hat in the winter. Even this baby who cannot articulate or even conceptualize what he is doing shows a determination not to be ruled from without. This foolishness is bound within his heart. Allowed to take root and grow for fourteen or fifteen years, it will produce a rebellious teenager who will not allow anyone to rule him. (Tripp, *Shepherding a Child's Heart*, 102–3)
>
> It is truly disheartening to see this author suggest that ominous deceptions lie behind the "sweetest little baby," "a tuft of rumpled hair," or the "smile of a baby"; let alone the horrendous example of a possibly uncomfortable, energetic, or irritated infant viewed as rebelliously resisting the wishes of the parent to change its diaper! Imposing theological constructs on babies can only distract the parents from responding to their real needs; and the child, lacking an experience of an efficacious love, will likely grow into the rebellious teenager that Tripp and others are trying to avoid. See Pearl and Pearl, *To Train Up a Child*, 17–19, in the section titled "When Drives Become Sin." On the positive side, the Pearls at least reference an age of accountability and suggest that God is sensitive to the meaning of the child's selfish behavior. James Dobson also refers to an age of accountability to mitigate the parents' anxiety. However, he makes disturbing comments about "rebellion" in an infant/toddler that can start as early as eighteen months old, using the classic image of the "temper tantrum" as evidence. Viewing a child's temper as primarily

Help from "The Study of the Soul"

Some forms of accommodation are necessary for all children as they grow up in a "community of others" that typically includes siblings and extended family members along with parents. All members of the family both contribute and sacrifice for the good of the whole. The danger lies in "pathological accommodation," as Brandchaft described it: unnecessarily limiting or refusing a child's essential vitality simply because it annoys, confuses, or challenges the parent in some way.

Being taught, either by reprimand or induced guilt, that his physical energy, inquisitiveness, or exploratory nature are not acceptable—or that her love of artistic expression, friendships, or active play are not appropriate—will leave any child confused and disappointed. Often the only explanation the parent may offer is that the child's actions inconvenience or disturb the parent on an emotional level; and those emotional reactions may even be disguised behind some philosophy of parenting and child development. If the parent operates from a Christian perspective, convenient uses of proof-texting Scriptures may be employed to shut down any dissension.[15]

Attachment theory speaks to a carefully-observed understanding of relatedness between mother/parent and child. Healthy attachment promotes the well-being of each, but especially of the child and his growth to maturity. Clinton and Straub, both psychotherapists and Christians, describe the importance of this attachment bond:

---

a moral issue again misses the point of the toddler's own perceptions and the actual motivations for the emotional storm. If a parent defines a tantrum as rebellious and therefore sinful, she may well take an approach that is more punitive than if the action was defined differently. When an adult cries and screams in either anger or pain, he or she is not perceived as being in sin; at least not until the reasons for the episode are discerned! See Dobson, *Parent's Answer Book*, 15–17.

15. A noteworthy example appears in Gary Ezzo's book *Preparation for Parenting*, 122. The scripture is Matt 27:46: "My God, my God, why have You forsaken Me?" Earle Morgan of Focus on the Family, in an e-mail to the Christian Research Institute, says of Ezzo,

> In support of their teaching that mothers should refuse to attend crying infants who have already been fed, changed and have had their basic needs met. "Praise God," writes Ezzo, on page 122 of, *Preparation for Parenting*, "that the Father did not intervene when His Son cried out on the cross." completely disregarding its original context and we see no way to make such an application without completely disregarding its original context and purpose. (Quoted in Kathleen Terner and Elliot Miller, "Cultic Characteristics of Growing Families International," Christian Research Institute, 2009, www.equip.org)

Part III: All in the Family

> In our most important relationships in the first years of life, we form implicit emotionally charged *core beliefs* about ourselves. We learn which emotions are acceptable and which are off-limits for our parents, and the lessons we learn in those years form our most fundamental assumptions about the reality of feelings, the expression of them, and the validity of emotional needs. The assumptions we develop form a powerful interpretive grid that can determine how we respond to our own emotions and others' feelings for the rest of our lives.[16]

These core beliefs about which emotions/reactions are acceptable and which are not become affectively "laid down" in memory. The feeling-intensity shapes the ability to express or not express certain aspects of the self. The quality of the attachment bond (i.e., the parents' acceptance, empathy, protection, and enthusiasm) fosters this freedom to develop one's particular way or bent.[17]

ATTACHMENT STYLES

Ainsworth postulated three "styles" of attachment and attachment behaviors: secure, ambivalent and avoidant.[18] A fourth style, called "disorganized," was identified by Mary Main, another important contributor to attachment theory.[19] The four styles have been divided into two categories based on their outcomes for children: secure attachments (based on the secure attachment style), and anxious attachments (resulting from ambivalent, avoidant, or disorganized attachments).

Only the child who experiences a secure attachment will have an optimal opportunity to live out his potential. That child will have the freedom and permission to develop her own natural inclinations, aptitudes, physical prowess, or temperament in the context of a long and loving acceptance. Healthy attachments also incorporate guidance and limits, along with the encouragement to persevere when the going gets tough. As Clinton and Straub state, the securely attached child could conclude, "My needs are legitimate and my parents are glad to meet them."[20]

---

16. Clinton and Straub, *God Attachment*, 57, italics original.
17. Ibid., 66–67.
18. Ainsworth et al., *Patterns of Attachment*.
19. Main and Solomon, "Procedures for Identifying Infants," 121–60.
20. Clinton and Straub, *God Attachment*, 69; the authors further describe the securely

Help from "The Study of the Soul"

By contrast, the affective outcomes of anxious attachment are not so harmonious. The three styles of anxious attachment were highlighted in a study called "The Strange Situation"[21] which explored children's responses to separation and reunion. During the study a mother would leave her toddler alone in a playroom. A "strange woman," whom the child had seen earlier, then came in to sit with her. After a few minutes, the mother returned to the room and made visual and verbal contact with her offspring. How would the infant respond both vocally and physical? How would she cope with the loss of mother's presence, touch and soothing voice? The children's affective states could be discerned in their reactions to the mother's reentry and renewed availability.

Children who fell in the category of "avoidant attachment" were evasive toward the mother when she returned to the playroom. They did not hold the mother's gaze; often they did not walk or crawl to meet her. They showed more interest in the toys around them than in their parent. They seemed to demonstrate a passive resistance to the reuniting and restrained emotional expressions when the mother made physical contact. Brisch describes the avoidant child in the Strange Situation as follows:

> These children react to separation with little protest and display no clear attachment behavior, such as following the mother to the door and crying. In general, they continue to play, although perhaps with less curiosity or persistence. Occasionally they follow the mother with their eyes when she leaves the room, so it is clear that they do register her disappearance. After her return, they are

---

attached child (69–70):

> He realized that the most important authority figures in his young life—mom and dad—are trustworthy, and since they aren't threatened by his expressions of emotions, he isn't threatened by them, either.
>
> As secure children grow up, they feel equally comfortable with intimate relationships and their own sense of autonomy. That is, they aren't too needy or too independent. They develop wisdom in relationships, perceiving who is trustworthy and who isn't, but they aren't black-and-white thinkers; they are secure enough to look at shades of gray in people and situations. They have emotional integrity, admitting the reality of the full range of emotions—both positive and negative emotions—and they engage in a healthy emotional regulation and aren't dominated by their emotions. Under stress they have the ability to think clearly, seek advice from trusted friends, and respect authority without engaging in blind obedience.

21. Ainsworth et al., *Patterns of Attachment*, and Ainsworth, "Patterns of Infant-Mother Attachments."

apt to react to her with avoidance and they do not ask to be taken into her arms. Usually there is no intense physical contact.[22]

This response by the child is self-protective. It signals a relationship where her emotions have not been clearly and consistently responded to by the mother/parent. The child resists the invitation to "reconnect" with her mother since she does not expect a vibrant welcome based on past experience. She avoids being traumatized by a crushed hope for an emotional response. The child has cut herself off from her genuine feelings and her genuine need for care.

If these children continue their experiences into adulthood they will face difficulties trusting any other person to connect with their emotional needs. Their conflicts may be expressed by a fundamental emotional denial: they decide that experiencing affects is not important or just too uncomfortable, especially regarding vulnerable emotions such as sadness, joy, or love. They take action to avoid "feeling encounters," creating serious obstacles to living a healthy life. Strong emotions, whether they are seen as positive (compassion, tenderness, affection, excitement, concern) or negative (remorse, self-pity, loneliness, insecurity, dejection, hopelessness) must be rejected as threats to the person's self-cohesion. Embracing any of them would usher in the dread of falling apart.

The second anxious attachment style has been labeled "ambivalent." These infant/toddlers responded to the mother's return to the playroom with determined efforts to reconnect. They came to the mother, signaled that they wanted to be held, and began to be soothed. However they soon became fussy and pulled away from the mother's embrace and cried more intensely. They then made another movement toward reconnection and comfort, followed by another pulling away. Only after multiple iterations did the children calm down and return to a pre-abandonment state. The cycle or tension in the movements toward or away from the mother signal the child's ambivalence about what he can do to quell his anxiety. As Brisch explains,

> These children demonstrate the greatest distress after separation and cry intensely. Their mothers upon return are not able to calm them quickly. It generally takes these children longer to achieve emotional equilibrium. Sometimes they are not able to return to play, even after several minutes. When their mothers pick them up, the children express a desire for physical contact and closeness

22. Brisch, *Treating Attachment Disorders*, 27.

while at the same time behaving aggressively toward their mothers (kicking, hitting, pushing, or turning away).[23]

These children are reluctant to trust that their mother's presence and ability to soothe them will be sufficient for them, or that it will last. They have been let down too many times in the past. The parent's inconsistency in addressing the needs of the moment has left a troublesome impression. Intermittent expressions of attachment in the midst of misattunement become confusing and disturbing for the child.

Later in life these kinds of inconsistencies again lead to difficulties in trusting the care or love of another who is supposed to be trustworthy. After growing up with perceived irregularities in their parenting, adults demonstrate a pronounced need for reassurance and quick assuring responses. This type of need often lies behind the seemingly endless churning and to-and-fro in romantic relationships that drives couples crazy!

The third type of insecure or anxious attachment, identified by Mary Main, is called "disorganized." As the name suggests, these children's response to the mother's reconnecting ministrations are highly disorganized to the point of being chaotic. As Karl Brisch describes them:

> [They] demonstrate short periods of disorganized behavior, such as running toward the mother, stopping short halfway, and then turning around and running away from her, increasing their distance. That is, the movements of such children may appear to "freeze." In addition, Main and Solomon observed repetitive stereotyped behavior and movement patterns. They interpreted these behaviors as a sign that the child's attachment system had been activated but could not express itself in clear behavioral strategies.[24]

This "freezing" behavior—stopping and going and repetitive movement—betrays an extreme level of anxiety. Children from high-risk homes where extremes of neglect and violence are perpetrated upon family members often display the disorganized attachment style. Though the response from his primary caretakers may have been barely adequate, the child still seeks to maintain some measure of attachment through his signaling behavior. Clinton and Straub, who call this style "fearful attachment," describe the kinds of environments that evoke this kind of reaction in the child:

23. Ibid.
24. Ibid., 27–28.

Part III: All in the Family

These homes may have been physically, emotionally, and sometimes sexually abusive. Instead of love and stability, the child often experienced parents who exhibit out-of-control rage, fierce demands, or soul-numbing isolation. The child doesn't enjoy a safe haven, the joy of exploration, or the confidence of reattaching when times are tough. That's because the source of the child's comfort is also the source of pain and hurt![25]

Living in this kind of early environment devastates the child's ability to trust others for the consistent care that he needs. Many adult psychiatric problems are rooted in a fearful attachment pattern. Depression, severe anxiety, interpersonal conflicts, personality disorders, and many other internal conflicts may mar the existence of adults raised in these kinds of homes.

The securely attached child responds very differently in the "Strange Situation."

He will be saddened when his mother leaves the playroom. He may cry a bit when he notices that she is not returning right away. He will allow himself to be soothed by the other woman who comes to sit in the room. When his mother returns he may cry a bit more but quickly calms down and soon either enters into either active play with his mother or goes exploring in search of a new toy, looking back at mom for her watchful eye and approval. He is reconnected and ready to experience the rest of his day.

The literature offers abundant analyses of the reasons why particular attachment styles develop and their probable affects on adult functioning.[26] A test called the "Adult Attachment Inventory" has been helpful for diagnosing various psychological disturbances, from relatively simple problems to full-fledged personality disorders.[27] Living in a milieu where the responses to one's emotional and sometimes physical desires are confusing, intermittent, insufficient, or even hostile inevitably generates a sense of anxiety. The anxiety may be circumstantially specific, such as during an actual separation, or it may permeate the life of the child each and every day.

---

25. Clinton and Straub, *God Attachment*, 73.

26. Three books on attachment worthy of exploration are: Akhtar, *Mother and Her Child*; Newton, *Attachment Connection*; Grossman et al., *Attachment from Infancy to Adulthood*.

Another helpful book, written with a Christian perspective, is Clinton and Straub's *God Attachment*. The authors effectively review the psychological data, always integrating it with biblical and theological perspectives.

27. George et al., "Attachment Interview for Adults."

Help from "The Study of the Soul"

The latter outcome is most likely produced by the chaos of a disorganized early attachment relationship with parents.

The development of a faith relationship with the God of the Scriptures, the Father of our Lord Jesus Christ, relies on trust. We must be capable of accepting and receiving on an affective level the kind of love that God the Father offers us. Interestingly, much of what Scripture tells us about this love would be described by attachment theorists as "having a secure base." For example:

> Let us therefore draw near with confidence to the throne of grace, that we may receive mercy and may find grace to help in time of need. (Heb 4:16)

> Come to Me, all who are weary and heavy laden, and I will give you rest. Take My yoke upon you, and learn from Me, for I am gentle and humble in heart; and you shall find rest for your souls. For My yoke is easy and My load is light. (Matt 11:28–30)

> Now may our Lord Jesus Christ Himself and God our Father, who has loved us and given us eternal comfort and good hope by grace, comfort and strengthen your hearts in every good work and word. (2 Thess 2:16–17)

> Do not fear, for I am with you; do not anxiously look about you, for I am your God; I will strengthen you, surely I will help you. Surely I will uphold you with My righteous right hand. (Isa 40:10)

> For as high as the heavens are above the earth, so great is His lovingkindness toward those who fear Him. As far as the east is from the west, so far has He removed our transgressions from us. (Ps 103:11–12)

These are only a smattering of statements concerning God's loving care for his children. It is a unique aspect of the God of the Bible that he intimately attends to his creation and those whom he has created. As one theologian puts it, "Other religions with their many ceremonies are commonly occupied with the business of making God care, 'of awakening by sacrifice and prayer or act, the slumbering intent of the deity' (Masterman)."[28] The Christian, by contrast, is called to approach God with the attitude described by the Apostle Peter:

---

28. Stibbs, *First Epistle General of Peter*, 171; quoting J. H. B. Masterman, *First Epistle of St. Peter* (London: Macmillian, 1912).

Part III: All in the Family

> Humble yourselves under the mighty hand of God that He may exalt you at the proper time, casting all your anxieties upon Him for He cares for you.

It is right and good and appropriate to submit or acquiesce to the Lord since he is God and he knows all. He will take you to a better place in due time. He will do this simply because he already cares for you, not as a response to any action you performed or merit you may think you achieved. This marvelously describes the experience of the securely attached child with parents who know their child's individual issues and understand which needs should particularly be addressed. Their understanding and attention bring their child to a better place than he was before.[29]

1 Peter 5:7 tells us that we can unburden our anxieties and cares onto the Lord because we know he cares about us individually and intimately. The phrase "he cares for you" may be better rendered, "there is a care for him concerning you."[30] Or possibly, "'it is a care to him' what transpires in the life of a believer."[31] What concerns you concerns God; whatever makes you feel troubled, God cares about it. Not only is he concerned about you, he is engrossed in what troubles you. The nuances of 1 Peter speak to the kinds of involvement that good parents practice with their children, in order to remedy their problems or help them tolerate them.

Since children remember and internalize the dominant caring styles of those who love them, the quality of that care becomes all important. Anxious attachments effectively impose a distorted template of expectations for all of the child's close relationships. The template includes particular "rules" the child believes he must follow in order to achieve even an insecure attachment (which at least avoids the dreaded sense of being unattached or abandoned—a fate worse than death for most children). In

---

29. William W. Meissner, Jesuit priest and renowned psychoanalyst, said in his book *Psychoanalysis and Religious Experience*, 138:
   > Certain aspects of the child's developmental experience seem particularly relevant for the shaping of his religious experience and ultimately for his experience of relationship to God. At the most rudimentary level, the child's early experiences of "mirroring" in interaction with the mother provide the basis for important elements in the structuring of his concept of God. In his experiences of the mother as a loving and caring presence in nursing ... by which the child finds himself narcissistically embraced, admired, recognized, and cherished, he finds a symbiotic union with the mother that can serve as the basis for an evolving sense of trust, acceptance, and security.

30. Lenski, *Interpretation of the Epistles*, 224.

31. Cramer, *First and Second Peter*, 71.

adulthood, drawing emotionally closer to another person may spark fears of losing one's ability to choose for oneself, or a conviction that loving another will require one to accommodate completely to that person. It is easy to conclude that the costs of entering into in-depth relationships are too high to make them worthwhile.

For the anxiously attached child there will come a time when all active protests cease. Any hope of using crying, kicking, arguing or resisting as effective responses will end in the child's mind. He may still offer verbal complaints but internally he will have given up hope for genuine recognition of his unique personhood. He will feel guilty for desiring to oppose the decrees of his parents and an even greater sense of remorse for acting out any of those wishes. The only remaining emotional option is to accommodate, comply and give up all offending notions. This is not an adaptive or adjusting kind of accommodation that aims to salvage some personal space. It is compliant, submissive, and conforming, a tragic abandonment of his original desire or longing, no matter how important it was to him or intrinsically right it may have felt.

BEING YOUR TRUE SELF

Contemporaneous with Bowlby's and Ainsworth's work on styles of attachment was that of Donald Winnicott, a pediatrician turned psychoanalyst. Winnicott played a major role at the British Psychoanalyst Institute in London before the work of Bowlby became better known. He had always been sensitive to the early influence of the relationship between mother and child though his focus was not shared by the majority of his peers. In ascendency at this time (1940–1965) were the works of Anna Freud, who championed her father's classical analytic theories, and Melanie Klein, who restructured Sigmund Freud's work into her own understanding of intra-psychic conflict.[32] Both of these approaches to psychological disturbances pointed to the child's innate propensities or internal biological constraints as their origin. The actual relationship between parent and child was largely shaped by, or served to exacerbate, the underlying dynamics.

Winnicott began to view child development as much more dynamic and intersubjective than the Freudians believed. Was a particular mother a "good-enough mother"; that is, did she pay attention to her child's needs

---

32. Hughes, *Reshaping the Psychoanalytic Domain*, 1–26.

and address them in timely, thoughtful and nonintrusive ways?[33] Could she resist the temptation to do "everything" in her power to perfectly meet her infant's demands, thus allowing some inevitable (and manageable) frustration in her child's life? Could she also attune herself to the requirements for soothing and restoring an emotionally injured child?[34]

Winnicott described the mother at the end of her pregnancy as entering into a "primary maternal preoccupation."[35] This construct is characterized by the mother's heightened sense of unity with the infant, a sort of harmonious identification that guides the mother in addressing the baby's dependencies. Howard Bacal calls this a "state of enhanced maternal empathy"[36] which becomes a "holding environment" for the newborn. Bacal further comments,

> The *holding environment* is Winnicott's term for the overall technique of good-enough mothering of the infant, the provision of which is determined by the mother's ability to empathize with her baby's needs. . . . Winnicott stresses the importance of the quality of the mother's physical holding of her infant, which must entail an identification with the baby . . . provided by the mother's empathy with her baby's needs. . . . The mother's ability to meet the needs of her young infant derives from a state of *primary maternal preoccupation*. . . . At this time, when the infant is maximally dependent, his world must be maximally adaptive to his needs. In this very early phase of life, if the mother fails to adapt in these ways or if she intrudes substantially with her own needs ("impingement"), the infant's reaction to her intrusions breaks up his "going-on-being."

---

33. Winnicott, "Ego Distortion," 140–52. See also his *Home Is Where We Start From*, 142–49. He says that the good-enough mother

> starts off with a high degree of adaptation to the baby's needs. That is what "good-enough" means, this tremendous capacity that mothers ordinarily have to give themselves over to the identification with the baby; towards the end of a pregnancy and at the beginning of a child's life, they are so identified with their baby that they really practically know what the baby is feeling like, and so they can adapt themselves to the needs of the baby in such a way that the baby's needs are met. Then the baby is in the position of being able to make a developmental continuity of growth which is the beginning of health. The mother is laying down the basis for the mental health of the baby, and more than health—fulfillment and richness. . . .
>
> So the mother . . . has this ability to identify with the baby without resentment, and to adapt to the baby's needs.

34. Seinfeld, *Interpreting and Holding*, 105–6.

35. Winnicott, "Primary Maternal Preoccupation," 300–305.

36. Bacal and Newman, *Theories of Object Relations*, 193.

Help from "The Study of the Soul"

If *reaction to impingement* becomes a characteristic pattern in his life, it will seriously interfere with the integration of his self.[37]

In essence Winnicott describes a kind of dance between the mother and her child in which the mother both leads and follows her offspring. She leads in that she understands the kinds of emotional resources that the relationship requires; she anticipates when they will be needed and prepares herself to use them. She follows in that she gives careful attention to the many different ways her baby presents his needs to her and she develops the ability to adapt to his cues.

What the baby needs to see when it looks up into the mother's (or father's) face is its own reflection in the appreciative gaze of their eyes. The mother's attunement to her child and her delight in meeting his needs is expressed in her eyes, and the child sees his own face mirrored in his mother's contentment.[38]

This visceral experience spurs the development of an internally congruent fundamental sense of self-acceptance—what Winnicott calls the "true self."[39] Simply stated, the child begins to develop a healthy self-esteem. Over time, as the relationship grows, the child will gain an inner sense of "okay-ness" in being herself; an ability to express that self in activities and relationships; and a freedom to make mistakes and learn from them without suffering undue self-denigration. Stephen Parker has recently described this true self

> as something inviolable in humans, a sense of aliveness and realness that made life worth living, a sacred center that was incommunicable. . . . It represented the creative potential of humans; a desire to be who they truly were rather than comply with external impositions . . .
>
> The true self originated in early infant movement ("spontaneous gestures") . . . as these spontaneous gestures were appropriately attended to by the mother, the true self emerged as the center of aliveness and realness for the infant. A *failure to respond appropriately* to these early gestures, either *though neglect or through asserting the mother's needs over the infant's* caused a *compliant false self to arise*.[40]

---

37. Ibid., italics original.
38. Green, "Analytic Play," 216.
39. Bacal and Newman, *Theories of Object Relations*, 191–92.
40. Parker, *Winnicott and Religion*, 202, emphasis mine. Parker goes on (214) to explain this truly dynamic side of Winnicott:

Part III: All in the Family

Winnicott's parents were deeply religious people with roots in the Wesleyan tradition in Great Britain. Judeo-Christian understandings of human nature and "the world in which people live, implicitly found their way into [Winnicott's] theorizing."[41] Marie Hoffman goes so far as to say,

> For Winnicott, the loving, immanent relationship between a caretaker and an infant is strongly in the foreground. . . . Whether one speaks of Winnicott's "holding environment," "good-enough mothering," or the "facilitating environment," this foreground good object who is loving is analogous to the Wesleyan loving God, one whose grace is abundant and whose provision is bountiful.[42]

Once again, the biblical depiction of God's compassion and insight into the nature and plight of his children can be seen in the parents' compassion for their own (Ps 103:13–14). However, Winnicott's description of the breakdown of this relationship and its impacts in adulthood draws us back again to the issue of parental impingements. Winnicott implicitly gives credence to both Brandchaft's concept of "pathological accommodation" and my own examination of the encumbrance of parental disregard.

In Winnicott's terms, impingement by the mother/primary caretaker/parents on the infant's "spontaneous gestures" creates disruptions in the child's "going-on being"[43] (i.e., the child's free-feeling experience of himself in his surroundings). Impingement here means to interfere by limiting

---

> Winnicott's answer to the questions of what made life worth living was the feeling of being alive or real. This quest to feel real or alive is a complex concept that is interwoven with several of Winnicott's key ideas. . . . it is connected with the emergence of a sense of "self," or a "subjective sense of being. . . ." Much of Winnicott's work was devoted to unfolding the richness of this concept of feeling alive or real and its connection to a sense of being, to creativity, to an ability to "play" and surprise oneself. The richness of this yearning to be alive led Winnicott at one point to remark that "we are poor indeed if we are only sane." Real life is more than just an absence of problematic symptoms. Winnicott also spoke of this quest to feel real and be alive in his work on the true and false self. People yearn to be the true selves they feel themselves to be. The true self, with its inviolable, yet fragile core that must be protected and whose gestures must be nurtured is a way to feel real.

For comparison, Richard Rohr offers another perspective in his book *Immortal Diamond*. Coming from an overtly theological perspective, Rohr sensitively describes the outworking of the true self.

41. Ibid., 193, 193–222.
42. Hoffman, *Toward Mutual Recognition*, 141.
43. Bacal and Newman, *Theories of Object Relations*, 193.

another's free flow of expression, encroaching or interrupting with the aim of advancing one's own agenda. For a mother with her child, it can be as dramatic as a collision of wills that ends in the child's total frustration or as subtle as using manipulation to alter the child's actions or responses.

The actions of the impinging parent can begin very early in a child's life, and for my purposes it is important to know that they can continue throughout the entirety of the parent/child relationship. They can start as early as the initial plans for the infant's feeding. How attentive is the mother (or father if bottle feeding) to the baby's subjective states of discomfort or anxiety, driven by his increasing hunger and need to be fed?[44] Do the parents respond to signals and cues the child uses to indicate his desires to play, to gaze, to be held, or to sleep? Do the parents overstimulate because they are not paying attention, or do they ignore motor movements from the child that signal a desire to be noticed?

Critical to this discussion are the parent's motivations for choosing whether or not to respond to their child's "requests." Do they share a predisposition or some sort of bias that requires the baby to conform to the adult's needs, schedules, or priorities? Obviously that child will experience a different kind of care than one whose parents are attuned to their child and responsive to her needs. Parker speaks of the "environmental failure" suffered by some children as the driver of one of Winnicott's most important insights: the development of the "false self."

> Winnicott's central thrust is his understanding that a lack of health in humans (being less than humans are destined to be) is due to breakdowns in environmental provision. This breakdown might be framed as a breakdown in relational functioning; this leads in turn to breakdowns in the emergence of healthy patterns of relating in the individual . . .
>
> If the origin of sin is environmental failure, then the chief way sin manifests in the daily life of the person is through the emergence of a false self. The *false self is the result of a lack of responsive attunement of the infant's gestures.* In such situations the infant's sense of self becomes "split" with a false self emerging to protect or hide the true potential. . . . This failure in care that contributes to the emergence of the false self produces a "fall" from one's potential. The presence of the false self stands at some level as a betrayal of the true self.[45]

---

44. Green, "Analytic Play," 216.
45. Parker, *Winnicott and Religion*, 216, emphasis mine.

For Winnicott, the false self arises from the child's accommodation to the requirements of the parents (especially the mother) when they fail to respond to her need signals. It may begin as a moment of confusion, sometimes seen in the eyes of the infant, or in an averted gaze. When the misattunement continues too long for the infant to tolerate, she ceases any protest behavior such as crying or fussing. She becomes compliant and does not offer any other challenges; she accommodates herself to the parent's message of "no."[46] The risk and terror of abandonment, which could increase if the child ramps up an affective storm, must be mitigated at all costs!

We should be clear that this experience is not a matter of the child failing to get what it desires; it would be profoundly unhealthy for any child to get everything that it wants. Rather it's the child's painful discovery that his felt needs are not okay and his natural self-expressions are not acceptable to those he trusts for his care. The false self develops out of that deeply personal sense of rejection.

By the time such a child is seven years old he will have become so accustomed to his parents' rejection of his felt needs that he will not regard them as needs anymore.[47] In the life of the adult, Winnicott sees this reaction as

> [a] relationship to external reality which is one of compliance, the world and its details being recognized but only as something to be fitted in with or *demanding adaptation. Compliance carries with it a sense of futility* for the individual and is associated with the idea that nothing matters and that life is not worth living. In a tantalizing way many individuals have experience just enough of creative living to recognize that for most of their time they are living uncreatively, as if caught up in *the creativity of someone else, or of a machine.* (emphasis mine)[48]

If we believe that all we are permitted to do is what others want us to do, life can easily look like a machine that has trapped us. We have no freedom to be ourselves, there is no safety in attempting to change, and we can't see a way out.

---

46. Gerhardt, *Why Love Matters*, 25–27, 130–31.

47. I am relating this to the so-called Catholic (Jesuit) maxim, "Give me a child until he is seven, and I will give you the man."

48. Winnicott, *Playing and Reality*, 65.

Help from "The Study of the Soul"

STRUCTURES OF PATHOLOGICAL ACCOMMODATION

Concerning these levels of personhood, psychoanalyst Donna Orange says,

> It may be worth noting that the "compliance" of which Winnicott speaks refers to more than simple compromise or Piagetian accommodation that is part of all learning and life in a social world. Instead, like Brandchaft's "systems of pathological accommodation" . . . *compliance here means a life so profoundly lost* that a radical restart is required.[49]

While Bowlby/Ainsworth's secure and insecure attachments and Winnicott's true self/false self dichotomies are largely concerned with internal affects and attitudes, Brandchaft's "structures of pathological accommodation" point to the resulting external behaviors that can mar a person's life. To express it schematically, at the risk of oversimplification: insecure attachments lead to false-self defensive reactions which manifest as pathologically accommodating responses to the injunctions of authority figures.

As Brandchaft explained it, when caretakers do not understand, attend to or support a child's emotional gestures, creative playfulness, and/or concentrated endeavors, the child's sense of self will be wounded. Like other analysts, Brandchaft is not referring to caretakers' responses to dangerous actions by the child that arise from his ignorance of situations or the possible outcomes of his behavior. Rather, when parents continually reject the child simply because of their own psychological limitations, the child will inevitably be emotionally injured. To protect the security of the relationship, the child, even as an infant, will "give up" her personal expressions and accommodate to her parents' attitudes. Brandchaft says of this reaction,

> When the child consistently is unable to communicate such experiences without perceiving that he is damaging or unwelcome to the caregiver, a watershed in the relationship occurs where by a painful inner conflict becomes structuralized.[50]

Brandchaft means that the child's repeated experiences of misattunement, lack of interest, or rejection by the parents will be reconstructed mentally in his own self-awareness. This revised self-understanding does not depend on reinforcers from the surround since the child has

---

49. Orange, *Suffering Stranger*, 148, emphasis mine.
50. Brandchaft, *Toward an Emancipatory Psychoanalysis*, 79.

internalized it as a personal frame of reference. He cannot benefit from his own self-determined actions even when they feel congruent with who he actually is (his nature, bent, or way). His driving need for his parents' approval, in whatever form he can evoke it, will affectively overrule any self-articulative desires or actions. Brandchaft, using the term "self-objects" to refer to the child's caretakers, says:

> Whatever early failures a child experiences in his developmental course with his self-objects they frequently include the denial of perceptions and the discounting of experience disjunctive to the parent's subjectively necessary picture of themselves. The child then learns what he is supposed and not supposed to think, feel, and do. The child, to whom the stability and approving responses of his self-objects are urgently necessary, adapts himself to the conditions required.[51]

Because of the tremendous importance of these day-to-day events, Brandchaft implores all parents to understand children's needs to be affirmed in their self-expressions!

> Parents must be capable of the profound shift in perspective that marks their own psychological differentiation from their child. They must have relinquished their need for the child to be the ideal child if they are to be able to appreciate and respond to the *unfolding of the child's intrinsic endowment.*[52]

The parents' appreciation of their child's "intrinsic endowment" is so essential to his dynamic makeup that he cannot grow up whole without it. Experiencing this appreciation strengthens his self-cohesion. He finds greater freedom and enjoyment in exercising his abilities, along with freedom from debilitating shame states. He knows he is cherished by his involved and observing parents because he can see their smiles, their enjoyment in his accomplishments, and the gleam in their eyes.

Brandchaft warns parents that this approach is not optional. Since mindful and responsive reactions to a child's genuine self-expressions help to feed her emotional soul, parents who are continually non-responsive can expect serious repercussions.

> Finally the caretakers possess enormous power to inhibit, undermine or destroy the development in the child of his innate capacity

---

51. Ibid., 36.
52. Ibid., emphasis mine.

for self reflection, which might afford him the opportunity for correction, choice, and independent judgment ... the child becomes incapacitated because he cannot integrate experiences that contradict the constructs of the parents.

The result is what I have come to believe is the most pervasive and disabling disorder of our times. *The tormenting doubt, never settled, about who and what one is, the absence of sustaining internal referents for one's sense of one's own self, and the lack of confidence, courage, and freedom to choose a course of one's own* are all rooted in this existential conflict.[53]

This lack of "confidence, courage and freedom" is the true cost of the long-term damage.

Without these qualities in a person's character, life becomes more difficult by an order of magnitude. A faith relationship with Christ is said to help develop these capacities in the life of the believer.[54] Yet to genuinely welcome and accept the love of God we must be capable of trusting in the reality of his goodness and affectively embrace the truths of the Scriptures. As has been said, the dimensions of God's love are not abstract but existential; they are to be grasped through the sinews of the heart (O taste and see that the Lord is good!).

The damaged mind-set says, "For reasons I don't understand, I am not allowed to be what I want to be, I cannot express what feels intrinsically good for me, and I don't know how to choose a different way." That mindset is fundamentally hostile to developing the confidence, courage and freedom to live affectively and effectively for Christ. This, I believe, is the reason why so many believers express their faith in forms that are purely abstract, legalistic or judgmental.[55] They lack the capacity to experience the

---

53. Ibid., emphasis mine.

54. See Eph 3:12; Heb 4:12; 1 John 4:17 for "confidence"; Josh 1:9; Ps 31:24; 1 Cor 16:13 for "courage"; John 8:32, 36; Gal 5:13; 2 Cor 3:17 for "freedom."

55. As described in Kinnaman and Lyons, *Unchristian*, 181–204. Dorothy L. Sayers, in *Creed or Chaos?*, 23, supports this by asking, "What are the seven Christian virtues?" Her answer: "Respectability; childishness; mental timidity; dullness; sentimentality; censoriousness, and depression of the spirits." She then explains,

> Whenever an average Christian is represented in a novel or a play, he is pretty sure to be shown practicing one or all of the *Seven Deadly Virtues* listed above, and I am afraid that this is the impression made by the average Christian upon the world at large. (emphasis mine)

Sayers wrote her comments in 1949, sixty years before Kinnaman and Lyons' book. It is disturbing to note how little has changed in that time!

PART III: ALL IN THE FAMILY

truth that the Lord is *for* us, that our concerns are his concerns, and that he wants to fulfill in some way the desires of our hearts because we love him (Ps 56:9; 118:6; 1 Pet 5:7; Ps 37:4–5). Without understanding the developmental injuries of pathological accommodation and how they can affect one's felt-understanding of God, the damaged mind-set will predominate. The power of this "weight" depends on the severity of the experience of parental disregard.

Believers mired in legalistic and judgmental expressions of faith tend to experience their submission to God as a kind of compulsive accommodation. Again Brandchaft describes the dilemma:

> Accommodation out of love, with a respect for the legitimate needs of one's partner, is the successful outcome of healthy development and remains the sine qua non of any wholesome relationship. Pathological accommodation, by contrast, show the continuing influence of traumatic developmental attachment experience and is marked by its essentially compulsive quality.[56]

In the early church the apostles sometimes contended with false teachers who promoted a "compulsive" understanding of obedience. Paul vividly portrayed the conflict in the book of Galatians. A group of believers from the church in Jerusalem taught that obedience to the Lord (and therefore the believer's expression of love) required complete submission to the Mosaic Law, just as the Jews did in Palestine. Paul said that if these teachers were correct, Christ sacrificed himself on the cross needlessly (Gal 2:21). Was God a taskmaster who imposes demands for compliance on his children? Paul reminded the Galatians that they received the empowering of the Holy Spirit through a faith relationship, not by following rules (3:2–3). Compulsory compliance simply would not do for those who were new creations in Christ. The false teachings only generated rivalries, envy, and contentious boasting about empty achievements in self-righteousness (5:26).

In his response, Paul spoke about the true righteousness nurtured by God's gracious relationship with the believer (2:16–21). The Holy Spirit comes to the believer through a faithful hearing of the gospel and performs his work within her (3:1–5). The fruit of the Spirit's work in the believer's heart, mind, and actions provide the evidence for God's holiness (5:22–25). All of these things are accomplished in the love relationship between God and his child.

56. Brandchaft, *Toward an Emancipatory Psychoanalysis*, 200–201.

Help from "The Study of the Soul"

Paul describes this as "freedom" for the believer. She has been freed to express her deepest inner truth. She does not follow the dictates of other human beings or allow herself to be enslaved by them (5:1). She is a new creature who follows the Word of the Spirit in the outflowing of her life (6:15; 5:22–23). Her motivation to lovingly serve springs forth from her freedom, not from legalistic compulsions (5:13).

A RAY OF HOPE

An ongoing experience of parental disregard creates a great weight in the life of the Christian, a psychological and emotional drag that hinders him from keeping his eyes on Jesus (Heb 12:1–2). Sometimes Christ's love seems too impenetrable; sometimes the early resentments that still dominate his emotions bleed over to his image of God the Father, making it very difficult to trust him for essential aspects of one's life. In my clinical practice I have worked with Christian people who have suffered the fallout that the apostle warned about. They have lost heart; they have not been able to reach the goals they strived for or follow God in the way they believed he was leading them. They could not find the capacity to receive love from others in any way that resembles the gifts the Scriptures promise.

Their stories are both heartbreaking and hopeful, real-life narratives with consequences that have sometimes left the protagonists in great anguish. Any psychotherapist who is a Christian can tell you dozens of these tales. In the next chapter I will offer three stories from my case histories to illustrate the impacts of parental disregard and the deeply personal work that believers have done to find freedom under the invited presence of the Lord.

CHAPTER SEVEN

The Embittered Christian and Trusting in God

> This father uses the Bible
> abuses the Bible
> to justify his unholy temper
> to cover up his sin
>
> As he quotes and preaches
> The child suffers the death of the father
> and the death of God the father ...
>
> "Abuse"
> (Ulrich Schaffer, 1980)[1]

William Barclay, the much-loved New Testament expositor, once said of Martin Luther's relationship with his father:

> It is one of the tragic facts of religious history that Luther's father was so stern to him that Luther all his days found it difficult to pray: "Our Father." The word *father* in his mind stood for nothing but severity.[2]

---

1. Schaffer, *For the Love of Children*, 68.
2. Barclay, *Letters to the Philippians, Colossians, and Thessalonians*, 195, italics

Commenting on Colossians 3:21, Barclay said, "The duty of the parent is not only discipline—it is also *encouragement,* and discipline and encouragement must walk hand in hand.... Spare the rod and spoil the child. It is true. But beside the rod keep an apple to give him when he does well."³ Luther spoke of the canings and whipping he endured as a child and suggested that the disciplines may have influenced his decision to join a monastic order as a young man. However, as his biographer Roland Bainton has said,

> Unquestioningly the young were roughly handled in those days, and Luther may be correctly reported as having cited these instances in order to bespeak a more humane treatment, but there is no indication that such severity produced more than a flash of resentment. Luther was highly esteemed at home. His parents looked to him as a lad of brilliant parts who should become a jurist, make a prosperous marriage, and support them in their old age.⁴

Luther's personal history shows that the outcomes of harsh parental correction are not always predictable. They may negatively affect the child's image of God as Father, but the damage may be mollified by other aspects of the relationship between the child and earthly father. In some cases negative impacts may be minimized over time only to reappear much later in painful "transferential" feelings when the young person experiences similar forms of reproach.

In this chapter I will share stories from three of my patients, drawn from my practice of over thirty years, which shed light on the experience of parental disregard in its many manifestations. They illustrate the long term outcomes of rejective "nonlove" with its insecure attachments and pathological accommodations, often leading to struggles in adult relationships with God as Father.

ODD MAN OUT: LEON'S STORY

Leon⁵ moved to Los Angeles from rural Indiana when he was twenty-four. He came with a friend to look for work in Hollywood and found success

---

original.

3. Ibid., italics original.

4. Bainton, *Here I Stand*, 17.

5. All names, occupations, and other relevant data has been changed to protect the identities of the people profiled.

Part III: All in the Family

as a television scriptwriter. Now thirty-seven, he is bright, creative, and excellent at what he does. Nonetheless he came to see me because he felt miserable about himself and had experienced repeated rejection in romantic relationships.

Leon's first words to me were, "My whole life has been an appeals case." He explained that the primary drive in his life was a need to prove that his parents had misjudged him. During his formative years his mother and father did not seem to understand boys in general and the kinds of activities they required to feel good about themselves as they grew. His mother, a very timid woman, saw the world as fundamentally dangerous. Leon considered her socially awkward, "not an example of how to live life." She placed her son and younger daughter in small private Christian academies up through their early teens. After middle school Leon enrolled at the local public high school, where he hoped to find a "few more girls to meet." However in the middle of his freshman year, much to his dismay, his mother decided to start homeschooling him. Throughout his remaining high school years he had few opportunities for normal peer group experiences.

Leon's father did not appear to be involved in these decisions. Leon recalled him as an intelligent man, a hydro-geologist by vocation, but largely "distant, not really there not a teacher." He was also "a disapproving dad, anger [being] the prevalent emotion," and rarely if ever offered words of affirmation or endearment. Looking back, Leon deeply regretted the absence of a genuine relationship with his father. Even today he sees no signs that his father actively loves him and he feels little love for his father.

The word that best summarizes his parent's attitudes was "insensitivity." They were insensitive to Leon's concerns about things important to him, unaware of how their self-imposed ignorance degraded his self-image, and uncaring about how their disdain would impact his confidence in relationships, especially with women. Leon once said of himself, "I am not worthy or interesting or cool enough to be known and related to."

Leon did not say that his parents were awful or abusive. Rather he believes they simply did not give serious thought to his experiences, his desires, or his longings. He expressed these themes repeatedly: "I am not allowed to get what I want; I am not allowed to make anyone angry"; and above all, "don't hope because you'll be disappointed." Beyond those maxims, he described his life in terms of stories, events burned in his memory as signposts of frustrations. Even in his late thirties he continued to relate stories from his childhood with deep emotion.

First and possibility most illustrative was the "squirt gun birthday party." At seven years old a friend invited him to a birthday celebration where the main event would be a huge squirt gun battle. The invitation clearly laid out the plans and asked that kids bring their own "hydro-weapons." But Leon's mother did not make sure her son was properly prepared, and she left the party without asking whether the birthday boy's parents had any extra equipment. None was available, leaving Leon the only unarmed child out of ten or more boys. As odd man out, in pure "Lord of the Flies" fashion, he was designated the stooge of the party. The other boys relentlessly soaked him, chased him, pushed him around, then soaked and chased him again. He had to shove one of the boys off his feet and threaten to fight him before it ended. He went back into the house, called his mother, and left the party humiliated and enraged.

Leon could not recall whether his mother upbraided the adults at the party for not intervening in the bullying that happened in their backyard. He did not know if his mother even understood the pain he experienced. (Leon learned that his mother could not remember the incident when he asked her about it after relating the story in our session.) He shared with me that he also had no recollection of any response from his father whatsoever. The incident left him with a devastated sense of insecurity and vulnerability: if terrible things happened to him, he was afraid his parents simply wouldn't care.

Later events reinforced Leon's uneasy awareness of parental misattunement and his inability to fix it. At thirteen he was thrilled to receive the Christmas present he'd been hoping for: a new CD player. When he tried to express his delight and excitement his father yelled at him to cut it out and quit acting like a child; there was no room in that house for spontaneous expressions. At sixteen Leon wanted to learn the guitar and practiced regularly in his room. One Saturday as he was trying to master some chord changes, his father stomped into the house from the backyard and barged into Leon's room, demanding, "When are you ever going to learn to play that thing!?" Shocked by his father's annoyance and disgust, Leon said of his guitar, "I never picked it up again." At seventeen he wanted to learn the martial art of Taekwondo and his parents gave approval for him to join a class. In his isolated home school environment, Leon hoped that the skills would help build his confidence and self-esteem. But when it was time to move beyond the beginner's stage and start sparring with other students, his parents refused to help purchase the necessary equipment and would not advance him the funds so that he could repay them later. He had no choice but to drop the class.

Along with many others, those stories told the tale for Leon of his parents' lack of interest in his life. Their implicit messages seemed to be, "You are not valuable enough for us to pay attention to what is important to you," and, "Life is just too difficult for you to get anything that you really want." After a particularly insightful session, Leon said, "I have often wondered why there has been this undercurrent of anger and sadness [in my life]." Psychoanalyst Chris Jaenicke suggests an answer:

> If a child's self-object needs for affective attunement remain consistently unmet, he or she will eventually withdraw to a vacuum-packed state of needlessness that matches exactly his or her surround. It is the only way to stay sane in order not to break apart on the rock of discrepancy between his or her perception of the world and the way the world presents itself. It is as if the child says to him- or herself, "If you give me nothing, then that's what I will become." As if by becoming invisible, it hopes to be seen.[6]

In psychoanalytic terms, "self-object needs" necessitate responses from caregivers that promote the stability and vitality of the self (the inner life of the person).[7] In everyday language they refer to a child's needs for security and significance, which are most often met through the soothing, encouraging, and protecting that a good enough parent provides for the child on a regular basis.

Leon's parents, by all accounts, either failed to understand these essential needs or simply ignored them. In Leon's words, "We were abandoned as children; my father saw something he didn't like in me, there was nothing there to see." When there's nothing to see, maybe it's best just to stay in the background. In present-day relationships Leon described himself as "retardedly shy and awkward; the curse of my family takes over." His "family curse" manifested as a pronounced ineptitude in interpersonal encounters, a social clumsiness joined with a fear of doing the hard work of getting past it. Speaking to women, Leon would be overcome by self-consciousness to the point of blanking out and not knowing what to say. This young man so knowledgeable in so many fields would become embarrassingly quiet in the presence of a woman he found attractive. He wanted to withdraw, become invisible and hide his shame. He could not recall a single positive

---

6. Jaenicke, *Risk of Relatedness*, 107.
7. Livingston, "Reflections of Selfobject Transferences," 156.

experience in his attempts at dating; but he did not really have the option to "withdraw to a vacuum-packed state of needlessness," in Jaenicke's terms. His career in the entertainment industry and his involvement in the Southern California church scene both drew him into regular social interactions. He was continually reminded of his loneliness and frustration, particularly as he watched many of his friends embark on successful relationships that culminated in marriage.

Leon's frustration and anger took a toll on his relationship with God. In the very conservative denomination where he was raised one learned to obey God and worship him appropriately. Leon developed a highly intellectualized faith with few if any personal dimensions. He described feeling "alone and isolated" in church as a teenager, believing that "everyone else is worshipping and I'm feeling despair!" He resisted attempts at being alone with God out of fear that he would only be disappointed. More than once he asked during therapy, "Where is God, isn't he supposed to be loving to me?" Perhaps his most revealing comment was, "Feeling God's love for me is unreal, it has all the involvement of imagining a triangle in my head." I doubt that I have ever heard a confession so thought-provoking and stunning in its honesty. In Leon's cerebral approach to experiencing his faith, God's love for him had become so abstract that it was literally nonsensical.

The kinds of emotional pain that Leon shared with me impact every facet of a person's life. The mind struggles constantly with troubling thoughts and false beliefs; the emotions become susceptible to threats from living in a stressful and unforgiving world; the will lacks the courage to stand up against injunctions that were internalized while growing up. Naturally these struggles can shape the believer's faith relationship with his Heavenly Father. The damage cannot be undone just by thinking differently about one's past or acquiring more cognitively based information about God's love or Christ's commitment to us. Real change requires new experiences that nourish a sensitivity and awareness about being loved and cherished for who we genuinely are.

In Leon's case he has worked diligently on his own issues. He changed his appearance, cutting his shoulder-length hair to a cleaner look that better frames his expressions. He now speaks with more ease with women and even initiates conversations with them. He sees that he cannot change the idiosyncrasies of the Los Angeles dating scene but he can learn to navigate them more effectively. I have encouraged his new active approach in relationships and I've seen him gain a willingness to explore the possibilities.

Rather than defining himself as incapable, unwanted, or outcast before an encounter, he waits to see how things play out. He feels more strongly that *he* has something to offer. As for his own trust in God the Father, who has compassion on him because he is "intimately acquainted with all his ways" (Ps 139:2), his progress has been slower and more difficult. Even so his attention and personal investment in church worship have increased, and he finds himself exploring the dimensions that a love relationship with God may open up for him.

THE MAN WHO WASN'T THERE: CHARLEY'S STORY

The terrible consequences of violent child abuse are well known to most of us. But what might happen to a child who is not abused or even seriously punished, but essentially dismissed emotionally? Could a neglect of this kind make a person so passive and ineffectual that they almost cease to exist?

Charley was four years old when his father divorced his mother and moved away. He has no clear recollection of the event, only a story from his grandmother about his dad giving him a large toy fire engine just before he left. His grandmother said that after his father left, Charley "came in [the house] and cried, then never spoke of it again." He also never saw his father again. Charley's mother fell into a period of depression and despondency so severe and prolonged that she had great difficulties caring for her only child. She remarried a couple of years later, and when Charley was nine his mother and stepfather had their first child together. By the time Charley was eleven he had two half-brothers who needed their mother's attention.

A striking feature of Charley's story is that he has little narrative memory of his relationships with his mother or stepfather during all those years. Where Leon's parents showed little understanding of the desires and endeavors that were important to him, Charley's parents seemed largely unaware that he had any depth of feelings and offered little or no emotional expression. Though recollecting only a few instances of harsh discipline, Charley said, "I was never hugged or told 'I love you.'" He could not recall any physical expressions of affection, even from his mother.

One evening in his teens Charley sat on his front lawn and eavesdropped on a neighborhood party that was happening below his house, using a device called "The Big Ear" to try to overhear the conversations. Even at the time he realized that this long-distance eavesdropping was an awkward attempt to allay his loneliness. He told me in session, "I felt a little embarrassed with myself." The incident served as a model in miniature for all of his teenage years. Though not entirely without friends, he remembers himself as a solitary boy disconnected from the main stream of adolescence.

During his adulthood Charley has spent much of his life moderately depressed, sometimes reaching depths that inhibit normal functioning. He becomes fearful of falling into a debilitating anxious state that would humiliate him in front of others. Often when under pressure or facing tight deadlines at work, his anxieties interfere with an already compromised memory, sabotaging the job he is trying to complete. Perennially underemployed, he has struggled with frustration at his "hamstrung" mental processing.

Charley sought out a connection with God over the years and has attended evangelical churches most of his entire adult life. Though he hoped his faith would be rewarded by a Heavenly Father who would come through for him, his perceptions slowly changed. Living through various life events in which he felt unaided or unprotected, his overriding sense became that God was largely uninvolved or uninterested in his life—mirroring the disconnect he had experienced with his parents. In romantic involvements Charley's life was largely nondescript. His confusion about healthy relationships culminated when he agreed to marry a woman because he thought it was his Christian duty: she needed love and a husband and Charley believed he should make the sacrifice. But his bride was morbidly obese, Charley felt intimidated by her emotionally, and he was not at all attracted to her physically. He pitied her but never felt in love with her. Not surprisingly, the ensuing marriage was difficult on all sides, ending tragically after sixteen years with his wife's sudden death from complications of obesity. Charley felt dismayed by her death but also a guilty sense of release.

What could make a difference in the kind of hollowed-out life that Charley was living? After passively giving up so much of himself, both personally and professionally, was it too late to expect anything better—let alone the "abundant life" the Lord seemed to have promised?

Charley did not give up trying. Starting during his college years and into his marriage he pushed himself to seek out therapists and Christian advisors, looking for some sort of substantive help that would make an impact on his situation. Nothing seemed to work. He came to me, finally, by referral from his pastor, who was deeply frustrated with his inability to address Charley's problems in the standard paradigm for pastoral counseling.

Part III: All in the Family

I was the first clinician with a psychoanalytic viewpoint that Charley had met.

In a few of our early sessions Charley said, "God must either be angry at me, disapproving of my life, or he does not enter into our lives to specifically help us." He is intelligent and he knows the Scriptures, including Proverbs 3:5–6: "Trust in the Lord with all your heart, and do not lean on your own understanding. In all your ways acknowledge Him, and He will make your paths straight." He most certainly knows Matthew 6:33–34:

> But seek first His kingdom, and His righteousness; and all these things shall be added to you. Therefore do not be anxious for tomorrow; for tomorrow will care for itself; each day has enough trouble of its own.

Yet Charley would have said that the absence of concrete, effectual responses from God in his circumstances had been destructive to his faith. He could not trust that God will help him or that "all these things shall be added" to him because, by all that Charley had been able to see, God did not actually care for him.

In our work together, Charley began to understand that the neglect he experienced as a child amounted to an implicit dismissal of the importance of *feeling* loved. Though not subjected to harsh punishments, his relationship with his mother and stepfather was still fundamentally punitive. A child between the ages of four and nine in those circumstances would internalize a profound sense of disillusionment, lacking so much of the nourishing, active expressions of love that all children need for personal growth. And since Charley's caregivers offered no explanation for their apparent lack of enthusiasm or interest in him, his sense of abandonment was compounded by the confusion and guilt that naturally follows when children reproach their parents for their upbringing. In Gerald Newmark's book *How to Raise Emotionally Healthy Children*, he speaks to a child's needs in this area:

> If children do not feel important and useful (and this is a major problem for our young people today), if they don't develop a sense of importance in constructive ways, they may seek negative ways to get attention. They may become rebellious, outrageous, antagonistic; they may engage in constant testing and struggling for power. . . . At the other extreme, they may become apathetic or withdrawn; they may lack initiative and ambition or they may become overly dependent on others.

> Children need to be included. They need to be brought in, to be made to feel a part of things. Children often feel left out and unwanted; when this happens they feel as if they are outsiders rather than part of the family.[8]

Over the years with Charley I have aimed to provide a presence in his life that affirms the insecure and demotivated aspects of himself, even while he works to clarify his strategies for tackling personal and professional conflicts. Nothing about this has been simple. He has been afraid I will abandon him, leaving him even more isolated and alone with his confusion, or that his sense of shame about his feelings will drive him to keep them obscured and difficult for me to understand. These are natural responses for someone confronting their own structures of pathological accommodation. Growing up, the safest course for Charley was to utterly avoid taking risks or moving in a new direction unless he had clear support from the authorities in his life. Brandchaft warned of powerful emotional consequences when a person violates the norms of their parental impingements. The "dictates of antiquity" are hard psychological habits to break.

> Any experience of success or steps toward strong, proud adult fulfillment may trigger a retreat to self-debasing self-criticism or to debilitating worries about the object's response in someone who has formed pathological structures of accommodation.[9]

Even in the face of those obstacles, persistence counts for something. Charley has not experienced a "breakthrough"—an event much rarer in real life than in the movies—but his progress has been real and practical, even if he doesn't always see it himself. Recently in his work as a film editor he completed the editing of his first feature film, working with more confidence and avoiding most of his old struggles against crippling anxiety. He has gained a better reputation in the industry and now just needs a few more breaks to get his career where he wants it to be. Spiritually he's begun to embrace the idea that even though the deficits in his upbringing may have damaged his understanding of God, along with impacting much of his personality, there may be a change brewing. He finds it possible now to ponder the truth that God has been continually involved in his life in ways that he has been unable to recognize. I look forward to hearing and experiencing the discoveries he makes as he learns to "see with new eyes."

---

8. Newmark, *How to Raise Emotionally Healthy Children*, 15, 25.
9. Brandchaft, *Toward an Emancipatory Psychoanalysis*, 194.

Part III: All in the Family

A FATHER'S DEATH: HOWARD'S STORY

Any man in his forties would be happy to be as widely respected as Howard, a schoolteacher who had taken on the vocation of working exclusively with special education children. He dealt with difficult situations every day with kindness and conscientious attention to the particular needs of his students. Parents felt relieved and fortunate that their children were under his instruction and care. Away from the classroom he was a member of an evangelical church, well-known for his understanding of theology, philosophical questions, and current affairs. He was particularly recognized for engaging and confronting the status quo about living out the Christian life in the local congregation. He could hold dialogues on almost any topic, leaving friends and acquaintances impressed (and sometimes confused!) with the depth and relevancy of his thinking.

Howard had another side that he rarely brought to light—and if not exactly a "dark side," it was more conflicted than anyone realized. Though a good-looking man with a respectable career, he had never married or been able to sustain a serious long-term relationship. It didn't help that his younger brother had gotten married for the first time at age forty. But his romantic frustrations are only aspects of a deep bitterness that often turned inward into self-denigration. He castigated himself for his inability to live a "successful" life despite everything he'd accomplished. His frustration often threatened to turn outward into critical and damaging attitudes toward people around him. He battled that impulse, knowing it was unfair to inflict it on people who had not caused his pain, but he did not always succeed. Every failure only seemed to confirm that affectionate and caring relationships with other human beings were simply not an option.

Each day he carried out his responsibilities and performed the tasks that kept his life in order. Inwardly he had given up on desiring any of the "big things" for himself. By some sort of inexplicable external fiat, he would not be able to achieve the things in life that mattered to him most.

There was no particular breaking point for Howard when he decided to look for help. He came to me seeking relief from an ongoing depression over the seemingly intractable negativity in his life. As often happens, our work consisted of creating a safe place for him to feel the potency of his feelings and the legitimacy of his hurt.

I found him unusually insightful about his own history and the impacts that have carried through to the present. He knew that a defining moment, after all this time, had been the death of his father when he was

The Embittered Christian and Trusting in God

close to five years old. The death seemed to come suddenly though Howard realizes now that his father had been sick for some time. He was left with a mother who, as he sees it, was so "afraid of life" that "everything was suspect."

"There was no grace for me as a human being," he said. "I did not grow up with a voice of reason, I grew up with a voice of warning." His mother seemed frightened of his entire boyhood and warned him about things constantly. Her implicit injunction seemed to be, "Don't have any desires for yourself." She never remarried and never gave Howard, as far as he could remember, any heartfelt demonstrations of affection. She also never told him stories about his father. Despite all that must have happened during Howard's first four years of life, he could not recall a single story from his mother about anything his father said to him or about him or activities they had done together.

As he put it, looking back: "I got my legs cut off when my father died." He believed he lacked a viable "inner man" because his father was not around for his childhood. An evocative term he once used for himself was a "goo you," someone who lacked basic substance or backbone. Without parental affirmation of his abilities or aspirations, he was left with a pervasive feeling of "you just can't do it."

In all of this Howard also battled with God about his life. Who was God to him? What did God want from him? Why hadn't he helped Howard with his life since God took away his father at such a young age?[10] Wasn't God supposed to fill in the gap; wasn't he his Heavenly *Father*? During young adulthood Howard saw his trust in God wane with each successive relational or financial breakdown. He once said of Proverbs 13:19, "If 'desire realized is sweet to the soul,' so the opposite must be true, 'desire unrealized is bitter to the soul.'" He struggled against a demeaning self-concept, fearing that God would never get involved in the parts of his life that were most painful for him. In anguished moments he spoke of the "pain of nonexistence," that he was "completely undeserving of love and warmth and connection." Perhaps his most devastating expression of despondency came during a Christmas season (just before a two week break

---

10. In truth Howard has always "remembered" that his father's death was not talked about at all. He was never allowed to express how he much missed his daddy. The enforced silence contributed to the internalization of depression and its many symptoms. For an excellent discussion on grief in preschool children (like the 4+ year-old Howard) see Crenshaw, *Bereavement*, 40–68. Also see Winter, *When Life Goes Dark*, 70–107, for a Christian perspective on death, grief, and depression in children.

in sessions), when he described himself standing before a "dark hole" in his life and peering into it. He knew that his despair was rooted in a fear of always being alone, without anyone in his life who he could love and who would love him in return, and without any capacity for changing his state.

Even in those dark times Howard continued the work of examining his life and the actions he'd taken, looking for ways to understand his woundedness and work through it to something better. Like anyone else, his condition was shaped not only by the events of his life but by the interpretive grid he used to evaluate those events and make sense of his past. It takes a particular kind of courage to reexamine that grid and consider other ways of understanding the choices available to us.

Our work became more focused as Howard's conflicts came to light. Even though he was aware of the damage caused by his father's death, he had not yet grieved for his loss and the hole it had left in his life. Allowing himself to grieve, finally, was essential for coming to terms with his pain. We also focused on developing a more forgiving spirit for other Christian people. Howard complained that he had rarely experienced genuine warmth from others, just a surface-level quasi-Christian kindness that was not interested in knowing how he felt inside. He had sought a receptive environment where "if one member (of the body) suffers, all the members suffer with it" (1 Cor 12:26). But the structures of a typical church ministry can make it difficult for single adult males to find fellowship. Sunday school groups cater to married couples of different ages and the worship services usually do not serve as a sharing time with other parishioners. Adults who do not fit the standard patterns can feel left out or marginalized.

Recently my own church invited Dr. Chap Clark of Fuller Seminary to share his concept of "sticky faith." He suggests that the entire body of Christ in the local church should aim to "hang out together," joining in different church ministries and talking in relaxed contexts with adequate time to get to know one another.[11] The Apostle Paul saw this kind of fellowship as natural for the people of God. The Greek word translated as "fellowship" *(koinoneia)* suggests a closeness that reminds us we have all been bought with a price (1 Cor 6:20). We are all in need of understanding and kindness and forgiveness; we have all been shown mercy by a brother or sister in Christ who offered real love and relevant care. In the early church, the Lord's days were structured so that this kind of human relatedness could take place.[12]

---

11. Clark and Powell, *Sticky Faith*.

12. My thoughts are inspired by the Apostle Paul's description of events on the Lord's

The Embittered Christian and Trusting in God

Even in the third century unbelievers would say of the Christians, "see how they love one another."[13]

Howard and I examined Paul's exhortations about genuine "body-life" found in Philippians 2:1–4:

> If therefore there is any encouragement in Christ, if there is any consolation of love, if there is any fellowship of the Spirit, if any affection and compassion, make my joy complete by being of the same mind, maintaining the same love, united in spirit, intent on one purpose. Do nothing from selfishness or empty conceit, but with humility of mind let each of you regard one another as more

---

day in the church at Corinth. In chs. 11, 12, and 14 of 1 Corinthians he speaks about preaching (prophesying), teaching, communion, a fellowship meal, and the manifestation of other spiritual gifts. These things would not have taken place during an actual worship service. See Wilken, *Spirit of Early Christian Thought*, 25–49. A particularly valuable insight about early church worship is found on p. 36:

> Before there were treatises on the Trinity, before there were learned commentaries on the Bible, before there were disputes about the teaching on grace, or essay on the moral life, there was awe and adoration before the exalted Son of God alive and present in the church's offering of the Eucharist. This truth preceded every effort to understand and nourished every attempt to express in words and concepts what Christians believed.

See also Banks, *Paul's Idea of Community*, esp. 52–61, and Martin, *Worship in the Early Church*.

13. "'See how they love one another,' these are words Tertullian noted (Apology [39.7]) in the Third Century, as spoken by some of the non-Christians of the time regarding Christian communalities. The 'love' they are referring to is the way in which the early Christian churches cared for each other, especially the poor." Taken from www.hoosiercatholic.org. See also Foster, *Freedom of Simplicity*, 66–67:

> In the period following the Apostolic Age, there was an exuberant caring and sharing on the part of Christians that was unique in antiquity. Julian the apostate, an enemy of Christianity, admitted that "the godless Galileans fed not only their (poor) but ours also." Tertullian wrote that the Christians' deeds of love were so noble that the pagan world confessed in astonishment, "See how they love one another." Exactly what is it that these Christians did which elicited such a response from their enemies?
>
> There was, first of all, an exceptional freedom to care for the needs of one another in the believing community. The Didache admonished Christians: "thou shalt not turn away from him that is in want, but thou shalt share all things with thy brother, and shalt not say that they are thine own."
>
> By A.D. 250 Christians in Rome were caring for some fifteen hundred needy people. In fact their generosity was so profuse that Ignatius could say that they were "leading in love," and Bishop Dionysus of Corinth could note that they were sending "supplies to many churches in every city."

important than himself; do not merely look out for your own personal interests, but also for the interest of others.

Clearly this was the touchstone for a healthy church when it comes to fellowship! Howard knew he would benefit from the kinds of encouragement, consolation, love and humility that Paul described, and he had a desire to minister to others in that same environment. There is much work to be done here in the congregations of the American church.

Over time Howard made continued progress. He began going on dates for the first time in seven years. As he feels stronger internally, he finds that he can be more open and accepting of the idiosyncrasies of others who he wants to know better. He understands that it's good for him to have goals or to want things for his life and to take action to accomplish them. Recently he was able to buy a house for himself for the first time—he made it happen by setting the goal and achieving it.

He continues to struggle with a propensity to interpret another person's concerns as critical and thus a denunciation; he automatically sees that attitude as disapproving and judgmental. The Apostle James says, "Is anyone among you suffering? Let him pray. Is anyone cheerful? Let him sing praises" (Jas 5:13). For Howard I would add, "Is anyone among you suffering? Let him share with the church and be encouraged. Let your story be known for you are loved!"

In his first letter, the Apostle John offers a truly astonishing insight about the fellowship of believers:

> By this the love of God was manifested in us that God has sent His only begotten Son into the world so that we might live through Him. In this is love, not that we loved God, but that He loved us and sent His Son to be the propitiation for our sins. Beloved, if God so loved us, we also ought to love one another. No one has beheld God at any time; if we love one another, God abides in us, and His love is perfected in us. (1 John 4:9–12)

John Stott says of that last statement,

> I would be hard to imagine the greatness of this conception. It is so daring that many commentators have been reluctant to accept it and have suggested that the genitive in *his love* is not subjective ("God's love") but objective ("our love for God"; cf. 2:5) or definitive (godlike love). But the whole paragraph is concerned with God's love, and we must not stagger at the majesty of this conclusion. God's love which originates in Himself (7, 8) and was

manifested in His Son (9, 10) is perfected in His people (12). It is "brought to perfection within us" (NEB). God's love for us is perfected only when it is reproduced in us or (as it may mean) "among us" in the Christian fellowship.[14]

The love of God comes to its fullness when we have the experience of *being loved by others* in the Body of Christ. His love becomes mature, complete, full-grown (that word *telos* again!). We all desire to experience this truth in the fellowship of believers, and I suggest that believers suffering from developmental woundedness need it all the more. Howard would thrive in the kind of environment that John describes and that Paul wishes for the church at Philippi, a place where believers can find healing and can offer love and healing in return.

N. T., ARE YOU RIGHT?

How should the church of Jesus Christ respond to people like Leon, Charley and Howard? They are not "special cases" and they are not mentally ill. Along with many others like them they have shown courage and perseverance in confronting their issues and their desire to grow in Christ. What sort of help or advice should the church provide?

The typical reaction from many traditional Christians has been to judge the lives of these people as spiritually immature, undisciplined, or mired in sin. Painful childhood relationships with parents should be remedied by "forgiving and forgetting." An individual may be reproved for holding his parents responsible for impacts on his life since Christians should never accuse their mothers or fathers of wrongdoing or neglect.

Eminent biblical scholar N. T. Wright, whom I have referenced repeatedly in these pages, provides an example of this mentality. In several of his works Wright comments on issues of familial and developmental conflict and the Christian life. He describes a particular person named Ben, who grew up in an environment of parental mistreatment,

> surrounded by selfishness, abuse and violence. . . . Paul's answer would be, without a doubt, that this is beside the point when it comes to the Christian character of virtue. "Those who belong to the Messiah Jesus crucified the flesh." There are no exceptions, no categories of people who can, as it were, slide sideways into the holiness which the gospel generates without going the painful

---

14. Stott, *Epistles of John*, 164, italics original.

route of crucifixion with the Messiah and then the hard moral effort needed to cultivate the virtues in all their fullness.[15]

Wright's account suggests that Ben was subjected to extreme forms of abuse, probably physical and even sexual. To remedy Ben's resulting conflicts Wright says that he must "crucify his flesh" and go "the painful route of crucifixion with the Messiah,"[16] clearly referencing Galatians 5:24: "Now those who belong to Christ Jesus have crucified the flesh with its passions and desires" (cf. Rom 8:13-14). Any other approach would be to "slide sideways into holiness."

Though we must be careful not to overanalyze such a brief passage, it is disturbing to see Wright seemingly make light of the terrible damage caused by child abuse in its various manifestations. He says of the one "surrounded by selfishness, abuse and violence,"

> Ben glimpsing the difference between his background and the life of genuine Christianity [he] may take a flying and grateful leap into the new world.[17]

Presumably when Ben takes a "flying and grateful leap into the new world," he will "crucify his flesh" concerning the old world he grew up in. Dr. Wright's genial imagery does not take into account how Ben's abuse may have affected his ability to grasp and act on those theological truths. Adults with comparable upbringings find themselves susceptible to depression, chronic self-deprecating thoughts, crippling anxiety when dealing with authority or close relationships, and difficulties following through on endeavors important to them. Wright's crucifying admonishments are directed to people with those states of mind or attitudes of heart. He does not explain how their internal obstacles might be overcome, except to say:

> This is not a matter of preformed character, but of choices thought through, reasoned out, and implemented, of the new language learned, practiced, and spoken, at first stumblingly and then, gradually, with increasing fluency.[18]

In lieu of self-awareness, Wright recommends self effort: choosing to acknowledge the grace of God and learning to speak "the new language."

---

15. Wright, *After You Believe*, 205.
16. Ibid.
17. Ibid.
18. Ibid., 206.

He offers no understanding of the burdens that years of abuse may place on the Christian who seeks to take in and believe the truths of God's love. Theological language becomes a facile method for obscuring the effects of child abuse in adulthood.

The fundamental point is that living out the impacts of an abusive childhood differs *in kind* from acting out the "deeds of the flesh." The damaged Christian who is frightened, depressed, cynical, hesitant, petulant, or even lethargic in his faith is displaying scars, not emblems of sin. His weaknesses may become sinful if unloving responses like those described in Galatians 5:21–23 develop from his symptomatic attitudes; but even this emotional state of being differs markedly from "walking in the flesh." In short, Wright's remedy—and the traditional reaction of many Christians—is either misinformed or a confusion of categories. Crucifying the flesh is a proper means for dealing with sin in one's life, but human responses to damages from child abuse are suffering, not sin.

EVERYBODY DANCE!

The three men profiled in this chapter continue to experience the consequences of various forms of parental disregard. During their formative years their individuality was not recognized by those who mattered most; their particular bents or inclinations were squashed or ignored; their desires or goals were marginalized; the only choices left to them were anger or anonymity. Each of them now longs for and works toward a new experience of God's compassion and encouragement. They understand that their trust in God as their Heavenly Father has been compromised and that they sometimes approach the Lord through the transferential lenses of their damaged upbringing. But their scars are genuine and the pain runs deep. They have struggled to develop the kind of faith that confidently believes that God hears their prayers and will come through for them.

Recently Leon told me about a movie that speaks to his sense of loss: *Billy Elliot*,[19] the tale of an eleven-year-old English boy who wants to become a ballet dancer. Billy begins the story in the school gym with other boys learning how to box, while on the other side of the gym girls are dancing in ballet class. Billy finds he's more interested in the dancing than the boxing. He gravitates to the ballet side of the gym and attempts some of

---

19. *Billy Elliot*, written by Lee Hall, directed by Stephen Daldry (BBC Films, Working Title Films, Universal Pictures, 2000).

the moves, showing enough talent and energy that the ballet teacher enlists him into the class. He quickly gains confidence, saying that when he dances it's like "I'm flying, like electricity is going through my body." His coal-miner father, predictably, takes a different view: ballet is not a manly activity and he refuses to allow Billy to participate, to the point of striking him in anger. But with the help of the ballet teacher and a timely viewing of his son's dancing skills the father begins to change his mind. He sees that he was not paying close enough attention and had not made an effort to understand why his son's natural abilities and desires drove him to dance. He raises money for Billy to take part in tryouts at a prestigious ballet school in London. He travels to the school with Billy, sits with him through the long delays, encourages him when he is down and speaks to the administrators on his behalf. He provides all the care and support that one would hope to see from a loving father.

Leon saw in this movie an image of the love and affirmation that he had never been given; he wished that Billy's experience could have been his own, even with the drama it entailed. Better to suffer and win the father's love than never to find it at all.

But for Leon as for most of us, life did not provide a sudden change of heart or a Hollywood ending. For most people, dealing with the fallout of significant parental disregard is hard work. Growing past those archaic and destructive ways of experiencing ourselves and the world around us takes concerted, corrective effort. It requires remedial and renewing strategies that encompass things we can do for ourselves and also effective ideas for enlisting the aid of others. We'll explore these kinds of strategies in the next two chapters.

PART IV

On the Road Again
Undoing the Burdens

CHAPTER EIGHT

A Path to Healing

> Thy word I have treasured in my heart,
> That I may not sin against Thee.
> Thy word is a lamp to my feet,
> And a light to my path.
> The unfolding of Thy words gives light;
> It gives understanding to the simple.
> I rejoice in Thy word,
> As one who finds great spoil.
>
> (PSALM 119:11, 105, 130, 162)

For any person who struggles with instabilities and personal obstacles rooted in incessant parental disregard, there are no easy answers. Mental quick fixes, such as attempting to reframe our identity (even as Christians) without the exacting work of self-examination, usually produce little more than self-denigrating attitudes that compound the problems. Protected by years of subtle yet pervasive rationalizations, the conflicts become deeply ingrained and even more troublesome by the time a person reaches adulthood.

But we are never without hope. As people such as Leon, Charley, and Howard have shown, growth and healing can occur even in the most difficult cases. Christians can have confidence that the grace of God and the love of God are at work in our lives, both "to will and work for His good pleasure" and to shape us into people of faith who know the joy of his salvation.

Even with that confidence, there's no alternative to hard work. The sufferer must take steps, on his own and with the help of others (whenever possible), to gain greater understanding of their deficient sense of self and the actions they can take to cooperate with Christ in his work of healing.

PREPARING TO LAY ASIDE

Self-awareness in these matters begins with gaining clarity about the influences that have shaped us and the impacts we still experience in adulthood.

If we were fortunate as children, our caregivers were wise enough and healthy enough to give us "good-enough" parenting, with a reasonable balance of guidance and freedom. We had practical limits to keep us safe as well as support and encouragement for our creative expressions and explorations of the world. Sue Gephardt provides a valuable description:

> The qualities of good parenting (and of close relationships in general) are essentially *regulatory qualities*: the capacity to listen, to notice, to shape behavior, and to be able to restore good feelings through some kind of physical, emotional or mental contact, through a touch, a smile, a way of putting feelings and thoughts into words. These capacities are personal ones, but they cannot be expressed fully in a culture which relegates children to the margins. To be able to notice and respond to other's feelings, takes up time. It requires a kind of mental space to be allocated to feelings, and a willingness to prioritize relationships. This is a challenge to a goal-oriented society.[1]

Note Gephardt's use of words such as "regulatory" (or regulate), "shape," and "restore." These are terms of guidance and tutelage, the kind of authority that aims to guide and protect something that is already in motion, like steering a ship through a narrows. A child who experiences that kind of parenting grows up with a sense of security about the world and his place in it, with confidence in the skills he has to offer and the contributions he can make.

---

1. Gerhardt, *Why Love Matters*, 214, emphasis mine.

A Path to Healing

But many have not been so fortunate. Perhaps our innate desires and inclinations were not given their due or our caregivers seemed incapable of paying attention when it mattered most; perhaps our thoughts and ideas about our own lives were treated as insignificant. Vital self-expressions evoked only annoyance and irritation. Our parents made decisions based on their desires for control or approval from their peers without considering our concerns, and our expressions of disappointment were squashed with harsh responses. We had no choice but to deny our affects, choices, and abilities while trying to regulate or tolerate our own emotions, all in the midst of anxiety and turmoil.

As we've seen, a Christian who regularly experienced these limiting injunctions early in her life will face ramifications for her faith. I have suggested that we can view these spiritual/developmental conflicts in the light of the admonitions in the book of Hebrews:

> Therefore, since we have so great a cloud of witnesses surrounding us, let us also lay aside every encumbrance, and the sin which so easily entangles us, and let us run with endurance the race that is set before us, fixing our eyes on Jesus, the author and perfecter of faith, who for the joy set before Him endured the cross, despising the shame, and has sat down at the right hand of the throne of God. (Heb 12:1–2)

Followers of Christ are to run the race of life with their focus on Jesus; they are not to become sidetracked or entangled in sinful distractions. Believers should likewise shed any "encumbrance" (*ogkos*) that might tire or exhaust them, making it difficult to trust in Christ's love and grace. The word *ogkos* suggests a "bulk, a weight, a burden, or an impediment," something that can weigh down the believer until he threatens to fall under the load, defeating his efforts to finish the race.[2] As we've discussed, these encumbrances are not necessarily sins or sinful, but they can become so if they cause us to turn away from the Savior and his grace to help us in time of need (Heb 4:16).

There may be no greater spiritual encumbrance than the yoke of parental disregard that burdens so many people today. It fatigues believers with unexamined and unresolved pains of self-doubt, leaving them incapable of internalizing any love that accepts them for who they are. They

---

2. So stated by Erdman, *Epistle to the Hebrews*, 113. For an excellent theological and historical exposition of this section, see Witherington, *Letters and Homilies*, 292–325, and Hughes, *Commentary on the Epistle to the Hebrews*, 437–517.

feel that their deepest aspirations are not worthy of accomplishment and they see no hope for becoming something more. Bible studies and prayer sessions do not bring them any closer to God as Father. They fear they must not be pleasing to him since they lack the kind of dynamic faith that seems to make a difference. They become tired, worn out, tripped up and falling down over the deceits of the "world the flesh and the devil." In everyday language, they live a life of discouragement and defeat wondering why God does not help them.

Yet I would suggest the apostle's admonition, in itself, offers a sign of hope. If we are called to "lay aside" any encumbrance, surely God has made it possible for us to do it. We are given no guarantee that it will be quick or painless, any more than for other aspects of growth to maturity. Yet we have grounds for trusting that grace will be there for us when we are ready to open ourselves to the work God seeks to do.

FIRST STEPS

When I work with believers who may be burdened by a history of parental disregard, I often begin by asking basic questions about the substance of their faith. The responses and reactions help heighten awareness about how their anxieties and the devaluation of their personhood may have impaired their walk with Christ.

My first question is, "*Where does the message of God's grace disconnect with you? Or, what great themes of the faith or common beliefs of Christianity seem to have little or no resonance in your life?*" It is important to identify any aspects of the message of the gospel that do not impact us emotionally. Does the fact that you are justified, redeemed, reconciled, and regenerated make any concrete difference in your disposition or your behavior? Do you experience them as personal realities or as abstract propositional beliefs? Responses such as, "I do not sense God's forgiveness for me as a person who sins," or, "I feel little or no trust in Christ's cross for my salvation," or, "I feel little or no joy in being a child of God," can point in important directions or offer clues to the aspects of faith that have been shut down.

If the first question evokes a negative or tentative response, I then ask, "*How are you affected by the descriptions of Jesus' love for those he ministered to? Where do those descriptions hurt you the most?*" For Christians with healthy faith, the accounts of Jesus' treatment of those he met in his public ministry inspire both joy and longing: they trust that the Lord would treat them with similar workings of love in their own moments of need. For Christians with impaired faith, the stories are often a source of pain. They may respond that "I do not feel that God understands me," or "I don't feel lovingly known by the Lord," or "I don't feel accepted by Jesus just being myself." The hurt springs from an absence in their lives, a sense of sadness, disappointment, or even anger because they have not experienced a gracious response to their own needs. "Is it really possible to believe that Jesus would respond to me in that way?"

These negative responses may be signs of a "transference reaction." As an example, a believer reading the story of Jesus' encounter with the woman caught in adultery (John 8:1–11) may find himself frustrated by the seeming naiveté of Jesus' offer of forgiveness. After all, we don't know the woman's attitude about her own sin before she was dragged into the public square. Was she a victim, or a willing participant? Did she actually want forgiveness, or was she just trying to save her own skin? Did Jesus really forgive her, or was he only making a point about the self-righteousness of her accusers? One way or another the believer cannot reconcile himself to the idea that Jesus would so easily forgive the sin of that person caught in the very act.

With further questioning or deeper self-examination, we might find that this believer's reaction to the Lord's graciousness resonates with past experiences. It may be that his parents were not forgiving people and did not offer grace or empathy in any measure. As a young man he felt scrutinized and picked on for every foible, and when genuinely guilty of some infraction, his parents disregarded any explanation that might mitigate the discipline they imposed. Though burdened and exasperated he never fundamentally rejected his parents' judgments; they were pious, righteous people who knew the Lord, and he inevitably integrated their beliefs about right and wrong. Small wonder, then, that he cannot embrace the ease of the Lord's forgiveness for the woman caught in sin. He has transferred to Jesus (and indeed to anyone in position of authority) the harsh and unforgiving judgments he learned from his caregivers.

Though unearthing of these kinds of reactions may seem problematic and painful, they are important first steps. Even more, the gospel stories that evoked the pain can also provide a pathway to healing.

For those caught up spiritually in transference reactions, my advice is: *go deeper*. Find a particular account of an encounter with Jesus that you find troubling, perhaps for reasons you don't quite understand. Instead of moving on, *take a closer look*: study the story with an open and inquisitive mind about what the evangelist is teaching about the love and grace of Jesus Christ. And once you've gained a clearer picture of what's happening in the text, *enter into the narrative*. Approach the story from a very personal or even existential perspective and see what you discover. Since Jesus treats people today through his Spirit as he treated them in his earthly ministry (Heb 13:8), you may well uncover truths that upend old assumptions and help you begin to "lay them aside."

JESUS AND THE LEPER

Let's consider one instance of "going deeper." Suppose as you read the first chapter of the Gospel of Mark you find yourself surprised or oddly disturbed by the healing of the leper in vv. 40 to 45. The story is simple enough: a man very ill with a disease that has left him physically debilitated and ritually unclean hears that Jesus is truly able to heal the sick. He approaches Jesus and his followers and begs the Lord to heal him.

For reasons that aren't clear, you find yourself closely identifying with the leper for the first time. You find it hard to grasp why someone in that condition—not only deathly ill but an utter social outcast—would be bold enough to approach someone like Jesus and ask for help. You don't understand why Jesus would choose to heal that man, or you may feel somewhat disturbed that this particular leper was healed while others were left without help. What's going on here, what do your reactions mean?

Your confusion and internal disturbance are good reasons for *taking a closer look*. You may find answers by exploring the personal and social dimensions that affected or motivated the people in the story, from the leper to the disciples to Jesus himself.

As a resource for this work, I recommend *The Great Physician: The Method of Jesus with Individuals*, by G. Campbell Morgan. The book offers outstanding explorations into Jesus' interactions with people during his public ministry and an entire chapter is devoted to the encounter with the leper. Morgan opens it by saying,

> It is quite impossible to over-estimate the value and importance of this story of the cleansing of the leper. Taken as a separate story, it is full of light, and indeed presents the evangel in a picture. If,

however, it be taken in connection with the ethical manifesto of Jesus, it is even more suggestive, and more wonderful.[3]

The "ethical manifesto of Jesus" is Morgan's evocative title for the Sermon on the Mount. His discussion draws on Matthew's version of the incident with the leper, which places it just after the completion of the sermon: "And when He had come down from the mountain, great multitudes followed Him. And behold, a leper came to Him" (Matt 8:1–2a). Morgan sees the situation as an immediate, practical demonstration of Jesus' teachings about the righteousness of God's people. He had just spoken of a righteousness that "surpasses that of the scribes and Pharisees" (Matt 5:20a) and of the blessings that come to the merciful (Matt 5:7). Righteousness was not found in platitudes or even in truthful exposition of godly principles; it was shown in acts of love. And now, just after completing an exhausting act of ministry to enormous throngs of people, Jesus is confronted by a genuine tragedy in the life of a fellow Jew. The leper was a child of Israel, a son of Abraham who was stricken with a disease that many of his countrymen viewed as God's curse.[4] He was required by law to remain at a distance and call out "unclean, unclean" so that others could hide from his contagion.[5] He was hideous to the eyes and grating on the ears.

The scribes, in their narrow understanding of righteousness, would not have helped the leper, and the Pharisees likely would have judged him a sinner. What would Jesus do? Morgan comments about this scene,

> It is evident that this carries us at once far beyond the presentation of some ideal. The presentation of an ideal is one thing, and the taking hold of a derelict human being outside the pale of religion and civilization, and restoring him, is quite another matter. Here our Lord is revealed in an entirely new aspect. We heard Him

3. Ibid., 97.
4. Ibid., 99.
5. See Hendriksen, *Exposition of the Gospel according to Matthew*, 391:
   We gather that the erroneous but almost universal notion . . . according to which a bitterly afflicted person must be notoriously wicked, a superstition refuted by Jesus, was prevalent also among the Jews. We can well imagine therefore, that if the leper . . . should have attempted to approach the average Jew, the latter, unwilling to become ceremonially "unclean" or to be seen near an individual *upon whom the dreadful curse of the Almighty* was thought to rest, would have rushed for shelter. . . . Most lepers, accordingly, would have despaired of ever being cleansed. Even those few who dared to hope would have "stood afar off" (Luke 17:12) as they cried out for help. (emphasis mine)

enunciate the final ethic. Descending from the mountain we see *Incarnate Purity and incarnate pollution* brought face to face, and there we have an illustration of the whole Christian enterprise.[6]

In Mark's account, we are invited to view the "incarnate pollution" from Jesus' own perspective. As he watches the leper draw closer to him, begging him, imploring him, even falling to his knees in homage to him, he is "moved with compassion" (Mark 1:40). That Greek word *splagna* (compassion) provokes the Lord into doing what love inspires him to do. It suggests great impact and depth of feeling; literally to the point of nausea when faced with another's suffering. Again Morgan:

> Now we turn to look at the Lord in the presence of the man, and to watch carefully His attitude towards him. We are first arrested by the fact that there was no manifestation of fear in the presence of leprosy. It is evident that He knew perfectly what power was resident within Himself, and therefore there was no fear. Moreover there was nothing of contempt in His attitude, and certainly there was no suspicion of despair.[7]

We know the outcome. Jesus expresses the depth of his compassion by reaching out a hand and touching the man who was untouchable, according to his society's standards of righteousness. As he told the crowds earlier that same day, the righteousness and mercy of the Lord far surpasses anything that human society can comprehend. He speaks the words "I am willing. Be clean!" and immediately the man's disease leaves him and he is cured (Mark 1:41–42).

Jesus instructs the man to keep quiet about his experience and avoid becoming a public spectacle. But the man, overwhelmed with ecstatic gratitude for his deliverance from a living death, found this restriction impossible to obey. As Mark tells us:

> He went out and began to proclaim it freely and to spread the news about, to such an extent that Jesus could no longer publicly enter a city, but stayed out in unpopulated areas, and they were coming to Him from everywhere. (Mark 1:45)

---

6. Morgan, *Great Physician*, 100. Emphasis mine. Actually commanded in Lev 13:45: "As for the leper who has the infection, his clothes shall be torn, and the hair of his head shall be uncovered, and he shall cover his mustache and cry, 'Unclean! Unclean.'"

7. Morgan, *Great Physician*, 102.

A Path to Healing

By "taking a closer look" at this account, we have opened up aspects of the story that may not have been clear. We saw vividly that the driver for the healing of the leper was Jesus' compassion in the face of human need—and not, as far as we can tell, any merit on the part of the man who was healed. Moreover, the action for Jesus was not as simple as it appeared: in choosing to touch the leper and to heal him, he overcame social and personal obstacles that would have stopped a person with shallower reservoirs of righteousness and love.

These are valuable truths and helpful for our appreciation of Christ's compassion. Even better, they prepare us for the second movement in the remediation of our wounded faith. We are ready to personally "enter into the narrative"; to *become* the leper in order to better understand the grace of God. We may discover what can happen when we are willing to bring our own disease to Jesus.

BECOMING THE LEPER

When I speak of "entering into the narrative," I have in mind the classical Benedictine method of scriptural meditation known as *lectio divina* or sacred reading. It is a contemplative approach for deepening one's understanding of a particular passage of the Bible and awakening to its personal application. As Eugene Peterson says,

> Lectio divina isn't a methodical technique for reading the Bible. It is a cultivated, developed habit of living the text in Jesus' name. This is the way, the only way that the Holy Scripture becomes formative in the Christian Church and becomes salt and leaven in the world.[8]

The "movement" of lectio divina has four parts. *Lectio*, the slow reading and rereading of the passage; *meditatio*, reflecting on any word or phrase that draws attention; *oratio*, talking through our thoughts with God; and *contemplatio*, clearing our mind for restfulness in God's presence.[9] Larry Warner says that lectio divina

---

8. Quoted in Wakefield, *Sacred Listening*, 22.
9. Warner, *Journey with Jesus*, 35.

takes you out of the place of being in control as you read the Scriptures and turns you into a listener waiting to hear the still small voice of God guide and direct you during your time in the Word.[10]

We are told that the Scriptures are the living Word of God, "sharper than any two edged sword and piercing as far as the division of soul and spirit, of both joints and marrow, and able to judge the thoughts and intentions of the heart" (Heb 4:12). Yet how can we hope to experience the full truth of this description unless we attend to the Scriptures with intense focus?[11] Richard Foster, in his wise and thorough explanation of lectio divina, provides valuable perspective:

> What does lectio divina mean? Well, it means *listening* to the text of Scripture—really listening, listening yielded and still. It means *submitting* to the text of Scripture, allowing its message to flow into us rather than attempting to master it. It means *reflecting* on the text of Scripture, allowing both mind and heart to be fully engaged in the meaning of the passage. It means *praying* the text of Scripture, letting the biblical reality give rise to our heart cry of gratitude, confession, lament and petition. It means *applying* the text of Scripture, seeing how God's Holy Word provides a personal word for our life circumstances. It means *obeying* the text of Scripture, turning, always turning away from our human ways and into the way everlasting.
>
> Most of all lectio divina means seeing the text of Scripture; *engaging the sanctified imagination* in the full drama of God's Word.[12]

By "engaging the sanctified imagination," in Foster's terms, we place ourselves into the text and open ourselves to whatever the Lord might teach us or show us or evoke in us by his grace. When the text at hand is an account of Jesus responding to people who met him during his earthly ministry, we have the opportunity to encounter him and hear his words as though he were meeting us at the same point of need. So how might lectio divina help us "enter the narrative" of the healing of the leper?

My resource in this case is *Journey with Jesus: Discovering the Spiritual Exercises of Saint Ignatius*, by Larry Warner. (By way of disclosure, I served

---

10. Ibid., 35–36.
11. Bruce, *Epistle to the Hebrews*, 80:
    God is not to be trifled with; His word cannot be ignored with impunity, but must be received in faith and obeyed in daily life. God's "To-day" has arrived; let us take His word seriously and make haste to enter His rest.
12. Foster, *Sanctuary of the Soul*, 40–41, emphasis mine.

in ministry with Larry Warner in the 1970s and we remain close friends after nearly forty years. At various times Warner has served as a church pastor, a seminary professor, an author, and a mentor for spiritual directors.) In a chapter titled "God's Love," Warner offers guidance for reflection and meditation on several Scripture passages—including the story of the leper in Mark 1:40–45.

I cannot hope, in these pages, to suggest what insights the reader might discover in a personal session of lectio divina around this story; but I am happy to quote Warner's guidance as a starting place. Here is how he directs us:

> Put yourself in the story as the leper.
> Imagine that you have been viewed with disdain and disgust all your life so that you have been and are an outcast. People turn away from you and keep their kids from you. You are viewed as one cursed by God.
> Now you come face to face with Jesus.[13]

It's a shocking statement. Outcast and lost, a pariah, abandoned by the people who once loved us and gave us a sense of our worth, we are suddenly face to face with Christ himself. How would we react, and what would happen next? Warner offers some questions to guide our meditation, a few of which I've listed below.

> What do you see in Jesus' eyes as He looks at yours?
> What does it feel like to be touched by Jesus, touched for the first time in years, touched by one who can heal you?
> What does it mean to you that, while you are still a leper, Jesus feels compassion for you?
> What does this tell you about how God sees you?[14]

As Warner says elsewhere in the chapter, "The grace you are seeing is a deeper awareness of God's love for you."[15] He continues his guidance by saying,

> Conclude your time by talking with Jesus about the feelings that arose within you toward him as you imagined your encounter with him as the leper.
> Now stop imagining you are a leper, and go back to being you.

---

13. Warner, *Journey with Jesus*, 68.
14. Ibid., 70.
15. Ibid., 71.

> Is it more difficult for you to internalize Jesus' love for you as yourself than it is when you imagined yourself as a leper? Why, or why not?[16]

Here Warner asks the crucial questions for those who suffer from a deficient sense of self. If you can imagine Jesus loving you and touching you and healing you even in the depths of leprosy, how is it that you struggle to believe it when you "go back to being yourself?" Why do we project onto Jesus attitudes and judgments we have learned from others who did not comprehend his depths of compassion? Is it possible to allow him, in our ordinary lives, to love us simply as he loved all the others who came to him in their damage and pain? Can we begin to let go of anything that prevents it?

In any of the stories of Jesus' encounters that we might choose for looking closer and entering the narrative—the healing of the paralytic, the calling of Zacchaeus, the woman at the well, and so many more—we see again and again the giving of new life and new freedom in ways that were not possible before. Jesus does not judge these people for the maladies they have contracted in their lives; instead he sets them free. For many modern Christians, to be released from the shackles of hopeless self-denigration and turned loose to finally live as God originally shaped them would be freedom indeed.

THE REDEMPTIVE FELLOWSHIP

So far I have been speaking as though a believer may be working alone in dealing with problems that arise from developmental breakdowns. But of course this is not ideal or even desirable. The value we receive from personal meditation should be strengthened and magnified by sharing our situations with other believers who support one another both in times of struggle and times of insight. Scripture encourages us to rejoice with those who rejoice and weep with those who weep (Rom 12:15). Dallas Willard calls the local congregation "a spiritual hospital,"[17] a place where conflicts or damages that may derail us from growing in Christ can be clearly and lovingly addressed.

In his book *Building Up One Another*, Gene Getz identifies twenty-one exhortations from the epistles regarding relationships between believers in

---

16. Ibid.
17. Willard, *Renovation of the Heart*, 234.

A Path to Healing

the local fellowship.[18] They call us to accept, edify, bear with, be kind to, and care for one another—behaviors that make no sense if Christians do not share their sufferings with each other. Paul makes the same point when he writes to the Corinthians:

> Blessed be the God and Father of our Lord Jesus Christ, the Father of mercies and God of all comfort; who comforts us in all our affliction so that we may be able to comfort those who are in any affliction with the comfort with which we ourselves are comforted by God. (2 Cor 1:3–4)

Believers are to comfort each other in any affliction with the comfort they themselves have received from the Lord. God uses the redemptive fellowship of the church to do his work.

Of course, congregations often fall short of Paul's ideal. Believers who have developed attitudes of mistrust and self-doubt from years of conflicted family relations are sometimes judged by other Christians as immature or even sinful. Compounding the damage from childhood experiences, sufferers are wounded again by these criticisms from other believers. We would be wise to bear in mind Paul's admonition in 1 Corinthians:

> Therefore do not go on passing judgment before the time but wait until the Lord comes, who will both bring to light the things hidden in the darkness and disclose the motives of men's hearts; and then each man's praise will come to him from God. (1 Cor 4:5)

Setting aside the eschatological aspects of this imperative,[19] Paul indirectly describes the type of ignorance that informs judgmental attitudes. Those who quickly pass judgment do not know "the things hidden in darkness" or "the motives of men's hearts." They have not taken time to understand either the significant historical circumstances that impacted the people they are judging or the motivations that drive them.

In Paul's terms, sufferers from parental disregard have become weak in faith (1 Thess 5:14; Rom 15:1). Their doubts about God's love and concern for their lives have torn them apart emotionally. What better place for these people to find a path to healing than in the body of Christ, the fellowship of the church? As Daniel Taylor explains it,

---

18. Getz, *Building Up One Another*. On p. 5 Getz lists 22 positive "one another" realities and actions of the body of Christ (contrasted with only 12 negative ones).

19. See Mare, *1 Corinthians*, 211.

Part IV: On the Road Again

> This idea is so appropriate for a community of believers yet so foreign to active practice. We are to be . . . burden bearers for one another, and doubt is one of those burdens.[20]

In his letter to the churches the Apostle Jude says, "And have mercy on some who are doubting" (v. 22). Those stronger in their faith should offer doubters mercy and tender understanding rather than judgment.[21] Again, Daniel Taylor sensitively explores the importance of the redemptive community:

> Sometimes life's troubles may so overwhelm me that I cannot for a time sustain a belief in God's loving concern for me and my fellow creatures. In my humanity I may, like many of my biblical predecessors in the faith, despair or even rage against God. At this point you must believe for me. Do not insist that I still believe. Do not whip the mule that has collapsed under the burden. Do what you can to lighten the burden and wait patiently until I have regained my strength. And someday I will do the same for you.[22]

The people Taylor wishes to connect with are "safe people," believers who genuinely seek to live out the Beatitudes as imitators of Christ.[23] They are "first responders" when affliction strikes fellow Christians and they seek first of all to empathize with those who are suffering. Safe people do not pass judgment and do not criticize or blame the weak for their pain. They offer to the wounded the comfort that they themselves have experienced from the Lord through his church. By grace may we all find safe people in the congregations where we fellowship; over time, may we all grow to become safe people for others.

In this chapter we have explored a range of resources for those suffering from parental disregard. If one or more of them proves valuable for a believer as she begins or follows her path to healing, well and good. When a sufferer's problems are particularly challenging or complex, it may be best to seek a more specific kind of help, in the form of one-on-one interventions with an experienced and compassionate counselor. We will examine the options for that kind of assistance in the next chapter.

---

20. Taylor, *Myth of Certainty*, 110.
21. Wolff, *General Epistles of James & Jude*, 111.
22. Taylor, *Myth of Certainty*, 110.
23. See Cloud and Townsend, *Safe People*, for a very usable description of the development of safe relationships.

CHAPTER NINE

The Power of Witness

*A wise man will hear and increase in learning
And a man of understanding will acquire wise counsel.*

(Proverbs 1:5)

*But God, who comforts the depressed, comforted us by
the coming of Titus.*

(2 Corinthians 7:6)

With the complexity of thoughts and feelings that damages from parental disregard can entail, many sufferers will feel the need for guidance and assistance in their journey of discernment and healing. Ideally the help would be provided by a caring advisor or counselor who is particularly knowledgeable and experienced in dealing with the challenges of developmental woundedness.

In this regard, three approaches or disciplines have demonstrated their value for the believer's healing process: spiritual direction, pastoral counseling, and psychotherapy (specifically, the subcategory of psychoanalytic psychotherapy). We will examine each of them in relation to the particular out-workings of parental disregard in a Christian's life.

SPIRITUAL DIRECTION

In recent years many Christians have explored spiritual direction as an avenue for deeper growth in their faith. Various expressions of this discipline have been practiced throughout the history of the church. The book *Five Models of Spiritual Direction in the Early Church* offers Athanasius, Gregory of Nazianzus, Augustine, John Cassian, and Pope Gregory I as major contributors to the development of the practice in the church's first millennium.[1]

Christian spiritual direction centers on the directee's relationship with God, often using a designed course of study and exercises to help strengthen his trust in God through Jesus Christ. The believer follows this path with the help and guidance of another, called the spiritual director. In the introduction to *Journey with Jesus: Discovering the Spiritual Exercises of St. Ignatius*, Larry Warner explains that the director seeks to help the believer

> enter into a holistic, life-transforming journey toward Christlikeness. This is not another book about the methods or techniques of Christian Formation but a vehicle that enables you to come before God through the Gospel narratives in order to meet Jesus again for the first time....
>
> A *Journey with Jesus* is not for spectators but for those with a hunger for something deeper, a yearning to walk with Jesus (not just read about Him), a desire to embrace more of what God has for you, a longing to be equipped to partner with what God is doing in and through you, a willingness to get down and get dirty with God, Jesus and yourself.[2]

Unlike pastoral counseling, spiritual direction does not primarily concern itself with emotional issues or conflicts in the directee's life. Rather it seeks to assist and support the believer along the path to God that she is already following. As Jeanette Bakke states,

---

1. Demacopoulos, *Five Models of Spiritual Direction*; see also Holt, *Thirsty for God*, 24–51.
2. Warner, *Journey with Jesus*, 9.

Spiritual direction is a kind of discernment about discernment. We explore what has seemed more or less important to us and how we are making choices and acting on our observations. We pay attention to how we interpret our experiences, thoughts, and feelings associated with our relationship with God and how that relationship influences our human relationships.[3]

The directee's life, in its various strengths and weaknesses, is viewed through the lens of her growth in grace. Bakke describes the purpose of spiritual direction as guiding believers to:

Nurture our dependency on God so that it permeates and takes precedence n our thoughts, attitudes, values, choices, and behaviors. (18)

Place our hope in God. . . . We long to experience God's presence in this shattered, exquisite world and need help to believe in our ability to recognize God's voice. (21)

Give caring attention to our relationship with God—attention that is focused on life's foundations underneath ordinary busyness. (22)

Pursue God with all our heart as a way to respond to God, who is pursuing us. In direction we gather many threads together. We bring diverse prayers, impressions, and experiences into direction conversations to invite the Spirit of God to reveal themes and patterns, movements and counter-movements that affect our spirit and life. (22)

The Holy Spirit's revealing presence enables and guides the exploration of the directee's personal conflicts, no matter their origin. In this respect, a person who finds it difficult to experience God's acceptance could benefit from direction by gaining a renewed appreciation of the gospel message. As Bakke comments further,

Spiritual direction is a process that often affects our point of view—the way we look at things. At times directors will ask questions that encourage exploration of a particular Scripture passage, concept, or way of praying or journaling. These suggestions are intended to help directees clarify and examine their own questions and considerations.[4]

---

3. Bakke, *Holy Invitations*, 18.
4. Ibid., 19.

For believers who have suffered intense and prolonged experiences of parental disregard, I have some cautions regarding spiritual direction. As we've seen, these believers may harbor strong feelings of resentment toward God. Parental impingements and the sufferer's pathological accommodative responses can generate a shameful despair that is humiliating to expose to others. Truths about God's love can be resisted not out of pride, but from a place of pain. This may be why Jeannette Bakke says, "Spiritual direction is for essentially healthy people."[5]

It may be necessary to investigate and confront these developmental injuries before a directee will be capable of welcoming the truth of God's love and grace. This type of work does not generally fall under the purview of spiritual direction, but it can certainly be labeled "spiritual." Under the authority of the Holy Spirit it shifts the focus, exploring the believer's formative experiences and examining how he reacted and developed in response to parental impingements and deficits. The believer "works through" his own history by experiencing, understanding, grieving and reframing the painful injunctions and judgments from his caretakers. The process motivates and empowers him to take ameliorative actions that can reshape his life and free him to genuinely grow in grace through practices such as spiritual direction.

PASTORAL COUNSELING

Counseling by clergy offers another approach to dealing with the woundedness of parental disregard. There are, of course, organizations that provide pastoral counselors with extensive professional training and guidelines for intervention.[6] But in this context I am primarily speaking of the everyday care of pastors for the members of a local church and others involved in its life. The issues discussed between a pastor and a congregant are typically viewed in light of the biblical teaching (i.e., practical theology) that is preached and taught at the church.[7]

Pastoral counseling from a caring minister can be efficacious for many kinds of personal problems, not simply those related to trusting God or understanding certain Christian doctrines. Whatever issue the counselee wishes to address should be lovingly accepted as a concern—though the

---

5. Ibid., 30.
6. E.g., see the American Association of Pastoral Counselors, http://www.aapc.org.
7. Browning, *Moral Context of Pastoral Care*, 109.

pastor is not obligated to "accept" all aspects of it. As Don Browning has said,

> Not only is care to be associated with love, forgiveness, and grace. Care in a Christian context also should exhibit a kind of practical moral inquiry into the way life should be ordered.... Only when our pastoral care contains within it dimensions of practical moral inquiry do we earn the right temporally to relax these moral concerns and concentrate specifically on the emotional difficulties and the unique feelings of the person for whom we care.[8]

The phrase "the way life should be ordered" presupposes a common reference point or point-of-view for personal issues. It does not suggest a judgmental dismissing of a person's needs; it merely clarifies where genuine wellbeing resides and how it can be sought. As Ray Anderson puts it,

> Before there can be competence in counseling, we must understand competence in being human, in living humanly, openly, and lovingly with others and with God.[9]

Anderson's phrase "competence in being human" presupposes a template for understanding our humanity. The practice of pastoral counseling unashamedly relies on biblical theology/anthropology as its templates. They enable the counselor to work with people "in an integrative way, as human persons first of all, based on a biblical anthropology rather than a cognitive belief system."[10]

The counselee's life is therefore primarily viewed in the context of her relationship to God and any specific problems are explored in relation to her moral and relational beliefs.[11] Pastoral counselors, of course, may have received training in psychotherapeutic methods, whether behavioral, humanistic, or analytic. They may also employ one of the various "biblical

---

8. Ibid., 15. See Townsend, *Introduction to Pastoral Counseling*, 75–103, for an in-depth presentation of the scope and methods of pastoral counseling. She writes,
> Pastoral counselors excel in identifying and mobilizing clients toward spiritually based self-healing in three ways: (1) they are highly attuned to listen for spiritual meanings in therapy and bring these into conversations; (2) they help clients evaluate "when religion gets sick" and is detrimental to mental health or coping; and (3) they value the process of personal growth and spiritual discovery.... Pastoral counselors often make no distinction between psychotherapeutic change and spiritual growth and discovery. (77)

9. Anderson, *Christians Who Counsel*, 17.

10. Ibid., 36.

11. Townsend, *Introduction to Pastoral Counseling*, 78.

counseling" approaches.[12] What defines the counseling as "pastoral" (apart from its context in a local church) is its grounding in the great themes of the Bible, whether they are expressed as "creation, fall, redemption," "sin, salvation, glorification," or some other construct. As the process develops, the counselees' personal narratives intertwine with their identity and growth as Christians.

Pastoral counseling naturally turns to Scripture for aid in understanding personal and moral conflicts, for resources to help counselees come to terms with their pain, and for encouragement about the love and forgiveness that God offers to the suffering soul. Anderson's words of advice for the psychotherapist also carry weight for the pastoral counselor:

> To be most effective, the counselor should be so familiar with Scripture that she can "tell" its basic stories or paradigms in the context of the therapy process without using the Bible itself. . . . It is up to each counselor to decide whether to use the Bible in therapy. There is, however, no reason not to use it, provided that this Word has not become "dis-incarnate" and is not brought in as something alien to the therapeutic creation itself. The Word of God should be a friend. If it sounds strange to the ear, the ear has become estranged from the heart. The Word, even in its strangeness, can provide healing and growth.[13]

The efficacy of Scripture is mediated through the care and respect that the pastoral counselor brings to the relationship. Evoked in this context, Scripture can genuinely help transform the "thoughts and intentions of the heart" (Heb 4:12).[14] Anderson calls this "the authority of the Word of God" which impacts the recipient by "its power to affect the 'hearing' which is the assimilation of the Word into one's own responsibility."[15]

For a person suffering the emotional and relational consequences of parental disregard, pastoral counseling can play a valuable role. The counselor can offer the counselee empathy and support while helping her understand that the Scriptures do address her issues. They illuminate the pain of

---

12. My recommendations for exploring this hybrid of psychotherapy and pastoral counseling would be as follows. To examine a particular approach by one author, see Watson, *Biblical Counseling for Today*. For an in-depth evaluation of the issues, see Clinton and Ohlschlager, *Foundation & Practice of Compassionate Soul Care*. For a helpful debate and contrast between different approaches, see Johnson, *Psychology & Christianity*.

13. Anderson, *Christians Who Counsel*, 133.

14. Ibid., 121–35.

15. Ibid., 126.

"losing heart" as a result of parental provocations (Col 3:21) and teach that all parents should treat their children as gifts from God (Ps 127:5). They can help sharpen the counselee's emotional responses to harsh memories as she is freed up from feelings of guilt and shame. As David tells us, "Behold, thou dost desire truth in the innermost being and in the hidden part Thou will make me know wisdom" (Ps 51:7).

Coming to terms with the "hidden truth" of parental disregard in a person's life is not an easy process. It draws out a complex mix of emotions such as anger, guilt, confusion, shame, regret, grief, disappointment, remorse, mourning, and forgiveness. Pastoral counseling can grapple with the complexities of these responses and especially address the disturbances they have caused in the counselee's relationship to God. The counselee needs to safely reflect on her sense of God's absence during the abusive situations in childhood and explore how she has come to view him since that time.

The weakness of pastoral counseling in these situations is that it may not provide a sufficient context or set of tools for changing deep-seated attitudes and decisions. A survivor of severe parental disregard may develop a mind-set of entitlement that puts him at odds with much of the Christian ethic. The pain from a "loss of heart" may render behavioral changes too frightening and therefore too dangerous to pursue. Structures of pathological accommodations can be protected by self-denigrating beliefs that are subtle, complex, and only partly understood.

Pastoral counseling at its best would center on the larger meanings behind the conflicts, supporting the counselee through his emotional suffering and giving permission to grieve through the guilt and blame—and over time, seeking to develop forgiveness for those involved. It would also be directive in problem-solving, charging the counselee to take an active approach with personal conflicts or relationships, always in light of the counselee's relationship with God and his desire to be right with him.

PSYCHOTHERAPY

In his aptly titled book *Psychotherapy: The Art of Wooing Nature*, Sheldon Roth defines the discipline as

> the study of and understanding of the vicissitudes of love. It entails finding the point at which development was frustrated and the adaptive patterns that were used to cope with this frustration.

> Aggression as it occurs either as anger and guilt . . . is most often secondary to the frustration of love, and the insecurity and aggressive disharmony emanating from such failure.[16]

In place of the caregiving love that every child needs, a child finds frustration, resulting in an insecure sense of self and "aggressive disharmony" in outward relationships. Roth's description echoes the patterns we have seen in the consequences of parental disregard. A child does not receive loving acceptance for his particular bent or way; his propensities or aptitudes for certain activities or expressions are rejected. The adaptive patterns that he uses to cope with his frustration are the "pathological accommodations" that Brandchaft describes. His strategies are necessarily adaptive and accommodative because every child fundamentally needs the loving support that only approving parents can provide.

Psychotherapy is the "study and understanding of the vicissitudes" of a person's emotional pain. What exactly is that pain, and why does it cause such distress? How did it start, and why has it maintained its presence in the person's life? Psychotherapy takes the patient's particular life story as the context for the clinical work. With the overwhelming evidence of the importance of early attachments, the person's primary relationships become a central focus of the field of study. The experience of these relationships and the "vicissitudes of love" within them are at the core of the exploration.

Psychotherapy aims to offer the person (client or patient) a safe place to examine their emotional landscape and begin to make sense of it. Speaking of the clinician's role in this endeavor, Karen Maroda says,

> The best thing we can offer is an opportunity for them to speak of their concerns as early as possible, and a demonstration of our ability to listen and be empathic. . . . . Unless we decide we cannot work well with a certain client, we need to help him overcome his fears of being vulnerable, weak, embarrassed, or ashamed.[17]

The dysphoric feelings described by Maroda (along with others such as guilt, shame, rage, terror and despondency) signal that injurious events have occurred in a person's life. The intensity of these affects disrupts healthy living. The circumstances where they erupt offer clues both to their origin and to the reasons why they have been maintained. An experienced

---

16. Roth, *Psychotherapy*, 17.
17. Maroda, *Psychodynamic Techniques*, 14.

and empathetic clinician can provide assistance in deciphering these clues. As Donna Orange explains,

> Psychoanalysis is primarily a collaborative effort to comprehend a person's emotional experience. Such comprehension means entering into and dwelling inside the experience of the patient, including the experience of the analytic relationship by both partners. Together patient and analyst struggle to make sense of the patient's experience of being the person she or he is, particularly but not exclusively in the analytic relationship.[18]

Psychoanalysis works within the relationship that develops between analyst and patient both to explore the emotional pain in the patient's life and to provide new experiences that can help ameliorate that pain. It offers the patient free movement and expression of memory, belief, and experience. The analyst promotes this freedom in order to expand the patient's awareness of her internal incongruities and lack of integration. Beliefs that are based in memory may conflict with present-day experiences; beliefs congruent with present-day experience may become unsettled when disquieting memories from a suppressed past come to light.

Christians seeking a path to healing may face additional obstacles in embracing a safe environment for sharing their stories. Many evangelical Christians have found it difficult to be honest about personal emotional pain, believing that people who belong to Christ should not experience anxiety or depression and should not hold grudges or assign blame to others, especially God.[19] Even if a person suffered deprivations in childhood and the lacerating messages from that time feel as though they are "written

---

18. Orange, *Emotional Understanding*, 6.

19. For a most disturbing yet profound example, see Heitritter and Vought, *Helping Victims of Sexual Abuse*. The authors relate the case of "Elizabeth," one of their patients, who had been molested for seven years by her uncle beginning at the age of ten. Below is their description of the parents' reactions when the abuse was disclosed; note that all parties involved were described as Christians:

> Elizabeth's parents reacted to the abuse disclosure by telling her it was, "all over now." She was to "forgive and forget," to "put it all behind her." Injustice raged within her. Why hadn't her Christian parents protected her from him in the first place? She had never even been told that something like this could happen. Why hadn't her mother listened to her when she first tried to tell her about the abuse? Why couldn't her parents understand how much pain she was going through now that her horrible shame was exposed? Why wouldn't they support her by at least *trying* to understand the intensity of the pain she had been enduring in silence for so long? (61, italics original)

in stone," a true Christian should have allowed the Holy Spirit to renew his mind and release him from his pain without outside intervention. When a believer does not experience freedom from the affective impact of past abuses, he may see himself as a spiritual failure, compounding the conflicts he has been unable to address.

Christians who oppose the whole concept of psychotherapy may protest that painful life events should be "dismissed" or "rejected," since the Apostle Paul said, "When I became a man I put away childish things," and, "Forgetting what lies behind and reaching forward to what lies ahead, I press on toward the goal for the prize of the upward call of God in Christ Jesus" (1 Cor 13:11; Phil 3:13b–14). It hardly needs saying that construing those scriptures in that manner distorts Paul's intentions: the apostle was speaking of the Christian's growing faith in the freedom of Christ, not a kind of intentional amnesia about formative experiences. Yet even if we allow the critics' application of the texts we face an issue of overriding importance. What if the Christian is unable to put away these "childhood" feelings because they are too disturbing and too disruptive in his daily life? Anxiety only deepens when there is little understanding of the etiology (i.e., causative beginnings) of the disruptive affects and why they continue to be experienced. Are they rooted in an internalized injunction that must be obeyed under penalty of some kind of internalized disapproval? Embedded in the stories of many sufferers are subtle motivations that stimulated particular actions or attitudes that then developed into discernible conflicts. The conflicted behaviors became the rationale for harsh attitudes of self-denigration or antisocial, antagonistic postures toward others. We cannot realistically expect a believer, or any other person, to magically resolve complex and deep-seated issues through a sort of willful "dismissing" or forgetting.

In his book *Theory and Practice of Counseling and Psychotherapy*, Gerald Corey says of psychoanalytic psychotherapy ("Psy. P" for short),

> Successful analysis is believed to result in significant modification of the individual's personality and character structure. Therapeutic methods are used to bring out unconsciousness material. Then childhood experiences are reconstructed, discussed, interpreted and analyzed. It is clear that the process is not limited to solving problems and learning new behaviors. Rather, there is a deeper probing into the past in order to develop the level of self-understanding that is assumed to be necessary for a change in character. Psychoanalytic therapy is oriented toward achieving insight,

but not just an intellectual understanding; it is essential that the feelings and memories associated with this self-understanding be experienced.[20]

Most contemporary schools of Psy. P view the experiencing and understanding of affects as the keys to successful treatment.[21] "Success" in treatment includes both a reduction of inimical symptoms such as anxiety and depression and a beneficial transformation in the ways the patient views himself and others in the world. As Psychoanalyst Sandra Buechler explains it,

> The emotional sources of the capacity to effect change are the same for the clinician as they are for the teacher, theologian, or political leader. . . . But I think I do not differ from many others in my belief that to be transformed in any meaningful way we need to be inspired by an emotional experience.[22]

Various practitioners have offered their own perspectives about essential aspects of Psy. P, and resources for further study can be found in the bibliography.[23] For my purposes, three aspects of this form of psychotherapy are most important for those damaged by parental disregard.

First is the insight that *conflicts result from lived experience*—which is simply to say that the actual events in a person's life are crucial to her development as a person. Impingements, deprivations, abuses, and traumas are the roots of psychological conflicts. People most often defend themselves against childhood suffering through various forms of denial, from "forgetting" the emotional potency of past relationships or events (a kind of disassociation) to "forgetting" the events completely (the action that Freud called repression). Other defenses attempt to ameliorate the misery or distract sufferers from their pain (addictions, compulsions,

---

20. Corey, *Theory and Practice*, 72.

21. A particularly important statement was made by Drew Westen in his book *Self and Society*, 49: "Where drive was, there shall affect be." This largely unrecognized aphorism points to the shift in understanding about the fundamental human motivations for living. In place of Freud's biological satisfaction of tension caused by sexual and aggressive drive derivatives, we now speak of "affect regulation" and spontaneity, both as by-products of human relationships and in service of them.

22. Buechler, *Making a Difference in Patient's Lives*, 24.

23. For a thorough and readable exposé, see McWilliams, *Psychoanalytic Psychotherapy*. Also see Cabaniss et al., *Psychodynamic Psychotherapy*, and Summers and Barber, *Psychodynamic Therapy*.

cause-orientations).²⁴ The key point in all these situations is that the person suffers because the affects that are sparked by the painful experiences are necessarily disruptive. They may take the form of settled emotional dispositions such as shame, guilt, or self-loathing, or evocative feeling states such as terror, rage, despondency or anxious bewilderment. Though the events occurred long ago, the emotional responses can be accessed today if painful memories become "too real." In treatment we allow these emotions to be reexperienced in all their turbulent power. The patient's fear of being overwhelmed by disorienting affects must be handled gently and safely by the clinician. The parental impingements must be reframed as events that occurred through no fault of the patient's. The pain must be understood for what it is, since the causes, no matter how heinous, are over and gone. Though the emotions are still relevant, the abuse has thankfully stopped.²⁵

The second essential insight is that *conflicts can become embedded in different levels of awareness* in a person's mind. The classic distinction between conscious and unconscious memory is fundamental to the psychoanalytic approach.²⁶ One reason that developmental conflicts affect people differently is that, to some degree, they are "remembered" differently. Research suggests that the more traumatic an event is, or the younger the

---

24. A key focus of current addiction studies is the "self-medication hypothesis," which identifies avoidance of suffering as the primary motivation for substance abuse (as opposed to a desire for pleasurable experiences). See Khantzian and Albanese, *Understanding Addiction as Self Medication*. As they explain in their introduction (xvi),

> The self-medication hypothesis gives a humanistic and understandable explanation as to why addictions are so compelling. It emphasizes that psychological pain is at the heart of addictive behavior and that vulnerable individuals resort to their addiction because they discover that the addictive substance or behavior gives short-term and otherwise unobtainable relief, comfort, or change from their distress.

25. In *Into Abba's Arms*, 158, family therapist Sandra Wilson describes the awakening of pain during her own treatment:

> I finally tapped into that soul-deep pool of pain. As wave after wave of grief and abandonment terror washed over me, I sobbed so convulsively that I had dry heaves. I broke blood vessels under both eyes! As unpleasant as this all sounds, God made that time one of the major milestones in my ongoing healing journey.

The intensity of Wilson's experience should not be taken as the norm. Successful treatment uniquely brings out each patient's particular memories, which the patient has long defended against examination or exposure. The patient protects himself precisely because he fears the kind of suffering that Dr. Wilson went through.

26. See Corey, *Theory and Practice*, 65–66.

age of the child when it occurs, the more likely the event will be relegated to "distant" memory even to the point of being forgotten.[27] Children can experience trauma from frightening events when parents do not respond to their needs with appropriate soothing and protection, both during and after the occurrence. The duration and/or speed of onset of alarming situations, and their cumulative impact over time, likewise play important roles in the development of the child's "dis-ease."

Understanding the specific reasons why a person feels the way they do is the keystone of the healing process. Psychoanalytic treatment investigates the causes behind difficult feelings and attitudes and promotes the expression of emotions that have been too raw to acknowledge. Sufferers may expend enormous effort in over-controlling or even stifling these gut-level affects, essentially "disowning" them when they become too dangerous to be communicated. In treatment, the terrifying childhood emotions can finally be expressed as the patient brings them under her adult understanding in the presence of the supportive witness of the therapist.[28] The clinician's encouragement validates the reality and significance of those feelings. The Christian knows that Jesus understands her anguish throughout this process since he is "a man of sorrows and acquainted with grief" (Isa 53a).[29]

This brings us to the third salient feature of Psy. P: *the relationship between the clinician and the patient is all important.* The value of that

---

27. In Meares, *Intimacy & Alienation*, 32–39, three kinds of memory are discussed. First is "procedural" memory, the nonverbal or preverbal recall of motor skills and repertoires. Second is "autobiographical" memory, the recalling of facts such as where one attended school and the names of the schoolteachers. Third is "declarative" or "episodic" memory, which is "made up of episodes of personal experience that have a sensory aliveness" (35). See also Baddeley, *Working Memory, Thought, and Action*, 335–50.

28. See Buirski, *Practicing Intersubjectively*, 109:

> An important function of the therapist/witness is facilitating the trauma survivor's capacity to put words to their frightening story by reconstructing it in the safe and supportive presence of an attuned other. Through the experience of sharing with the witness, the trauma survivor can gain access to disavowed or unformulated aspects of the experience. In the intersubjective field constructed with the particular therapist/witness, the survivor and witness together further the unfolding, illumination, and articulation of the meaning of the traumatic experience.

29. Consider Ps 22:1–21 (as a depiction the suffering of Christ on the cross) in light of Heb 2:18, where we are told that "since [Jesus] Himself was tempted in that which He has suffered, He is able to come to the aid of those who are tempted." The anguish of Christ's "forsakenness" is inchoate, much like the depth of terror sufferers can experience during the emergence of childhood traumatic memory.

relationship cannot be overstated. The therapist's role is crucial for the patient's healing because people often respond to others in ways that echo their responses to significant persons in their past, particularly those they see as authority figures. As we noted earlier, in psychoanalytic terms this reaction is known as transference. As one writer describes it,

> Transference is a psychological organizing activity. *In treatment, it refers to all the ways that a patient assimilates the analytic relationship into the affect-laden, archaically rooted configurations of self and other.* The transference is a microcosm of the patient's total psychological life. The analysis of the transference provides us with an understanding of the patterns that dominate his or her subjective world. So, while the transference refers to the unconscious organizing principles that crystallized out of the early formative experiences, it is an expression of the continuing influence of these principles rather than a regression to or a displacement from the past.[30]

In a therapeutic relationship, transference makes it easier for the clinician to perceive how the patient related to significant figures in their childhood. The reactions are sharpest when memories of past events that afflicted the patient are triggered during therapy. Particular sensitivities which cause the patient great suffering can be brought into the present so that their meanings can be unlocked. These and other aspects of transference have been the subject of a great deal of research over the years, and resources for further study are widely available.[31]

Another key aspect of the patient/clinician relationship is that it allows personal—and sometimes painful—changes to occur clearly and honestly in the presence of a caring other. Accepting the misery of past suffering and developing new beliefs about ourselves and others takes courage and determination. In his book *Intimate Engagements: The Collaborative Basis of Therapeutic Change*, Steven Frankel says of one of his patients,

> Analysis provided Andrew with the possibility of having his needs recognized and met. It also exposed him to enormous interpersonal risk. Part of my job was to create a steady environment. A sense of safety and the promise of a relationship with someone

---

30. Jaenicke, *Risk of Relatedness*, 117, italics original.

31. See Wachtel, *Therapeutic Communication*, 102–21, for a thorough explanation of transference in the clinical setting. Also see Grand and Crawley, *Transference and Projection*. For a more technical description refer to Gabbard, *Textbook on Psychoanalysis*, 65–92, 255–68.

committed to his welfare were basic ingredients for him to bring core needs and anxieties into our work. The transferences and conflicts that limited his progress could be interpreted as it became clear that they were blocking progress.[32]

This "sense of safety" with the committed other has become the basis of treatment in contemporary psychoanalytic psychotherapy. Before the clinician offers any interpretive statements or problem-solving strategies, this relationship must be comfortably established. As analyst Peter Buirski describes it,

> I remain convinced that one of the important promoters of growth and health is the inverse of what disrupted it in the first place: the quality of emotional relating between people who are important to each other. If *the consistent misattunement of the early caregivers* plays a large role in the child's emotional impairment, then repair must necessarily involve a new and *improved attuned relationship*.[33]

The new "attuned relationship" becomes a context where the patient is enabled to delve into primal and sometimes terrorizing feelings. For some patients it will be the first time that they can share their stories with complete honesty. Their attempts at expressing emotions with family members or friends may have left them feeling judged, disregarded, or let down by a non-comprehending response. Among Christians, they may have faced judgment for expressing anger, disrespect, or any other negative attitude toward someone in their past. The Apostle Paul (echoing Jesus' words in Matt 7:7) offers admonitions that I wish were practiced much more widely in the church:

> Therefore do not go on passing judgment before the time but wait until the Lord comes, who will both bring to light the things hidden in the darkness and disclose the motives of men's hearts; and then each man's praise will come to him from God. (1 Cor 4:5)

When "things [are] hidden in the darkness," it's very difficult to render sound judgment.[34] Paul addresses his words to the Corinthian church,

---

32. Frankel, *Intricate Engagements*, 180.
33. Buirski, *Practicing Intersubjectively*, xvii, emphasis mine.
34. Mare, *1 Corinthians*, 211, says "('What is hidden in darkness') are the acts and motives concealed in the inner recesses of a person's mind and heart." Morris, *First Epistle of Paul*, 76 refers to the counsel of the hearts as "men's secret desires and motives, good and evil alike." If people have such difficulty discerning their own desires and motives,

a notoriously immature and yet grandiose congregation of believers (cf. 1 Cor 3:1–3). Though he criticizes some of their actions he always seeks to know more of their story; he refuses to reach conclusions until he sees for himself what is going on (1 Cor 4:18–21; 2 Cor 12:20–21). Paul understood better than many that people have different reasons for doing things "hidden in the darkness." Some hide their actions out of shame, knowing that they are clearly wrong, sinful, or hurtful to others. Others act because they are personally in pain, confused or weakened to the point of desperation or clouded judgment. Many people, including many Christians, choose not to share their vulnerabilities, distress, shame, abuse, or anything that might subject them to humiliating reactions. Why should they risk being re-traumatized in by recounting their travail to someone who will only pass judgment? A relationship with a supportive therapist can resolve this dilemma for the sufferer, as Donna Orange explains.

> Remembering is experienced as dangerous partly because it includes the memory of being alone with whatever the trouble was, without the support and validation of witness. Not until the tie to the analyst is strong can vivid kinds of remembering be risked, for without a secure connection the patient's fear that the memories will be overwhelming and lead to psychosis or self-destruction prevents their emergence. The tie to the analyst makes it possible for the patient to discover and to survive realizing—making real—the full horror of what happened to her or him as a vulnerable child. Part of the horror was being alone.[35]

The promise and experience of no longer being alone in the grip of unresolved past abuse inspires the sufferer's courage to do the hard work of psychotherapy.

ANGELA'S PAINFUL PROGRESS

Several years ago I treated a woman named Angela who had been molested by an older relative for nearly eleven years beginning in childhood. The relative, an intimidating church-going man who worked in law enforcement, threatened to harm Angela's parents if she ever reported the abuse. She felt a searing shame over the sometimes nearly indescribable humiliation she

---

how much more problematic is it for an outsider to understand them well enough to pronounce judgment?

35. Orange, *Emotional Understanding*, 138–39.

experienced from her molester, along with a terrible guilt about not taking action about it until the middle of her adolescence.

When Angela came to see me nearly thirty years after the abuse ended, she understandably had very little experience of God's forgiveness for herself or anyone else. Her sense of self had been powerfully compromised, nearly shattered, and she was confused about most aspects of relationships, though she had been able to function fairly well in her marriage. Clearly Angela was not to blame for the abuse she had suffered, but she had no strength to advocate on her own behalf. She found it difficult to accept that she had been victimized entirely by a man who was in the family circle. She suspected that her mother knew something was amiss and possibly even colluded in some way with the perpetrator, or perhaps simply did not want to face the truth about the debauchery in her own family. Yet to a large degree Angela only blamed herself for not disclosing what was happening to her as she got older.

Many aspects of Angela's life had been stunted or radically altered by the emotional trauma of continuous molestation. She was a believer who attended an evangelical church almost every Sunday. But how could God forgive her for allowing the abuse to continue for so many years? How could she feel "joy in the Holy Spirit" (Rom 14:19) if the Spirit was not present when she was being cruelly exploited? Her Christian faith consisted almost entirely of head knowledge: she trusted the cross and resurrection of Jesus Christ for her salvation, but they had no practical presence in her life.

My treatment with Angela took the path of intense psychotherapeutic work around the trauma itself. Crucially, she had to learn to see herself in a different way; she needed to recognize that a six-year-old child did not have the resources to resist her adversary's advances. What could she do, knowing that the man carried a gun and that he threatened to use it on her parents if she revealed their secret? Beyond that basic acceptance Angela had to get free from the enormous burden of guilt she had placed on herself. Most of all she needed to detoxify the terrifying feelings she had experienced during the abuse and bring that historic, episodic memory into the wisdom and perspective of her adult mind. We explored all of those tasks, and others, during the years of her treatment.

For the strengthening of her faith, Angela's obstacles had much in common with others who have suffered abuse. God had to be understood anew, taking the vantage point of Angela's experience of his grace as she worked through her pain in the present. Her herculean efforts during treatment marked the first attempts she had ever made to face these issues squarely. One particular obstacle was her enormous sense of disappointment in her mother, who likely had some notion that her daughter was being molested yet did not question her about it or take any other action. This essential "protective layer" from God had failed. Why would God give Angela a mother who would not safeguard her own daughter? It's difficult to imagine a more severe example of parental disregard. Angela had to learn to see her mother as too fearful and intimidated to intervene in her torment. She had to understand that blaming herself for not revealing the abuse was an accommodation to her mother's own weakness.

Over time, Angela came to see that her work with me in treatment was under the domain and blessing of Christ's love for her. The Apostle Paul, feeling despondent over terrible reports he had received about the church at Corinth, said "God who comforts the depressed comforted us by the coming of Titus" (2 Cor 7:6). Titus brought better news and a renewed perspective to Paul about the Corinthians; he provided new insights into their commitment to the faith and their love and respect for Paul. Love and comfort and new understanding changed Paul's emotional disposition. Similarly, Angela achieved new insights about her former ways of viewing her life. She was taken seriously even in the most challenging aspects of her self-condemnation. She was supported, encouraged, and witnessed in the excruciating pain that she once suffered alone. God comforted her through my role as her therapist. What a privilege to have worked with her!

SEEKING HELP

With the choices available for outside intervention, what guidance can we offer a person who seeks assistance? I would suggest that sufferers begin by identifying the areas of their life that need the most attention or cause the most distress. Typically, the more intense and continuous the childhood rejections had been, the greater will be the psychological/emotional difficulties that a person must face.

For the Christian, we've seen that this fundamental ongoing misattunement can radically distort her experience of God. The spiritual problems caused by a faulty "transferential" view of God are legion; they may take the form of an overly legalistic faith (God will reject me unless I offer "total" obedience) or a morally lapsed faith (God really isn't interested in what I do or what matters to me). More common may be a nominal, colorless faith, since the believer's unacknowledged anger at his caretakers, including God, precludes any emotional investment in the relationship.

The spiritual problems naturally impact a Christian's self-image and self-awareness, often creating or amplifying depressions and anxieties. These in turn can increase the difficulties of establishing and maintaining healthy relationships. If the conflicts are not addressed, if they are left to multiply and reinforce each other, other types of spiritual, emotional, relational, mental, and even physical problems can result.

I would suggest, then, that attention should first be given to the sufferer's subjective experience of his difficulties and particularly to his own evaluation of them. The top priority should be the place where his heart feels most troubled. Does he feel so depressed that it colors his whole day? Does he fear authority so much that his anxieties interfere with his work or even make it difficult to stay employed? Does he spoil relationships because he uses the Bible in ways that burden the people close to him with guilt and condemnation (just as it was used on him when he was young)? Does he view God as distant and not interested in the crucial aspects of his life? An emotionally compromised sense of self can become manifest in these and many other types of disruptive reactions.

My recommendation for Christians dealing with these kinds of maladies is to begin by approaching the minister or other member of the pastoral staff at their own church. This presumes a viable relationship of trust and confidence in the maturity and wisdom of the pastor or minister,[36] but in most situations it's a sensible first step, particularly for Christians who are uncertain about psychotherapy.

During the interactions with the pastor as counselor, other courses of action can be explored. Most ministers are trained to recognize both the depth and seriousness of psychological symptoms. They also know how to discern problems related to faulty beliefs built on misunderstandings or misuses of the Scriptures. An effective, caring pastor should be able to recognize when a sufferer would likely benefit from a more in-depth and personally engaged out-working of his internal conflicts and relationship with God.

---

36. My concern is that church members should develop an appropriately biblical relationship with their pastor (or pastoral staff member). The Scriptures teach that the minister is responsible before God to act as a knowledgeable guide for those who place themselves under his leadership. Let them "shepherd the flock of God among you" as the Apostle Peter says in 1 Pet 5:1–3. (See also 1 Thess 5:12; Heb 13:17; Eph 4:11–13.)

Part IV: On the Road Again

Of course, if the believer feels confident in his discernment about the roots of his issues, he can choose his own course of action. The key is to be proactive about the challenges and seek outside opinions from trusted people. Be in prayer about the decision if you can be. If your current attitudes or feelings about God make prayer seem foolhardy, speak with your pastor or someone else you respect for their maturity and wisdom in the Lord. Most critical is to avoid closing down or ignoring the attitudes and beliefs that cause disruptive feeling states. Commit yourself to dealing with them, and consider entering into a process with someone who is both compassionate and trained to help with the problem areas.

Many have wondered whether, when a Christian considers therapy, it would be best to seek a psychotherapist who is also a Christian. Most Christian authors have recommended pursuing this kind of treatment with a professional who is also a believer, and I agree. For the Christian especially, the outcomes of parental disregard impact essential aspects of their faith. In most cases, it's beneficial to work through those conflicts with a clinician who understands and cherishes the importance of her relationship with God. Accepting and paying attention to the spiritual aspects of the patient's suffering by no means disrupts the developmental and clinical work of the psychotherapist, especially the psychoanalytic psychotherapist.[37]

It is certainly possible for a perceptive and sympathetic non-Christian therapist to recognize the importance of the patient's faith issues and work compassionately with her to resolve them. The patient's concerns in these areas need to be clearly discussed during the initial intake session. My own view is that, for holistic recovery and healing from the damage of parental disregard, a believer is best served by working with a clinician who is a Christian.

---

37. For a recent treatment of this subject I recommend Holeman, *Theology for Better Counseling*. In a section titled "Theologically Reflective Counseling in Action" (93–99) Holeman identifies four goals for the clinician who works with Christian clients:

Attending to theological echoes—What level of theological understanding is present?

Addressing salient theological themes—Such as forgiveness, justice, grace, etc.; applying relevant applications.

Aligning areas of life to be more theologically congruent—Help in bringing into line any unloving, or unChrist-like actions and attitudes that are contributing to areas of difficulty.

Attaining a deepening Christian character—Keeping in mind that Christ-like character makes for healthier living both individually and in relationships.

Conclusion

Christians believe that the world, in fundamental ways, is "not right." Theologically we express this by saying the world is fallen, a truth that carries ramifications for every human being, particularly in the whole realm of personal relationships. Even with the new birth, believers still face a continuing struggle against the inborn propensity to act out selfishly instead of living in the fullness of Christ, "to walk in the same manner as He walked" (John 2:6).

It comes as no surprise, then, that Christians who are parents face the same kinds of issues and dilemmas as all parents everywhere. There are no special privileges that make Christian parents more capable than other mothers and fathers who love their children and want to do good for them. Parenting is a daunting experience with a fluid array of costs and benefits that must be continually renewed and re-understood.

Yet the Christian parent has been given great gifts in the Word of God. Among its insights are Paul's words: "And fathers, do not provoke your children to anger; but bring them up in the discipline and instruction of the Lord" (Eph 6:4). Here Paul seems to expect that Christian parents can and should nurture their children and rear them tenderly. His particular intent is better expressed by the paraphrase of the same verse in the Living Bible:

> And now a word for you parents. Don't keep on scolding and nagging your children, making them angry and resentful. Rather

bring them up with the loving discipline the Lord Himself approves, with suggestions and godly advice.

Grace is certainly given to parents who are believers, the same grace that their relationship with Christ affords them in any aspect of their lives (1 Cor 15:10; Heb 13:21).

I have had no intention, in this book, of criticizing parenthood or the vast number of caring parents who love their children and guide them as they grow. My concern has been to alert the Christian community to the reality of developmental woundedness in our midst. Inside and outside of our churches we find men and women, raised in Christian homes, whose parents ignored Paul's warnings about exasperating children or arousing rage in them through harsh methods of correction or unrealistic expectations.[1] Those children suffered the experience of parental disregard and now struggle with its manifestations in adult life.

Though many today will find that observation self-evident, the insights about parental disregard continue to face opposition in some factions of the church, either through active rejection of their importance or passive denial of their existence. This despite the undeniable havoc the damages have wreaked and the obstacles they have created to experientially embracing the truth of God's love. Too many of my patients over the years have been believers living subjectively frustrating lives, struggling against the temptation to act out in various ways to soothe or distract themselves from the pain of their internalized self-rejection. N. T. Wright speaks to this:

> The answer to temptation is to find out, perhaps, painfully and over a long period, what it is about you that is at the moment *out of shape, distorted, in pain*. Then one may begin to find out, again often painfully, how it is that God longs to help you to get what is distorted *back into focus*; to get what is crooked back into shape; to get what is *bruised and hurt back into health*. That will take time; it will certainly take prayer. . . . There is excellent precedent for saying that you will need help. Wise spiritual and practical guidance is part of your birthright as a member of the body of Christ. . . . To grapple with temptation *knowing that its roots run deep into the person that you presently are is to engage with it realistically*.[2]

---

1. Another positive description of how a father should relate to his children can be found in 1 Thess 2:11, where Paul describes his ministry to the church by saying, "Just as you know how we were exhorting and encouraging and imploring each one of you as a father would his own children."

2. Wright, *Following Jesus*, 88, emphasis mine.

Conclusion

Temptation is often rooted in a desire to address painful and confusing personal needs through illegitimate means, i.e., methods that are contrary to the life of Jesus Christ. For my purposes, Wright's proactive stance speaks to the work of growing past the malignant belief systems that parental disregard implants in its sufferers.

Readers who wish to work on their own issues should seek wise counsel in choosing the modality best suited for them, as described in chapters 8 and 9. Whatever intervention is chosen, the work must be an authentic exploration of the conflicts and sorrow that have distorted the person's life. The pain may have been disavowed or suppressed until recently; it may have been a constant source of bitterness that has hobbled personal relationships. For Christians the pain must be brought into the light of self-understanding and of biblical intercession before God. Sandra Wilson comments,

> Such an unfathomable transformation comes when people bring their deep pain, anger and grief right into the presence of God. As they practice the real presence of God by being real, by honestly pouring out their anguish and doubts, and as they listen to God pour out his heart to them, intimacy builds. And as the *Person* which is Truth becomes real to them, his *promises*, which are true, become real to them. Thus, God's *Word* comes alive as never before because, in effect, *God* has come alive as never before.[3]

The wonderful outworking of God "coming alive" to the believer "as never before" warrants the effort required to do this work.

Several years ago I treated Betty, a woman in her mid-forties, for issues related to unresolved parental conflicts that were impacting her marriage. Her rather self-critical relationship with God had also affected her relationship with her husband. One distinctive thing about Betty was her admiration for Mary Magdalene. She saw Mary, from whom the Lord had cast out seven demons (Luke 8:2), as a person who had been freed from heavy burdens in her life. In some medieval traditions she was identified as the "sinful woman" in Luke's gospel (7:36–50) as well as the woman caught in adultery (John 7:53—8:11), suggesting that she had lived as a prostitute before being forgiven and restored by Jesus.[4]

---

3. Wilson, *Into Abba's Arms*, 39, italics original.

4. Witherington, *What Have They Done with Jesus*, 22–23. Witherington does not believe these scriptures are about Mary Magdalene or that she was a prostitute.

Part IV: On the Road Again

Betty was both astounded and encouraged that this woman became a trusted disciple of Jesus Christ, even a "first-tier" disciple who followed Jesus for much of his ministry. She was at the cross where he was gruesomely killed and at the tomb early Easter Sunday morning, where she became the first person to see and touch the resurrected Christ.[5] In Betty's view, Mary's relationship with Jesus—his gentle acceptance of her, not as an "unclean" formerly possessed woman but as a genuine disciple—inspired her to continue as his diligent follower. She had been freed from the burdens of her past, the sinful demonic involvement and possibly the immoral lifestyle and other choices that had weighed her down. Jesus healed her with his power and renewed her with his love. No wonder her devotion led her to become the marvelous witness to Christ that we still encounter in the Scriptures!

Every believer needs that kind of connection with Jesus: a relationship based in the truth of our unique situation, whatever we have experienced in our lives; and with all of the encumbrances we carry, whether sinful or not. We must each bring them to Jesus for his ministry and his love.

Ultimately it is the love of God the Father that "covers a multitude of sins" (Prov 10:12; 1 Pet 4:8; Jas 5:20), and it is our great fortune that his love can be manifested and expressed in more ways than we can imagine. In my own calling as a psychoanalyst, working with patients has always been a loving experience for me. I deeply respect the courage they have shown in the work of gaining freedom from the bonds of developmental woundedness. Those who know him have learned to surrender the truth of who they are to Jesus, coming to a place where they can finally experience the depths of his love and acceptance. Jesus is the lover of our souls. He gave his life on the cross in an act of eternal love that will one day heal all pain in those who believe.

> The cross reveals that Jesus has conquered sin and death and that nothing, *absolutely nothing*, can separate us from the love of Christ.

5. Ibid., 18. See also Morgan, *Great Physician*, 305–12, esp. 308ff. Morgan believes that Mary stayed near the tomb the night Jesus was crucified (from Matt 27:61) since the Roman guard was not present until the second evening. He bases this on the statement that the chief priests did not ask Pilate for a guard until "the next day" (Matt 27:62). Morgan (309) recaps Mary's actions:

> Thus we see Mary of Magdala in her deep sorrow standing by the Cross until her Lord was dead, carefully familiarizing herself with the place of the grave, watching as He was buried there, seeing the grave stone rolled to the opening of the sepulcher, and staying there all night. There were no Roman soldiers there during that night. *There were no disciples there.* (emphasis mine)

Conclusion

Neither the imposter [within] or the pharisee [within], neither the lack of awareness nor the lack of passion, neither the negative judgments of others nor the debased perception of ourselves, neither our scandalous past nor our uncertain future, neither the power struggles in the church nor the tensions in our marriage, nor fear, guilt, shame, self-hatred, nor even death can tear us away from the love of God, made visible in Jesus the Lord.[6]

---

6. Manning, *Abba's Child*, 156, italics original. See also ibid., 163–64, where Manning speaks of the believer as if he were "reclining on Jesus' breast" like the "disciple who Jesus loved" at the Last Supper (John 13:23).

> The moment you press your ear against His heart, you instantly hear *Abba's footsteps in the distance*. I do not know how this happens. It just does. It is a simple movement from intellectual cognition to experiential awareness that Jesus and the Father are one in the Holy Spirit, the bond of infinite tenderness between Them. Without reflection or premeditation the cry, "*Abba, I belong to You*," rises spontaneously from the heart. The *awareness of being sons and daughters in the Son dawns deep in our souls*, and Jesus' unique passion for the Father catches fire within us. In the Abba experience we prodigals, no matter how bedraggled, beat-up, or burnt out, *are overcome by a Paternal fondness of such depth and tenderness that it beggars speech*. As our hearts beat in rhythm with the Rabbi's heart, we come to experience a graciousness, a kindness, a compassionate caring that surpasses our understanding. (emphasis mine)

Bibliography

Ainsworth, Mary. "Patterns of Infant-Mother Attachments: Antecedents and Effect on Development." *Bulletin of the New York Academy of Medicine* 61 (1985) 171–91.

Ainsworth, Mary, et al. "Infant-Mother Attachment and Social Development: 'Socialization' as a Product of Reciprocal Responsiveness to Signals." In *The Integration of a Child into a Social World*, edited by M. P. M. Richard, 99–135. New York: Cambridge University Press, 1974.

———. *Patterns of Attachment: A Psychological Study of the Strange Situation*. Hillsdale, NJ: Erlbaum, 1978.

Akhtar, Salman, ed. *The Mother and Her Child: Clinical Aspects of Attachment, Separation, and Loss*. Northvale, NJ: Aronson, 2011.

Allen, Diogenes. *Love: Christian Romance, Marriage, Friendship*. Princeton: Caroline Press, 1987.

———. *Traces of God in a Frequently Hostile World*. Salt Lake City: Cowley, 1981.

American Psychiatric Association. *Diagnostic and Statistical Manual of Mental Disorders DSM –IV-TR*. 4th ed. Arlington, VA: APA, 2000.

The Analytic Greek Lexicon. Grand Rapids: Zondervan, 1977.

Anderson, Ray. *Christians Who Counsel: The Vocation of Wholistic Therapy*. Grand Rapids: Zondervan, 1990.

Anderson, Ray, and Dennis Guernsey. *On Being Family: A Social Theology of the Family*. Grand Rapids: Eerdmans, 1985.

Archer, Gleason. "Proverbs 22:6 and the Training of Children." In *Learning from Sages: Selected Studies on the Book of Proverbs*, edited by Roy B. Zuck, 273–76. Grand Rapids: Baker, 1995.

Augsburger, Myron. *Matthew*. Communicator's Commentary. Waco, TX: Word, 1982.

Bacal, Howard, and Kenneth Newman. *Theories of Object Relations: Bridges to Self Psychology*. New York: Columbia University Press, 1990.

Baddeley, Alan. *Working Memory, Thought, and Action*. Oxford Psychology. Oxford: Oxford University Press, 2007.

Bainton, Roland. *Here I Stand: A Life of Martin Luther*. New York: Mentor, 1950.

Bakke, Jeanette. *Holy Invitations: Exploring Spiritual Direction*. Grand Rapids: Baker, 2000.

Banks, Robert. *Paul's Idea of Community: The Early House Churches in Their Historical Setting*. Grand Rapids: Eerdmans, 1980.

Bibliography

Barclay, William. *The Letters to the Philippians, Colossians, and Thessalonians*. Daily Study Bible. Philadelphia: Westminster, 1959.

Barnes, Albert, et al. *Proverbs to Ezekiel*. Edited by F. C. Cook. Barnes Notes on the Old & New Testaments: An Explanatory and Practical Commentary. Grand Rapids: Baker, 1953.

Bauckham, Richard. *Jesus and the Eyewitnesses: The Gospels as Eyewitness Testimony*. Grand Rapids: Eerdmans, 2006.

Bauerlein, Mark. *The Dumbest Generation: How the Digital Age Stupefies Young Americans and Jeopardizes Our Future (or, Don't Trust Anyone Under 30)*. London: Penguin, 2008.

Beebe, Beatrice, et al. *Forms of Intersubjectivity in Infant Research and Adult Treatment*. New York: Other, 2005.

Bettelheim, Bruno. *A Good Enough Parent: A Book of Child-Rearing*. New York: Vintage, 1987.

Blaimes, Harry. *The Christian Mind: How Should a Christian Think?* Vancouver: Regent College Publishing, 1995.

Boman, Thorlief. *Hebrew Thought Compared with Greek*. New York: Norton, 1960.

Bowlby, John. *A Secure Base: Parent-Child Attachment and Healthy Human Development*. New York: Basic, 1988.

Brandchaft, Bernard. *Toward an Emancipatory Psychoanalysis: Brandchaft's Intersubjective Vision*. With Shelley Doctors and Dorienne Sorter. New York: Routledge, 2010.

Brisch, Karl. *Treating Attachment Disorders: From Theory to Therapy*. New York: Guilford, 1999.

Brown, Raymond. *Christ Above All: The Message of Hebrews*. Bible Speaks Today. Downers Grove: InterVarsity, 1982.

Brown, William *Character in Crisis: A Fresh Approach to the Wisdom Literature of the Old Testament*. Grand Rapids: Eerdmans, 1996.

Browning, Donald. *The Moral Context of Pastoral Care*. Philadelphia: Westminster, 1976.

Bruce, F. F. *The Epistle to the Hebrews*. New International Commentary on the New Testament. Grand Rapids: Eerdmans, 1977.

Buber, Martin. *The Knowledge of Man: Selected Essays*. Edited by Maurice Friedman. Atlantic Highlands, NJ: Humanities International, 1988.

Buechler, Sandra. *Making a Difference in Patient's Lives: Emotional Experience in Therapeutic Setting*. New York: Routledge, 2008.

Buirski, Peter. *Practicing Intersubjectively*. New York: Aronson, 2005.

Bulloch, C. Hassell. "The Book of Proverbs." In *Learning from the Sages: Selected Studies in the Book of Proverbs*, edited by Roy B. Zuck, 19–34. Grand Rapids: Baker, 1995.

Cabaniss, Deborah, et al. *Psychodynamic Psychotherapy: A Clinical Manual*. Chichester, UK: Wiley, 2011.

Clark, Chap, and Kara Powell. *Sticky Faith: Everyday Ideas to Build Lasting Faith in Your Kids*. Grand Rapids: Zondervan, 2011.

Clinton, Tim, and George Ohlschlager, eds. *Foundation & Practice of Compassionate Soul Care*. Vol. 1 of *Competent Christian Counseling*. Colorado Springs: Waterbrook, 2002.

Clinton, Tim, and Joshua Straub. *God Attachment: Why You Believe, Act, and Feel the Way You Do about God*. New York: Howard, 2010.

Cloud, Henry, and John Townsend. *Safe People: How to Find Relationships That Are Good for You and Avoid Those That Aren't*. Grand Rapids: Zondervan, 1995.

Bibliography

Cohen, Charles, and Vance Sherwood. *Becoming a Constant Object in Psychotherapy with the Borderline Patient*. Northvale, NJ: Aronson, 1991.
Cooper, Terry. *Sin, Pride & Self-Acceptance*. Downers Grove: IVP Academic, 2003.
Corey, Gerald. *Theory and Practice of Psychotherapy and Counseling*. 9th ed. Belmont, CA: Brooks/Cole, 2013.
Cramer, George. *First and Second Peter*. Chicago: Moody, 1967.
Crenshaw, David. *Bereavement: Counseling the Grieving throughout the Life Cycle*. New York: Continuum, 1990.
Dana, H. E., and Julius Mantey. *A Manual Grammar of the Greek New Testament*. Toronto: Macmillan, 1955.
Demacopoulos, George. *Five Models of Spiritual Direction in the Early Church*. Notre Dame: University of Notre Dame Press, 2007.
Dobson, James. *Parent's Answer Book: A Comprehensive Resource from Today's Most Respected Expert*. Wheaton: Tyndale, 2003.
Dunnam, Maxine. *Galatians, Ephesians, Philippians, Colossians, Philemon*. Communicator's Commentary. Waco, TX: Word, 1982.
Eadie, John. *A Commentary on the Greek Text of the Epistle of Paul to the Colossians*. Edited by W. Young. Grand Rapids: Baker, 1884, 1979.
———. *A Commentary on the Greek Text of the Epistle of Paul to the Ephesians*. Edited by W. Young. Grand Rapids: Baker, 1883, 1979.
———. *A Commentary on the Greek Text of the Epistle of Paul to the Philippians*. Edited by W. Young. Grand Rapids: Baker, 1884, 1979.
Eigen, Michael. *Toxic Nourishment*. London: Karnac, 1999.
Eldridge, John. *Epic: The Story God Is Telling and the Role That Is Yours to Play*. Nashville: Nelson, 2004.
Erdman, Charles. *The Epistle to the Hebrews*. Philadelphia: Westminster, 1966.
———. *The Epistles of Paul to the Colossians and to Philemon*. Philadelphia: Westminster, 1966.
Ezzo, Gary. *Growing Kids God's Way: Biblical Ethics of Parenting—Along the Virtuous Way*. Burlington, IA: Growing Families International, 2007.
———. *Preparation for Parenting: Bringing God's Order to Your Baby's Day and Restful Sleep to Your Baby's Night*. Simi Valley, CA: Growing Families International, 1990.
Fonagy, Peter, et al. *Affect Regulation, Mentalization, and the Development of the Self*. New York: Other, 2002.
Foster, Richard. *Freedom of Simplicity: Finding Harmony in a Complex World*. New York: HarperCollins, 1981.
———. *Sanctuary of the Soul: Journey into Meditative Prayer*. Downers Grove: InterVarsity, 2011.
Fowler, James. *Adult Development and Christian Faith*. New York: HarperSanFrancisco, 1984.
Frankel, Steven. *Intricate Engagements: The Collaborative Basis of Therapeutic Change*. New York: Aronson, 1995.
Friedman, Maurice. *Martin Buber: The Life of Dialogue*. 4th edition. London: Routledge, 2002.
Gabbard, Glen. *Textbook on Psychoanalysis*. 2nd ed. Arlington, VA: APA, 2012.
George, C., et al. "The Attachment Interview for Adults." Unpublished manuscript. University of California, Berkeley, 1985.

Bibliography

Gerhardt, Sue. *Why Love Matters: How Affection Shapes a Baby's Brain*. New York: Brunner-Routledge, 2004.

Getz, Gene. *Building Up One Another*. 2nd ed. Colorado Springs: Cook, 1976.

Goldberg, Carl. *Understanding Shame*. Northvale, NJ: Aronson, 1991.

Grand, Jan, and Jim Crawley. *Transference and Projection: Mirrors to the Self*. Buckingham UK: Open University Press, 2002.

Green, Andre. "Analytic Play and Its Relationship to the Object." In *In One's Bones: The Clinical Genius of Winnicott*, edited by Dodi Goldman, 213–22. Northvale, NJ: Aronson, 1993.

Green, Joel, and Mike Baker. *Recovering the Scandal of the Cross: Atonement in New Testament & Contemporary Contexts*. Downers Grove: IVP Academic, 2000.

Grossman, Klaus, et al. *Attachment from Infancy to Adulthood: The Major Longitudinal Studies*. New York: Guilford, 2005.

Guthrie, Donald. *New Testament Introduction*. Downers Grove: InterVarsity, 1970.

Hall, Douglas John. *God & Human Suffering: An Exercise in the Theology of the Cross*. Minneapolis: Augsburg, 1986.

Hauerwas, Stanley, and William Willlimon. *Resident Aliens: A Provocative Christian Assessment of Culture and Ministry for People Who Know That Something Is Wrong*. Nashville: Abington, 1989.

Heitritter, Lynn, and Jeanette Vought. *Helping Victims of Sexual Abuse: A Sensitive Biblical Guide for Counselors, Victims and Families*. Bloomington, MN: Bethany House, 2006.

Hendriksen, William. *Exposition of Ephesians*. New Testament Commentary. Grand Rapids: Baker, 1967.

———. *Exposition of the Gospel according to Matthew*. New Testament Commentary. Grand Rapids: Baker, 1973.

Hiebert, D. Edmond. *A Call to Readiness: The Thessalonians Epistles*. Chicago: Moody, 1971.

Hildebrandt, Ted. "Proverbs 22:6A: Train Up a Child?" In *Learning from the Sages: Selected Studies of the Book of Proverbs*, edited by Roy B. Zuck, 277–92. Grand Rapids: Baker, 1995.

Hoffman, Marie. *Toward Mutual Recognition: Relational Psychoanalysis and the Christian Narrative*. New York: Routledge, 2011.

Holeman, Virginia Todd. *Theology for Better Counseling: Trinitarian Reflections for Healing and Formation*. Downers Grove: InterVarsity, 2012.

Holt, Bradley. *Thirsty for God: A Brief History of Christian Spirituality*. Minneapolis: Augsburg Fortress, 1993.

Hughes, Judith. *Reshaping the Psychoanalytic Domain: The Work of Melanie Klein, W. R. D. Fairbairn & D. W. Winnicott*. Berkeley: University of California Press, 1989.

Hughes, Phillip. *A Commentary on the Epistle to the Hebrews*. Grand Rapids: Eerdmans, 1977.

Issler, Klaus. *Living into the Life of Jesus: The Formation of Christian Character*. Downers Grove: InterVarsity, 2012.

Jackson, Maggie. *Distracted: The Erosion of Attention and the Coming Dark Age*. New York: Prometheus, 2008.

Jaenicke, Chris. *The Risk of Relatedness: Intersubjectivity Theory in Clinical Practice*. New York: Aronson, 2008.

Bibliography

Jamieson, Robert, et al. "Jeremiah–Malachi." Vol. 2, pt. 2 of *A Commentary, Critical, Experimental, and Practical on the Old and New Testaments*, edited by A. R. Fausset. Grand Rapids: Eerdmans, 1978.

Jewitt, Paul. *Who We Are: Our Dignity as Human; A Neo-Evangelical Theology*. With Marguerite Shuster. Grand Rapids: Eerdmans, 1996.

Johnson, Eileen. *The Children's Bill of Emotional Rights: A Guide to the Needs of Children*. Plymouth, UK: Aronson, 2012.

Johnson, Eric, ed. *Psychology & Christianity: Five Views*. 2nd. Downers Grove: InterVarsity, 2010.

Jones, Joseph. *Affects as Process: An Inquiry into the Centrality of Affect in Psychological Life*. Hillsdale, NJ: Analytic, 1995.

Karen, Robert. *Becoming Attached: First Relationships and How They Shape Our Capacity to Love*. New York: Oxford University Press, 1994.

Keller, Timothy. *The Prodigal God: Recovering the Heart of the Christian Faith*. New York: Dutton, 2008.

Khantzian, Edward, and Mark Albanese. *Understanding Addiction as Self Medication: Finding Hope behind the Pain*. New Delhi: Good Times, 2008.

Kidner, Derek. *Proverbs*. Tyndale Old Testament Commentaries. Leicester, UK: Tyndale, 1963.

Kiel, James. *Leading Your Family to Water*. Maitland, FL: Xulon, 2003.

Kimnach, W., et al., eds. *The Sermons of Jonathan Edwards: A Reader*. New Haven: Yale University Press, 1999.

King, Patricia. *Overcoming the Spirit of Narcissism*. Maricopa, AZ: XP, 2010.

Kinnaman, David, and Gabe Lyons. *Unchristian: What a New Generation Really Thinks about Christianity . . . and Why It Matters*. Grand Rapids: Baker, 2007.

Kohut, Heinz, et al. *How Does Analysis Cure?* Chicago: University of Chicago Press, 1984.

Kreeft, Peter. *The God Who Loves You: "Love Divine, All Loves Excelling."* San Francisco: Ignatius, 1988.

Kruger, J. D. "Some Thoughts on the Education of Children" [in German: Gedanken von der Erziehung der Kinder]. 1752.

Ladd, George Eldon. *A Theology of the New Testament*. Grand Rapids: Eerdmans, 1974.

Lambert, Billy. "Proverbs 22:6: Train Up a Child." Chapter 7 of *Great Texts of the Bible Revisited: Faulkner University Lectures*, edited by M. Floyd Baily Jr. et al. Montgomery, AL: Faulkner University, 1993.

Lasch, Christopher. *The Culture of Narcissism: American Life in an Age of Diminishing Expectations*. New York: Norton, 1979.

———. *The Minimal Self: Psychic Survival in Troubled Times*. New York: Norton, 1984.

Lenski, R. *The Interpretation of the Epistles of St. Peter, St. John, and St. Jude*. Minneapolis: Augsburg, 1966.

Lewis, Clarence. *Death and Life Are in the Power of the Tongue*. Ministry, OK: Tate, 2007.

Lewis, C. S. *The Problem of Pain*. London: Bles, 1940.

Lewis, Michael. *Shame: The Exposed Self*. New York: Free Press, 1992.

Lincoln, A. T. *Ephesians*. Waco, TX: Word, 1990.

Livingston, Louisa. "Reflections of Selfobject Transferences and a Continuum of Responsiveness." In *How Responsive Should We Be*, edited by Arnold Goldberg, 155–73. Process in Self Psychology 16. Hillsdale, NJ: Analytic, 2000.

Lucas, R. C. *The Message of Colossians & Philemon: Fullness & Freedom*. Bible Speaks Today. Downers Grove: InterVarsity, 1980.

Bibliography

Main, Mary, and J. Solomon. "Procedures for Identifying Infants as Disorganized/Disoriented during the Ainsworth Strange Situation." In *Attachment in the Preschool Years*, edited by M. T. Greenberg et al., 121–60. Chicago: University of Chicago Press, 1990.

Manning, Brennan. *Abba's Child: The Cry of the Heart for Intimate Belonging*. Colorado Springs: NavPress, 2002.

Mare, W. Harold. *1 Corinthians*. Expositor's Bible Commentary. Grand Rapids: Zondervan, 1976.

Maroda, Karen. *Psychodynamic Techniques: Working with Emotion in the Therapeutic Relationship*. New York: Guilford, 2010.

Marshall, I. Howard. *Aspects of the Atonement; Cross and Resurrection in the Reconciling of God and Humanity*. London: Paternoster, 2007.

Martin, Ralph *Reconciliation: A Study in Paul's Theology*. Atlanta: John Knox, 1981.

———. "Reconciliation in Romans 5:1–11." In *Romans & the People of God*, edited by Swen K. Soderlund and N. T. Wright, 47–48. Grand Rapids: Eerdmans, 1999.

———. *Worship in the Early Church*. Grand Rapids: Eerdmans, 1974.

M'Caw, Leslie, and J. A. Motyer. "Psalms." In *The New Bible Commentary: Revised*, edited by D. Guthrie et al., 446–547. Grand Rapids: Eerdmans, 1970.

McGilchrist, Iain. *The Master and His Emissary: The Divided Brain and the Making of the Modern World*. New Haven: Yale University Press, 2009.

McKnight, Scott. *The Jesus Creed*. Brewster, MA: Paraclete, 2004.

McWilliams, Nancy. *Psychoanalytic Psychotherapy: A Practitioners Guide*. New York: Guilford, 2004.

Meares, Russell. *Intimacy & Alienation: Memory, Trauma and Personal Being*. London: Routledge, 2002.

Meeks, Wayne. *The Origins of Christian Morality: The First Two Centuries*. New Haven: Yale University Press, 1993.

Meissner, William W. *Psychoanalysis and Religious Experience*. New Haven: Yale University Press, 1984.

Miller, Alice. *For Your Own Good: Hidden Cruelty in Child-Rearing and the Roots of Violence*. New York: Noonday, 1990.

Moreland, J. P. *Love Your God with All Your Mind: The Role of Reason in the Life of the Souls*. Colorado Springs: NavPress, 1997.

Morgan, G. Campbell. *The Great Physician: The Method of Jesus with Individuals*. Old Tappen, NJ: Revell, 1937.

Morris, Leon. *The First Epistle of Paul to the Corinthians*. Tyndale New Testament Commentaries. Grand Rapids: Eerdmans, 1976.

Morrison, Andrew. *The Culture of Shame*. Northvale, NJ: Aronson, 1996.

Moule, H. C. C. *Studies in Colossians & Philemon*. Kregel Popular Commentary Series. Grand Rapids: Kregel, 1977.

Nee, Watchman. *The Normal Christian Life*. Fort Washington, PA: Christian Literature Crusade, 1957.

Needham, David. *Birthright: Christian Do You Know Who You Are?* Portland: Multnomah, 1979.

Newmark, Gerald. *How to Raise Emotionally Healthy Children: Meeting the Five Critical Needs of Children . . . and Parents Too!* Tarzana, CA: NMI, 1999.

Newton, Ruth. *The Attachment Connection: Parenting a Secure and Confident Child Using the Science of Attachment Theory*. Oakland: New Harbinger, 2008.

Bibliography

Ogilvie, Lloyd. *Autobiography of God: God Revealed in the Parables of Jesus*. Ventura, CA: Regal, 1979.
Orange, Donna. *Emotional Understanding: Studies in Psychoanalytic Epistemology*. New York: Guilford, 1995.
———. *The Suffering Stranger: Hermeneutics for Everyday Clinical Practice*. New York: Routledge, 2011.
Packer, J. I. *Knowing God*. Downers Grove: InterVarsity, 1973.
Paris, Joel. *Psychotherapy in an Age of Narcissism: Modernity, Science and Society*. London: Palgrave McMillan, 2012.
Parker, Stephen. *Winnicott and Religion*. Lanham, MD: Aronson, 2012.
Parsons, George. "Guidelines for Understanding and Proclaiming the Book of Proverbs." In *Learning from the Sages: Selected Studies on the Book of Proverbs*, edited by Roy B. Zuck, 151–68. Grand Rapids: Baker, 1995.
Pascal, Blaise. *Pensées*. Translated by A. J. Krailsheimer. London: Penguin, 1669, 1995.
Pearl, Michael. *No Greater Joy*. Vols. 1–3. Plesantville, TN: Pearl, 1997, 1999, 2001.
Pearl, Michael, and Debi Pearl. *To Train Up a Child*. Pleasantville, TN: Pearl, 1994.
Peck, M. Scott. *The Road Less Traveled: A New Psychology of Love, Traditional Values and Spiritual Growth*. New York: Simon & Schuster, 1978.
Pfeiffer, Charles. *The Epistle to the Hebrews*. Chicago: Moody, 1962.
Pinsky, Drew, and S. Mark Young. *The Mirror Effect: How Celebrity Narcissism Is Endangering Our Families—and How to Save Them*. New York: Harper Perennial, 2009.
Plantinga, Cornelius, Jr. *Not the Way It's Supposed to Be: A Breviary of Sin*. Grand Rapids: Eerdmans, 1995.
Pruett, Kyle. *Fatherneed: Why Father Care Is as Essential as Mother Care for Your Child*. New York: Broadway, 2000.
Reeves, Rodney. *Spirituality according to Paul: Imitating the Apostle of Christ*. Downers Grove: IVP Academic, 2011.
Rohr, Richard. *Immortal Diamond: The Search for Our True Self*. San Francisco: Jossey-Boss, 2013.
Ross, Allen. *Proverbs–Isaiah*. Expositor's Bible Commentary 6. Grand Rapids: Zondervan, 2008.
Roth, Sheldon. *Psychotherapy: The Art of Wooing Nature*. Northvale, NJ: Aronson, 1987.
Rutschky, Katharina. *Black Pedagogy* [in German: Schwarze Pädagogik]. Berlin: Ullstein, 1977.
Sayers, Dorothy L. *Creed or Chaos?* Manchester, NH: Sophia Institute, 1974.
Schaffer, Ulrich. *For the Love of Children: Meditations on Growing Up with Children*. San Francisco: Harper & Row, 1980.
Schore, Allan. *The Science and Art of Psychotherapy*. New York: Norton, 2012.
Seinfeld, Jeffrey. *Interpreting and Holding: The Paternal and Maternal Function of the Psychotherapist*. Northvale, NJ: Aronson, 1993.
Shabad, Peter. *Despair and the Return of Hope: Echoes of Mourning in Psychotherapy*. Northvale, NJ: Aronson, 2001.
Sherbondy, Steven. *Changing Your Child's Heart: Parenting Tools to Change Your Child's Attitude, Not Just Behavior*. Carol Stream, IL: Tyndale, 1998.
Siegel, Daniel. *The Developing Mind: Toward a Neurobiology of Interpersonal Experience*. New York: Guilford, 1999.

Bibliography

———. *The Mindful Therapist: A Clinician's Guide to Mindsight and Neural Integration*. New York: Norton, 2010.

Stern, Daniel. *The Interpersonal World of the Infant: A View from Psychoanalysis and Developmental Psychology*. New York: Basic, 1985.

———. *The Present Moment in Psychotherapy and Everyday Life*. New York: Norton, 2004.

Stibbs, Alan. *First Epistle of Peter*. Tyndale New Testament Commentaries. Grand Rapids: Eerdmans, 1959.

Stott, John. *Christian Counter-Culture: The Message of the Sermon on the Mount*. Downers Grove: InterVarsity, 1978.

———. *The Epistles of John*. Tyndale New Testament Commentaries. Grand Rapids: Eerdmans, 1964.

———. *Your Mind Matters: The Place of the Mind in the Christian Life*. Downers Grove: InterVarsity, 1972.

Sulzer, Johann G. "An Essay on the Education and Instruction of Children" [in German: Versuch von der Erziehung und Unterweisung der Kinder]. 1748.

Summers, Richard, and Jacques Barber. *Psychodynamic Therapy: A Guide to Evidence-Based Practice*. New York: Guilford, 2010.

Swindoll, Charles. *Parenting, from Surviving to Thriving Workbook: Building Healthy Families in a Changing World*. Nashville: Nelson, 2006.

Tasker, R. V. G. *The Gospel according to St. Matthew*. Tyndale New Testament Commentaries. Grand Rapids: Eerdmans, 1961.

Taylor, Daniel. *The Myth of Certainty: The Reflective Christian and the Risk of Commitment*. Downers Grove: InterVarsity, 1992.

Tenny, Merrill C., ed. *The Zondervan Pictorial Encyclopedia of the Bible*. 5 vols. Grand Rapids: Zondervan, 1975.

Thompson, Curt. *Anatomy of the Soul: Surprising Connections between Neuroscience and Spiritual Practices That Can Transform Your Life and Relationships*. Chicago: SaltRiver, Tyndale, 2010.

Townsend, Loren. *Introduction to Pastoral Counseling*. Nashville: Abingdon, 2009.

Toy, C. H. *Proverbs*. International Critical Commentary. Charleston: Nabu, 2010.

Tripp, Tedd. *Shepherding a Child's Heart*. 2nd ed. Wapwallopen, PA: Shepherd, 2005.

Twenge, Jean, and W. Keith Campbell. *The Narcissism Epidemic: Living in the Age of Entitlement*. New York: Free Press, 2010.

Vanhoozer, Kevin. "The Love of God: Its Place, Meaning and Function in Systematic Theology." Introduction to *Nothing Greater, Nothing Better: Theological Essays on the Love of God*, edited by Kevin Vanhoozer. Grand Rapids: Eerdmans, 2001.

Wachtel, Paul. *Therapeutic Communication: Knowing What to Say When*. 2nd ed. New York: Guilford, 2011.

Wakefield, James. *Sacred Listening*. Grand Rapids: Baker, 2006.

Warner, Larry. *Journey with Jesus: Discovering the Spiritual Exercises of Saint Ignatius*. Downers Grove: InterVarsity, 2010.

Watson, Jeffrey. *Biblical Counseling for Today*. Nashville: Word, 2000.

Wells, A. F. "Proverbs." In *The New Bible Commentary Revised*, edited by Donald Guthrie et al., 548–69. Grand Rapids: Eerdmans, 1970.

Westen, Drew. *Self and Society: Narcissism, Collectivism and the Development of Morals*. Cambridge: Cambridge University Press, 1985.

Wilken, Robert Louis. *The Spirit of Early Christian Thought: Seeking the Face of God*. New Haven: Yale University Press, 2003.

Bibliography

Willard, Dallas. *Renovation of the Heart: Putting on the Character of Christ.* Colorado Springs: NavPress, 2002.
Wilson, Sandra. *Into Abba's Arms: Finding the Acceptance You've Always Wanted.* Wheaton, IL: Tyndale, 1998.
Wilson, William. *Wilson's Old Testament Word Studies.* McLean, VA: Macdonald, n.d.
Winnicott, Donald W. "The Concept of a False Self." In *Home Is Where We Start From: Essays by a Psychoanalyst,* compiled and edited by Clare Winnicott et al., 65–70. New York: Norton, 1986.
———. "The Concept of a Healthy Individual." In *Home Is Where We Start From: Essays by a Psychoanalyst,* compiled and edited by Clare Winnicott et al., 21–34. New York: Norton, 1986.
———. "Ego Distortion in Terms of True and False Self." In *The Maturational Processes and the Facilitating Environment,* 140–52. New York: International Universities, 1960.
———. *Playing and Reality.* New York: Routledge, 1971.
———. "Primary Maternal Preoccupation." In *Through Paediatrics to Psycho-Analysis: Collected Papers,* 300–305. London: Hogarth, 1956.
Winter, Richard. *When Life Goes Dark: Finding Hope in the Midst of Depression.* Downers Grove: InterVarsity, 2012.
Witherington, Ben, III. *The Christology of Jesus.* Minneapolis: Fortress, 1990.
———. *Letters and Homilies for Jewish Christians: A Socio-Rhetorical Commentary on Hebrews, James and Jude.* Downers Grove: IVP Academic, 2007.
———. *The Letters to Philemon, the Colossians, and the Ephesians: A Socio-Rhetorical Commentary on the Captivity Epistles.* Grand Rapids: Eerdmans, 2007.
———. *What Have They Done with Jesus: Beyond Strange Theories and Bad History—Why We Can Trust the Bible.* New York: HarperSanFrancisco, 2006.
Wittner, Donna, and Sandra Petersen. *Infant and Toddler Development and Responsive Program Planning: A Relationship-Based Approach.* Upper Saddle River, NJ: Pearson / Merrill Prentice Hall, 2006.
Wolff, Richard. *General Epistles of James & Jude.* Wheaton, IL: Tyndale, 1969.
Woods, Guy. *Questions and Answers, Open Forum, Freed-Hardeman College Lectures.* Henderson, TN: Freed-Hardeman College, 1976. Available at www.theseeker.org/cgbin/bulletin/show.pl?Mike%20Riley/comment.
Woolfolk, Anita, and Nancy Perry. *Child and Adolescent Development.* New York: Pearson, 2012.
Wright, N. T. *After You Believe: Why Christian Character Matters.* New York: HarperOne, 2010.
———. *Following Jesus: Biblical Reflections on Discipleship.* Grand Rapids: Eerdmans, 1994.
Wuest, Kenneth. *Wuest's Word Studies: The Pastoral Epistles in the Greek New Testament for the English Reader.* Grand Rapids: Eerdmans, 1952.

www.ingramcontent.com/pod-product-compliance
Lightning Source LLC
Chambersburg PA
CBHW060607230426
43670CB00011B/2007